Bohemian Lives

Amy Licence is an historian of women's lives, from queens to commoners. Her particular interests lie in Modernism, specifically Woolf and the Bloomsbury Group, Picasso and Post-Impressionism. She has an MA in Medieval and Tudor Studies and has published several scholarly articles and books on the late fifteenth and early sixteenth century: focussing on gender relations, queenship and identity, rites of passage, pilgrimage, female orthodoxy and rebellion. Her magisterial study *Catherine of Aragon: An Intimate Portrait of Henry VIII's True Wife* was published in 2016 by Amberley.

Amy has written for the *Guardian*, the *TLS*, the *New Statesman*, *BBC History*, the *English Review*, the *Huffington Post* and the *London Magazine*. She has been interviewed regularly for BBC radio, including *Woman's Hour*, and made her TV debut in the BBC documentary *The Real White Queen and Her Rivals*. She also writes literary fiction and has been shortlisted twice for the Asham Award.

Bohemian Lives

Three Extraordinary Women
Ida Nettleship, Sophie Brzeska,
Fernande Olivier

AMY LICENCE

AMBERLEY

For Tom, Rufus and Robin

This edition published 2019

Amberley Publishing
The Hill, Stroud
Gloucestershire, GL5 4EP

www.amberley-books.com

British Library Cataloguing in Publication Data.
A catalogue record for this book is available from the British Library.

ISBN 978 1 4456 9440 5 (paperback)
ISBN 978 1 4456 7065 2 (ebook)

Typesetting and Origination by Amberley Publishing.
Printed in the UK.

Contents

To see her body flowering with her soul,
And grow, unchained, in awe-inspiring art,
Within the mists across her eyes that stole
To divine the fires entombed within her heart.

'The Giantess'

Alas my poor Muse, what aileth thee now?
Thine eyes are bedimmed with the visions of Night,
And silent and cold I perceive on thy brow
In their turns Despair and Madness alight.

'To the Sick Muse'

Charles Baudelaire, *Les Fleurs du Mal*

Preface

By 1959, Pablo Picasso was easily the most famous artist in the world. His precocious talent had developed quickly, bringing him financial reward early in life, his unique style becoming instantly recognisable, whether it was depicting cubist landscapes, monolithic women or weeping faces with the features rearranged. He had created one of the most famous images of war, *Guernica*, in 1937, as well as the iconic symbol of peace, the Dove of 1949, the emblem of the First International Peace conference. A Spaniard who made his name in Paris, he was now seventy-eight. His distinctive fringe of jet-black hair had turned white, but his eyes still burned with the intensity of his genius.

Four years earlier, he had left behind his studio in the seventeenth-century Hôtel de Savoie on the Rue des Grands Augustins, with its wrought-iron gates and spiral staircase, where he had lived for almost twenty years. After so long in Paris, he had left the city for Cannes, moving into the Villa Californie with Jacqueline Roque, who would become his second wife. Symmetrical and white, with stucco work and iron balconies, full of beautiful furniture and works of art, the villa overlooked the bay. It was a far cry from the dilapidated, leaking studio in Montmartre that Picasso had inhabited when he had first arrived in Paris as a young man, freezing in the winter as he picked the bugs out of his bed. The contrast between the past and present must have struck him as he sat down to watch a television documentary exploring his early years. Broadcast on 15 November, 1959, *L'Art et les Hommes*, directed by Jean Marie Drot, brought together some of Picasso's oldest friends to speak about their life in the artists' colony at Montmartre in the first decade of the twentieth century.

Before Picasso on the screen appeared a face he had not seen for forty-seven years. It was that of an elderly woman, her white hair falling in short waves, arched eyebrows pencilled in above her slanting eyes. It was the face of his first love, the beautiful chestnut-haired Fernande Olivier, to whom he had erected a little shrine in his studio at the age of twenty-three from scraps of her clothing, candles and sketches he had made of her. After living together for seven years, during which time Fernande called herself 'Madame Picasso', they had parted with bitterness on one side and indifference on the other.

Since their separation, Fernande had found life more of a struggle than Picasso. Whilst his career soared, she had tried a number of different jobs, never realising her early dreams to teach or paint. Just two years earlier, in a desperate condition, she had threatened to publish a second volume of her memoirs and Picasso had stepped in, paying her around $20,000 not to make the material public until after both their deaths. In 2001, when extracts from her writings were collected and finally appeared in print, it was discovered Fernande had written a touching message to Picasso:

> So I owe you more than life could ever have allowed me to hope
> for. The only thought that comforts me … is to remember you,
> and the remembrance of you finally brings me calm and peace
> and I fall asleep at dawn because I can forget my present life as
> I am cradled by the memory of you.[1]

Seeing her again in 1959, Picasso's response was 'a disgusting performance. She was too old and fat and toothless to make a spectacle of herself.'

Their responses to each other in later life could hardly have been more different. Yet half a century earlier, amid the winding, cobbled streets of Montmartre, Picasso and 'la belle Fernande' had been happy in the midst of poverty, valuing art and love over materialism and bourgeois signs of status and respectability. She had been his muse, his inspiration, his model, in the vanguard of shocking post-impressionist innovations that rewrote the artistic rules. Experimenting with different media, with new ways of living, with sex and drugs whilst eking out their bread, they had lived freely and bravely. Their choices, and those of others like them, contributed to a redefinition of the process by which individuals defined their personal and artistic freedoms. They had been true bohemians.

Introduction

Inevitably this book requires some attempt to define exactly what is meant by the concept of 'bohemianism'. Lately, the name has evolved into something of a cultural trope, appropriated by fashion magazines and clothing collections for a sort of 1960s hippy-revival style, a shabby-chic glamour or dandyism, typified by floppy hats, long dresses, flowers worn in the hair and cravats. It has been used interchangeably with the words beatnik, dilettante, free-spirit, artist, gypsy, iconoclast, flower-child. And, indeed, there were times when leading bohemians set new trends with their clothing, such as Augustus John's gold earrings or Nina Hamnett's colourful harlequin stockings, but the original bohemianism was more a philosophy of opposition than a certain kind of clothing.

Initially, the bohemian was simply a wanderer from Bohemia, located in the present-day Czech Republic, but this is a misnomer similar to the notion that gypsies came from Egypt. Yet both types of nomads were considered romantic and daring, glamorous and dangerous, for living outside conventional social rules and not caring about the resulting censure. In mid-nineteenth century Paris, bohemianism took a literary and artistic turn, synonymous with the rise of mass popular culture, making the transition from the serialisation of novels in newspapers to the stage and popular song. Parisian bohemians became the subject of art and were themselves transformed into artists. They appeared in Henri Murger's stories, which Puccini used in his hugely successful opera, *La Bohème* and in Prosper Mérimée's short story *Carmen*, later made into an opera by Bizet, whose heroine is described as a 'Romani woman'. They were the individuals glimpsed in the street by the flâneur poet Baudelaire, the novelist Emile Zola's prostitute Nana and his obsessive failure of an artist, Claude Lantier, as well as the circle of ex-pat British artists that appear in George Du Maurier's *Trilby*. It was a spirit of defiance against bourgeois values to be found among the Impressionist artists meeting at the Café Guerbois, but also among the English Pre-Raphaelite painters and the New York journalists meeting at Pfaff's Beer Cellar. It was behind Thoreau's impulse to go into the woods and 'live deliberately' and Whitman's command to 'resist much, obey little'.

In 1862, the *Westminster Review* suggested that 'the term "Bohemian" has come to be very commonly accepted in our day as the description of a certain kind of literary gipsy, no matter in what language he speaks, or what city he inhabits ... A Bohemian is simply an artist or littérateur who, consciously or unconsciously, secedes from conventionality in life and in art.' The *Review* was correct that Bohemianism's essential component was its cultural 'otherness'. It stood in opposition to, but it also became an essential part of, the Belle Époque, a flourish of the era, a romantic tale of the poet writing in his garret which the elite watched at the opera or discussed over dinner. In many ways, Bohemia was a fictional construct with real-life followers, located as much in bourgeois fantasy as in reality. It was a play, a fashionable disguise, the weaving of fact and fantasy, the change of identity, the evolution of the self, a game 'for rich young boys to play', giving rise to the scathing comment, 'scratch a bohemian, find a bourgeois.'[1] Undoubtedly, some flirted with the bohemian lifestyle, secure in the knowledge that they had sufficient funds to do so, and the safety net of a family home to which they might return, or one day inherit. Their terms were fluid, their identities interchangeable, their lines easily crossed. For others, though, it was a calling, where artists worked in poverty hoping for recognition that never came. They experienced real hardship, of poverty, conditions that made their lives unendurable and forced them to live hand-to-mouth.

Sophie, Fernande and Ida each chose some aspects of bohemian living but not others. In rejecting traditional marriage, they suffered jealousy and censure, in rejecting material wealth they struggled to keep themselves fed and clothed. They were by no means the only notable bohemians of their era; they belonged to a whole legion of women pursuing art and love on a mixed journey of dazzling highs and crippling lows.

Sophie Brzeska, Ida Nettleship and Fernande Olivier were born within a decade of each other in the 1870s and 1880s. When Sophie arrived in 1872, Charles Darwin's *Origin of the Species* was thirteen years old but, by the time of Fernande's death in 1966, mankind was only three years away from setting foot on the moon. They inhabited a world in unprecedented transition, where individual rights and personal freedoms were being redefined, where women like them were seeking new ways of arranging their private and professional lives, questioning the traditional roles of dependence and maternity. In the decades following their deaths, these women's trails have been shadowy, their names only remembered in certain artistic circles because of the men with whom they shared their lives. History has tended to focus on their gender rather than their achievements, relegating them to the culturally anonymous status of 'Mrs Artist,' instead of making them the heroines of their own tales. But Sophie, Ida and Fernande have stories to tell that reflect the experiences of all women of ambition, from the past, present and future. They also hold historical importance as figures of emergent new womanhood; individuals, but also symbols of the struggle of a generation.

Although they never met, Sophie, Ida and Fernande shared so many friends and locations that it is tempting to speculate on their proximity; perhaps they followed a similar route through the Luxembourg Gardens or met mutual acquaintances in the same Montparnasse café. Did Fernande and Ida stand side by side to stare in through the window of an art dealer or Sophie occupy a park bench that had once been Ida's favourite sketching spot? Was Sophie tempted into a little almond-scented patisserie to buy a bag of Fernande's favourite pastries early one morning? Distanced by a century, such speculations are enjoyable but must remain firmly in the realms of fiction. The three did not meet, which makes the similarities in their situations all the more interesting.

Contemporary accounts make clear the actual distance between them. The finger-tips of their worlds repeatedly and fleetingly touched, linking them by hearsay and the gossip of those proverbially distant 'friends of friends', of whom there were many. Below that ran the cross-currents of mutual admiration between their partners and many influential figures of the day: Augustus John called in at Picasso's studio; Ida was visited by Gaudier's fellow Vorticist Wyndham Lewis, who was in many ways John's stylistic antithesis; sculptor Jacob Epstein exhibited with Gaudier and shared patrons with John; American dealer John Quinn bought works by Gwen John and corresponded with Sophie about Gaudier's legacy; Gaudier heckled the Futurists, while Fernande left Picasso for one of them. The Edwardian cultural network was small and select, and its playground was Paris. These women criss-crossed the pavements and restaurants of London, Montmartre and Montparnasse. Their lives meander through well-known artistic and literary 'nodes' or memes of the day: the Slade School, Post-Impressionism, the Bloomsbury Group, Montmartre, Fauvism, Cubism, Vorticism, Futurism and 'Bohemianism'. In many ways, they are specific to their time, but their struggle to balance love, work and life, to navigate what Germaine Greer identifies as the 'obstacle race' faced by women artists, is timeless.

1

Sophie

The early life of Sophie Stephania (or Suzanne) Brzeska reads like an Eastern European folk tale, inspired by a magical landscape, superstitions and rituals, signs and symbols, angels and devils. It was a world of childish dreams and extremes, making it easy to imagine Baba Yaga lurking in the woods around Sophie's house, or Prince Ivan descending to light her darkness with a feather stolen from the firebird.

Born in the Polish countryside into an aristocratic family fallen on hard times, Sophie was the neglected daughter in a family of boys 'growing up like poor dogs', escaping into stories, dreaming of running away. Books were her only friends. She had a 'loving heart, ardent, a soul full of enthusiasm' but suffered intensely as her mother was 'monstrous ... unnatural', while her father squandered his inheritance on womanising, plunging his family 'into hell'.[1] Always superstitious, Sophie feared the moon, walking with her back or side to it, in case it 'cast an evil influence'[2] over her, yet she was also intelligent and passionate, a young woman who was exuberant, idealistic, likening herself to Cinderella, longing for love. Her childhood would not seem out of place in a Tolstoy novel.

But this picture of bucolic disharmony does stem from fiction. It may be that Sophie deliberately depicted herself as a latter-day Natasha Rostova, without that heroine's happy ending, or perhaps ever hopeful of finding it. Her confidant, Horace Brodsky, later wrote that she was 'a great admirer of Dostoevsky and the Russians'[3] and her accounts capture something of their bleak melodrama and sentiment. What is known about Sophie's childhood comes from the anecdotes she told to friends, largely recalled after her death, and from the fragment of autobiography that she named *Matka*, or 'Mother'. These few pages, in which she rejected her native Polish for English and French, remained forgotten in University archives until their transcription and publication in 2008.[4] For the first time, Sophie's personal writing became accessible: her voice was heard again over eighty years after her death. It told a string of sad and fantastic adventures, of frustration and ambition, love and loss.

During the First World War, suffering ill-health and poverty and grieving the loss of her companion, Sophie had sketched out her escapades in Poland, France, America, Austria and England, establishing the pattern for a biography where truth and make-believe are not easily separable. Her love of fantasy and secrecy makes discovering the truth of her life an investigative, rationalising exercise rather than straightforward narration. Recreated across time, the Brzeski family's extremes may have appeared more like caricatures to Sophie's friends, coloured by the depth of her youthful unhappiness.[5] Later, her autobiographical novel was narrated by a heroine named Pleurette, drawn from the French verb 'to weep,' making herself both the personification of grief and an abstract literary construction. Whatever the accuracy of family portraits she created, there is certainly an emotional truth to her account; a deep sense of grief, injustice and waste.

Sophie's fiction later came to cloud her reality. Descending into insanity and dying in an asylum in 1925, she ended her search for 'a room of her own' in the confines of the madwoman's attic. It was a poignant end to a tale of female creativity and repression. And yet she had constantly fought against the expectations of her family and society, determined to live her life on her own terms, making her a bohemian in aspiration and practice. Her tangled story is part of the exhilarating movement by which female identities were reshaped against the broader backdrop of historical emancipation. Women worldwide were re-writing their roles and Sophie's actual journey requires no fabrication to add to its innovation and variety. Yet she was not only content with emancipation, she lived a deeply unconventional private life, aware of social censure, amid chains of her own making. It is time to untangle the facts of Sophie's life.

Sophie was born on 6 June 1872, in the village of Laçzki Brzeskie in Galicia, 125 kilometres to the east of Krakow. It remains a tiny place, a long ribbon development, a scattering of houses along a winding country road, surrounded by wide, flat fields. The present Catholic church, dedicated to 'Our Lady Queen and St Jude Thaddeus', post-dates Sophie's residence, as do many of the houses, but the sense of isolation and empty space that she experienced prevails. A population of 1,072 was recorded in 2011 and many of the houses stand alone, or in groups of two or three.[6]

Her father, Mieczyslaw or Micislaus, Brzeski was born in 1840, possibly in Krakow, where he was listed as living with his younger brother Bronislaw, in 1863. Mieczyslaw trained as a lawyer. The young Bronislaw, born in 1848, so then aged fifteen or sixteen, would go on to be a notary in nearby Tarnow. They were listed as living in the Ul Jagiellonian, a narrow street of mixed brown-brick and stone buildings, on the eastern side of the old town.[7] An ancient city that sits at the foot of the Carpathian mountains, Krakow had experienced a 'golden age' during the Renaissance, before passing into rule by the French Valois family and later being captured by Napoleon. By the 1860s it had become known as the 'Polish Athens'. The city's population had expanded in recent decades, from 41,086 in 1850, to 72,025 in 1890[8] and, by the year of Sophie's birth, the School of Fine Art and the Academy of Learning were already established. The city's educational opportunities and cultural riches were later to prove decisive in offering the young girl a bridge to independence. However, national independence was more difficult to obtain.

As a young man of twenty-two or three, Mieczyslaw was involved in an uprising that broke out in protest against conscription to the Russian Imperial army. Tensions had been building between the two nations for years, with Russia declaring martial law in Poland two years earlier in response to rioting sparked by the desire to defend Polish national identity. It became illegal to organise and lead public gatherings or to criticise the Tsar. Across Poland, around 10,000 young men rebelled, largely from the lower middle classes and younger sons from the increasingly impoverished nobility. Soon after the uprisings occurred, when a revolutionary government had seized Krakow, Mieczyslaw became a delegate to the academic benches, which he followed by establishing a correspondence office, presumably to facilitate the rebels. He was arrested in May 1864 and was listed as a volunteer in the uprising and a 'commander of the Square'.[9] The Polish rebels fought several bloody encounters with the Russian army before the rebellion was finally crushed in 1864.

In the late 1860s, Mieczyslaw married Ida Witski, the descendant of a noble family line and the pair moved to Lączki Brzeskie and started a family. Ida bore Michael Georgius Brzeski – baptised on 13 April 1869 – and a second child, who did not survive. After the arrival of Sophie in 1472, Ida bore Johannes Simon Brzeski, baptised on 21 June 1874, Georgius Adamus Brzeski, baptised on 5 June, 1876 and Romanus Augustu Brzeski, baptised on 27 February 1881.[10] There were other miscarriages or stillbirths, as Sophie tells us in *Matka* that while five children survived, four others were lost.

Sophie's father was 'of a noble family, a lawyer, and highly cultivated' and their home had a library, placing them among the 'intelligentsia' of the town.[11] According to her friend Brodsky, Sophie regretted the loss of their 'former grandeur' and considered her father responsible for this loss of status. On 'periodic visits' to Krakow he squandered 'his money on women and riotous living',[12] having been given 'carte blanche to fornicate' by his wife and, although he was of a 'superior intelligence', he countered this with a 'brutal selfishness'. Brodsky relates, recalling his conversations with Sophie, that she inherited 'all those qualities of truthfulness and cultural sensitiveness' from her father, as well as his erratic nature.[13] Brzeski's frequent disgraces led to 'terrible scandals' at home.

Sophie paints herself as a Cinderella figure. Her mother Ida was 'monstrous' and 'unnatural,' with only the instincts of a 'low female' loving none of her children, whom she treated like 'poor dogs'. Given 'more blows and curses than bread', Sophie was picked on for being a girl and the weakest of her siblings, her gender meaning she was simply material for marriage and not the 'brilliant future' which would flatter her parents' vanity.[14] Her 'termagant' mother spent her days reading and studying 'without a system', while the four boys ran wild, indulging in what became the regular family pastime of bullying and belittling their sister. They 'persecuted me for my ugliness, my stupidity and my wickedness', which led her to conclude later in life that any 'wickedness' on her part 'only existed as a result of the bad treatment'.[15] Sophie recounted how her mother disliked her and, after her birth, 'lost all interest in her and handed her daily care over to others', probably servants. She was later to profess affection for the eldest brother, Michael, whom she described as 'sensitive and delicate', who also suffered as a result of their mother's neglect. There was also an elderly uncle to whom she referred as a substitute father and a cousin's house where she sought refuge from the 'nest of vipers'.[16]

Sophie had grander ambitions than the marriage her parents wanted her to make. Longing to learn, she was denied the boarding school education of her brothers and left to her own devices. Her avid reading laid the foundations of knowledge that later enabled her to earn a living as governess and teacher. From an early age she aspired to write but was scoffed at; her family told her there was no money for 'so stupid a person' and the best thing would be for her to marry to their financial advantage. At some point in her teens she was educated in a convent, probably on the Vistula, on the outskirts of Krakow. Here, under the tutelage of nuns, she may have escaped some of the worst reforms imposed upon the Russian education system by the Governor-General of Poland 1883-1894, Iosif Gurko, responsible for implementing the plans of Tsar Alexander III. As part of this process of Russification, the Polish language was banned in schools, to be replaced by Russian or German, as was Polish literature, and many convent schools were forced to close. Sophie's excellent grasp of Russian and German, as well as her love for Russian and European literature may have been inspired at this time, but it was also the era of self-education, of popular library associations disguised as welfare societies and the famous underground Flying University of Warsaw. During Sophie's youth, the Polish intelligentsia were engaged in a largely clandestine education system.[17] The drive to gain access and improve herself through study, in spite of the odds, was a quality that she never lost.

Sophie was back at the family home at the age of eighteen, after attending the convent. She was now 'a very beautiful woman, and certainly very attractive, and the Brzeskis were going to use her to restore the family fortunes'.[18] Having been neglected, ridiculed and abused throughout her childhood, Sophie suddenly found herself in an unexpected position of importance, but she despised the notion of being married off, of being sold to a rich bridegroom in order to pay the family debts. She never specifies exactly whether it is marriage she objects to, or marriage in this manner, although it seems likely to have been the latter. It was typical enough at the time for Jewish families to arrange suitable matches with the service of a matchmaker; the stories of Polish immigrant Anzia Yezierska show that many Jews who left their homeland for New York at this time were still using this system at the turn of the century.[19] Unwilling to sell herself for the benefit of her despised parents, she was also critical of their marriage, intelligent and widely read. Despairing at the future they had planned for her, and melodramatic as ever, she was determined to dig in her heels and remain free, or die in the attempt.

It is impossible to deny the 'romance' of the autobiography Sophie recast in the 1910s. At the time of writing it she was in her forties, alone and increasingly unwell. Deliberately seeking isolation, she felt misunderstood and was quick to take offence at her neighbours and individuals who might have otherwise proved friends. Retreating further into her poverty and self-pity, she defined herself as a bohemian by default, valuing intelligence above wealth, living a nomadic existence, establishing relationships that broke the rules, eccentric in her habits, excluded from mainstream and artistic society. This was the mindset that constructed *Matka*, in which she retrospectively sowed the seeds of her bohemian present. Her childhood must rest upon that slender narrative, even though its few pages are a mere glimmer of candlelight amid the gloom of what went unrecorded.

2

Ida

Ida Margaret Anne Nettleship's childhood could hardly have been more different from Sophie Brzeska's. She was born in late Victorian London to parents who valued, even encouraged, Ida's artistic ambition and permitted her an extraordinary degree of freedom when it came to furthering her talent. Hers was a cultured, urban upbringing, in a small middle-class family with privileged artistic and scientific connections.

In contrast to Sophie's obscure roots, Ida's family are easily traced, as many of them were innovative figures in their fields or held prominent positions in the public eye. Among her immediate relatives by birth, she counted an historian of the United States, two famous surgeons, a bigamous lawyer who wrote science-fiction and invented the 'jungle gym', a dressmaker to the stars, a painter of the animal kingdom, a solicitor, an Oxford professor of Latin, a philosopher, an ophthalmologist, the founder of mathematical logic, the first female Fellow of the Institute of Chemistry and a number of educators in different fields.

Ida's London was a city where rich and poor lived close together. As the work of philanthropist Charles Booth would expose, the lace-hung drawing rooms of the comfortable middle-classes in Shoreditch lay within spitting distance of the poorest slums.[1] This world was captured in a series of photographs taken by Henry Dixon in 1878, the year after Ida's birth, of buildings dating back hundreds of years, with a mishmash of architectural styles. From medieval overhanging houses in Gray's Inn to the neo-Classical

Temple Bar, from the Tudor gateway at Lincoln's Inn and the old cobbled coaching inns to the busy working docks, the images encompass grandeur and industry, beauty and dereliction, a city evolving into the modern world. A second book of photographs, of London street life, published in 1877, by journalist Adolphe Smith and photographer John Thompson,[2] give a different insight into the streets Ida would have known. There are flower sellers under the ornate lamp posts of Covent Garden, Hansom cab drivers wrapped up against the cold, an immigrant boy playing a harp while an old man in apron and top hat smokes a clay pipe, chimney sweeps with their emaciated apprentices, 'ladder-men' sticking up posters advertising new waxworks of famous murderers at Madame Tussauds, and some bearded 'nomads' sitting on the steps of a wooden caravan, which is something of a foreshadowing of Ida's unexpected future. Her London was the largest city in the world, the centre of the British Empire, transformed by its spreading networks of railways and sewers – and by its vocal campaign for suffrage.

Socially, the city was a network of overlapping groups, with the upper-class elite including members of the royal family, lords, baronets, wealthy gentlemen and those who had made a fortune through business. Their calendars were dominated by the annual 'season': the Royal Academy's Summer Exhibition, the Derby, Henley Regatta and invitations to the most exclusive salons. Next there were the ever-growing middle classes who were becoming increasingly educated but still needed to earn a salary, although they were not as poor as the working classes who might be skilled or unskilled and, below them, the underclass of the impoverished and the prostitutes, scratching together an existence in the East End. There were also separate religious and charity groups, societies organised according to mutual interest or philosophies, some taking an experimental approach to life, some united by an artistic or literary passion, or a mutual love of philanthropy, teetotalism, bicycling, music or vegetarianism. Ida's family came from a mixture of overlapping groups, almost entirely derived from the educated, artistic middle classes.

For generations, Ida's family had been advocates for personal freedom. They were among the first Victorian bohemians, tolerating individual autonomy under a social veneer, not quite as openly as the Pre-Raphaelite Brotherhood, but closer to the models offered by the Prinsep-Pattle families of the Little Holland House set, or the Camerons at Dimbola on the Isle of Wight, or the Anglo-Indian Stracheys, and the many artistic circles that were flourishing in Hampstead, Highgate, St John's Wood, Chelsea and Kensington. Sometimes such freedom was tolerated in upper class society under the broad umbrella of being 'artistic' or 'aesthetic' but this could not always override social prejudice, which could just as swiftly reject 'all the flattery and nonsense which (was) rife' among people of that temperament.[3] Yet Ida's relatives embedded their personal morality amid the bastions of Victorian society; the church, the universities, the leading professions. Her maternal great-grandfather was the Oxford-born John Howard Hinton, who became a zealous Baptist and attended the World's Anti-Slavery Convention of 1840, where he would have heard Prince Albert making his debut speech as President of the Society for the Extinction of Slavery. John frequently preached that the state should not punish lapses of morality but leave that up to an individual's faith; he was also a prolific author, publishing his sermons and *The History and Topography of the United States of Northern America*, co-authored with his brother.

His son, James Hinton, Ida's grandfather, proved to be even more of a libertarian. Born in 1822, he attended a nonconformist school in Hertfordshire but, after the family relocated to London, he was apprenticed at the age of sixteen to a woollen-draper in Whitechapel. Whilst working as an insurance clerk, he undertook an intensive programme of study in the evenings, marking him out as far more capable than his current job allowed. After discovering his plan to run away to sea, his parents enrolled James at St Bartholomew's Hospital to study medicine. Newly qualified in the late 1840s, he travelled to Sierra Leone and Jamaica, before establishing himself in London as a leading aural surgeon at Guy's Hospital. His private life was unconventional for a pillar of the medical establishment, as he was outspoken in favour of polygamy, although he believed women to be naturally monogamous. Conducting a number of affairs, he argued that it was for the woman to compromise her ideals for the sake of men's comfort and that moral codes needed to adapt to keep in line with constant social change and that the spirit, rather than the letter, of the law should be followed.[4] His ideas later inspired the circle of Havelock Ellis, a progressive social reformer, although Ellis' wife Edith was deeply critical of his ideals, pointing out that Hinton assumed that it must be the role of 'women to do all the sacrificing and serving, while men reaped the rewards'.[5] It was a position that Hinton's granddaughter Ida was to later find herself in, and to rebel against.

Hinton also struggled with his faith, turning to philosophy to find solutions to his moral dilemmas. He found some statements in the Bible to be 'opposed to the principles of truth and justice' but sought consolation in love, writing to Margaret:

> I have long been of the opinion that the love with which lovers love ought not to be regarded as anything peculiar and extraordinary, but only as the nearest approach which we can make on earth to the true nature of that love with which we ought to comprehend all our fellow creatures.[6]

James Hinton was an example of that particular wave of Victorian scepticism that had begun with Darwin's *Origin of the Species* in 1859 and Matthew Arnold's 1867 'Dover Beach' leading to an increased focus upon human relations rather than divine ones. Coupled with a new mood of emancipation, it led him to believe that any action might be justified so long as it gave pleasure to another,[7] embracing a sexual freedom that even his more enlightened peers did not always appreciate. Ida never met her maternal grandfather, as he died two years before her birth, but later she could have read his letters and the accompanying biography that were published when she was an infant.

Ida's mother, Adaline, or Ada, was James and Margaret Hinton's third child, arriving after Charles Howard and William. She was born at the end of 1855[8] or in the first quarter of the year 1856, at Holborn,[9] after her parents had been married for four years. A second daughter, Margaret, also called Daisy, would later complete the family but balancing their needs against the adult worlds of work and pleasure was not easy. In 1858, Hinton wrote to a friend that the children were mostly in the care of his wife, being 'almost, but not quite, too much for her.'[10] Around this time they had moved into a 'tiny house in Tottenham', the dimensions of which were so small that Hinton claimed he could open the door with one hand, poke the fire with the other and, if he had had a third, open the window, all without rising from his chair.[11] The census of 1861 pinpoints them at 84, Philips Terrace, with Charles aged seven, William aged six, Adaline aged five and no sign yet of Daisy. Their mother was then aged thirty-four and one housemaid, Emma Longford, also lived with them.

With only the one servant, Emma, Ada's mother often did the cooking herself, on one occasion accidentally putting peppercorns instead of currants into a cake. But Margaret Hinton was an economical housewife, reducing their expenditure to £200 a year, well within what her husband was earning. There was also a small 'patch' of a garden at the back of the house where Hinton's philosophical theories were inspired by 'the gathering of a few green peas'. Eventually, in 1862, their straitened circumstances were getting the couple down, so Hinton returned to work at Guy's Hospital as an aural surgeon. For a while he lived apart from the family, taking a house in George Street, Hanover Square, where he set up his doctor's practice. Not long after, he found a larger home near Regent's Park, but in 1865-6, when Ada was ten, one of her brothers being considered delicate, Margaret and the children moved to Brighton, where James visited them every Saturday.[12]

An affectionate letter survives from James to Ada, written in September 1869, in which he predicts that 'you and Howard will be the drawing ones, Willy and Daisy the musical ones, only you make such progress with your music you will belong to both divisions.' As the elder girl, aged thirteen, she would find that she would 'be looked up to for everything by those careless little creatures' and it was also her job to 'keep mamma from doing too much'.[13] In the same year, Hinton published a pamphlet advocating equal education for women, in favour of 'every girl being brought up, like boys, to a profession, so that every woman, whether she needed to earn her own bread or not, should have her own distinct line of service.'[14] He believed that nursing was their ideal profession but, if a woman married, her training could only make her a 'better wife and mother'.

In 1871, the census lists Hinton still practising as a surgeon, living at 18, Savile Row, London, where the presence of two guests was recorded, along with three servants. This separation of the private and professional allowed Hinton to distance his family from the additional liaisons in which he indulged. At the time of the census, Margaret and her younger daughter Daisy, were staying with James' parents at Clifton in Gloucestershire; William was at school in Windsor, perhaps Eton, Charles at Rugby and the 16-year-old Ada was listed as a boarder at a small school of ten girls in Croydon. By the following summer, James Hinton had become unwell. He was in a state of nervous tension, frequently becoming enraged by cases of injustice and in March 1874, he gave up his practice in order to focus on good works. The following year, Ada accompanied her father to St Michaels, in the Azores, where Margaret had been staying to improve her health. James died there, on 16 December 1875, from an 'acute inflammation of the brain'.[15]

Four months later, Ada Hinton was married. She was just twenty years old and her husband was John Trivett Nettleship, an artist and illustrator, aged thirty-five. It is not known how they met, but it may have been through the artistic connections of Ada's mother; only at the end of his life was she able to persuade James Hinton to attend the Royal Academy, where Nettleship had begun to exhibit his large animal canvases from 1874. Perhaps an introduction was effected while the young Ada was gazing upon the painting of a lion or tiger, or perhaps it was made by a mutual acquaintance in their wider social circle. Another likely connection was a medical one: John's younger brother Edward was beginning his career as an ophthalmic surgeon at the London Hospital, before moving to Moorfield. Perhaps Nettleship and his family had been known to James Hinton; maybe the match had been his final wish. There are no references in his surviving letters to Nettleship or an engagement. It wasn't considered desirable to marry during a period of mourning but, in practice, many matches were concluded during this time, born of anxiety about the need to provide for the future of an unmarried girl, especially if the lost relative was male. Virginia Woolf's sister agreed to marry in the days following her brother's death in 1907, even though she had previously rejected Clive Bell as a suitor twice before. Ada's wedding took place on

15 April 1876 at St Pancras' registry office,[16] conveniently quick and unceremonious, where Vanessa and Clive would later marry. In spite of all this, it may well have been a love match.

The year 1876 was to prove a significant one in Ada's life for other reasons. Her elder brother William appears to have died around this time, although it is not clear exactly when. There was also a family scandal when Ada's brother Charles left his wife, assumed another identity and went through a bigamous marriage ceremony. These family issues, following so soon after her father's death, may have prompted Ada to accept what was still considered the most desirable role for a woman in Victorian society: that of a wife. In spite of her father's views on polygamy and her brother's situation, Ada still chose marriage as a desirable institution, a unit of social and domestic currency that allowed women a degree of freedom whilst subjecting them to other constraints.

Marriage was still considered a sacred union but the extent of its power was being challenged. In 1857, the Matrimonial Causes Act had established a separate court to hear divorce and separation cases, which had formerly required an act of parliament, but it was still very difficult for a woman to initiate such action. Until 1870, a woman and all her possessions, were owned by her husband, but the passing of the Married Woman's Property Act that year prevented a man from claiming the earnings and property his wife had accrued through work and inheritance, meaning they might live independently and support their children for the first time. Victorian society was frequently scandalised by famous cases of couples cohabiting, or reaching an alternative arrangement to allow for their personal freedom but these were not the norm; they were either secret, or scandalous. However, a tacit acceptance of their existence was implied when steps were taken to provide for the offspring of such unions in 1872, with the passing of the Bastardy Act, compelling fathers to support illegitimate children.

In practice, Victorian minds were not so easily changed. Two years after the act, in October 1874, Elizabeth Wolstenholme, a member of the Married Women's Property Committee, became the wife of Ben Elmy at Kensington Registry Office. She was five months pregnant at the time, prompting some fellow committee members to call for her resignation, feeling that the scandal was harming the women's movement. Writing in defence of her friends, the social reformer Josephine Butler commented:

> They have sinned against no law of Purity. They went through a most solemn ceremony and vow before witnesses ... They blundered; but their whole action was grave and pure. The English marriage laws are impure. English law ... sins against the law of purity. It is a species of legal prostitution the woman being the man's property.[17]

While criticisms against rigid social codes were mounting, the reality was that cohabiting frequently evinced feelings of abhorrence. Those who made the deliberate choice to adopt alternative living arrangements could anticipate significant censure, from family, friends and strangers alike. Ada was not prepared to take such a risk, eighteen months after the Elizabeth Wolstenholme brouhaha.

Ada's husband, John Nettleship, had been born in Kettering in 1841. He was the son of a solicitor, his mother Isabella was the daughter of a schoolmaster and vicar. John was the second of four brothers who reached adulthood: Henry Nettleship was a fellow of Corpus Christi College, Oxford, soon to be promoted to a professorship in Latin, Richard Lewis Nettleship was a philosopher at nearby Balliol College, and Edward was an eye-surgeon. John had been an Oxford chorister, then a pupil at the Cathedral school in Durham before following his father into the law. Only a few years had elapsed, though, before he deserted that occupation to pursue art at Heatherley School in Chelsea, founded in 1845. Early alumni of the school included Edward Burne-Jones, Dante Gabriel Rossetti and John Everett Millais, who had formed the Pre-Raphaelite Brotherhood in 1848. Their intention was to encourage the personal responsibility of artists to determine and follow their own course, striving for a creative integrity that united freedom with the duty to art. Initially, the group's membership was kept secret from the Royal Academy, whose president openly attacked its principles, while a backlash against its subject matter and style, led by novelist Charles Dickens, ensured its early lack of popularity.

Twenty years after the Pre-Raphaelites, a new 'brotherhood,' was formed around 1867-8 by John Nettleship, Jack B Yeats, brother of the poet, Edwin Ellis and George Wilson during their time at art school, although their intention was not to celebrate the medieval, but to produce visionary and symbolic art inspired by William Blake. The brotherhood, as Ellis defined it, was united by 'personal friendship, not dogma … a handful of men … in London, who hold opposite opinions, who take each his solitary path in art, delight in the power and anxiously try to help on the progress of one another, and are in a perpetual state of artistic civil war'.[18] In Yeats' view, Nettleship was definitely their leader, charismatic and forceful in personality, enthusiastic and 'full to the brim of excitement', more 'versed in the ways of the world'.[19] He was also sexually experienced, or boasted that he was, shocking the others with tales of his 'exploits' and seeming, to Ellis, to comprise 'mystical religion and genius'. Edward Byrne-Jones referred to him as 'His Nettleship'.[20] John achieved some success in his twenties with large-scale, salon-style inspirational works of animals, epitomised by his painting 'God Creating Art', which William Rossetti, brother of the artist, praised as 'the most sublime conception in ancient and modern art'.

The new couple's first home was in Hampstead. Not so long before it had been a leafy town, separate to the city a short distance to the south, four miles from Charing Cross. Hampstead's connection to the city by railway in 1860 and an extensive building program in the following decades had led to such rapid expansion that it was included in the county of London in 1889 and reclassified as a metropolitan borough soon after. Ada was only twenty-one at the time of the birth and must have conceived on, or soon after, the wedding night. Ida arrived on 24 January 1877 and was baptised on 13 May at St John's Church, Hampstead. That same summer, Ada fell pregnant again, giving birth to a second daughter, Ethel, in May or June 1878. Being so close in age to her first sibling, Ethel would have shared a nursery, toys, dresses and many similar experiences with Ida.

The 1881 census lists the four-year-old Ida and her family as resident at 2, Melbury Terrace, St. Marylebone (now in Kensington). A two-storey red brick building, the house is the end of a Victorian terrace with imposing features and large windows. Different from its neighbours, it has the look more of a workshop than a home, with its double front door under a scrolled arch and light pouring into the high-ceilinged ground floor space. Above it, a row of three small windows might suggest the living quarters, or else these might have been located in the extended sections to the side and back. Today the house bears a blue plaque denoting the residence of sculptor Sir Hamo Thornycroft, a Royal Academician in the *fin de siècle* style. The door to Thornycroft's residence bears the numbers 2a and 2b, with the sculptor living at 2b, indicating that the property had been divided in two, appearing smaller than when Ida knew it. However, the presence of a second door, marked only as number 2, indicates that another home lies behind, invisible but for a door, windows and wall, stretching along the side and around the back. A little crenellated wall rises to a low roof with a window and steps lead down to a basement: perhaps Ida and her family were squeezed in here.

For some reason, though, John Nettleship was absent on that particular date in 1881. Ada, aged twenty-five, was listed as the head of the family, a 'seamstress employing ten women and two girls.' Along with Ida and two-year-old Ethel, she shared the house with two housemaids, the twenty-six-year-old Anne E Harrison from Nottinghamshire and Matilda Thompson, aged nineteen, and two boarders, a dressmaker of twenty-three named Mary W Haward and a fourteen-year-old apprentice called Florence E Taylor. It was not unusual for couples to live apart, temporarily, for purposes of work, just as Ada's parents had done. John may have been staying with friends or family at the time, or even travelling abroad, just not present on that particular day. The marriage was still clearly a viable one, as their continuing life together proved. On 4 April 1886, their third and final child, Ursula Mary, was baptised at St.John's, Marylebone.

By 1891, the family had moved to 58-60 Wigmore Street, where their large double property contained John's fine art studio and Ada's thriving dressmaking business, as well as the living quarters where they welcomed visiting artists and poets. The red brick building stands five storeys high, on either side of a central white portion containing three bay windows. The Nettleship family rooms were on the fourth floor, in fairly primitive conditions, dimly lit by gas jets and lacking the separate bathroom that was being introduced into middle class homes.[21] It became a significant social hub in their mid-Victorian art circle, heady with poetry, romance and pre-Raphaelite ideals of beauty, as well as the smells of prepared canvases and tubes of oil paint. The young Ida would have seen in her father's studio artists and poets including Walter Sickert, William Rothenstein, Max Beerbohm, the Yeats brothers and Robert Browning. Ida was never allowed to forget how Browning had scooped her up as a baby and enthusiastically planted her face with kisses, a memory preserved in the biography her father wrote after the poet's death. By the early 1880s the intensity of this youthfully enthusiastic group had dispelled and Nettleship's subject matter became more restricted, to the point that, a decade later, Ida would introduce herself to friends as 'the daughter of the animal painter'. His lions and tigers were sensitively executed in the tradition of artists such as J M Swan and Briton Rivière but didn't sell well. Rossetti's earlier approval was lost and, to Nettleship's dismay, he began referring to his friend's later work as 'pot-boilers'.

Fifteen years younger than her husband, Ada Nettleship was initially a mother to her three young daughters, before becoming a successful and independent businesswoman in her own right. Part of the house in Wigmore Street was given over to her dress-making business, run with an air of ruthless efficiency by a figure dressed in heavy black brocade, decked with ribbons and lace, an outfit of her own devising made from a single piece of cloth, the fabric rustling as she moved about. In one portrayal, by the young Augustus John, Ada seems to come straight from the pages of a Dickensian novel: 'fat and soft and contrived to look older than she was … a slow-moving dumpling [with] Queen Victoria hands' and a temper that was 'certain, but bad'. Observing her in the role of employer, John saw her 'Spartan discipline' as part of the key to her success, 'peppered with fines and instant dismissals'.[22] But it was these qualities, as well as her imaginative creations that won her the patronage of influential women such as Ellen Terry and Constance Wilde, and the most famous actor of the day, Sir Henry Irving.

In June 1892, Irving wrote to Ada regarding a silk supplier and expressing his gratitude 'at the prospect of her undertaking more for them' and a month later, Ellen Terry asked her whether she had enough silk left to make another cape for Irving. He wrote to Ada that October, describing how he would not require a clasp for the cape, but would prefer to throw it over his shoulder, and referring to an imminent meeting with the seamstress, when they could discuss the details. In the autumn of 1892, Ada was working on a Cardinal's costume for Irving, probably for the role of Cardinal Wolsey in Shakespeare's *Henry VIII*, worn during his American tour of 1893; she was also producing costumes for *King Lear*, which opened at the Lyceum Theatre on 10 November.[23] In December 1894, Ellen and Ada were corresponding again, about a purple and green dress with a blue bodice that Ellen had had altered, possibly for a performance of King Arthur, for which dress rehearsals were being held the following January. Her next letter comments that her white Guinevere dress is much improved. Ada also appears to have been making items to supplement Ellen's personal wardrobe as well as her public performances. Early in 1895, the actress requested a 'cool spring coat' and asking for a 'black poplin', on which Ada was then started work, to be ready for the following week.[24] From 1895 to 1902, Ellen continued to order costumes and personal items, adding in more intimate comments about her long rehearsal schedule that suggest the two women had become friends. In October 1896, Ada was planning to visit the theatre and Irving wrote to reassure her that she was welcome to bring as many friends as she liked. Perhaps Ida and her sisters accompanied their mother to see the costumes they had witnessed her making paraded on the stage.

Ada was also responsible for creating one of the most famous theatrical costumes of the nineteenth century, Ellen Terry's emerald and sea-green Lady Macbeth dress, which was immortalised in a painting by John Singer Sargent in 1889. The work shows the actress wearing long, red plaits, with her arms raised above her head to hold a crown, a look of madness or terror in her eyes. The dress, in medieval style, with long, flowing, embroidered blue sleeves, folded back to reveal the green hem and lining. The bodice is clasped by a belt and girdle of gold leaves and the sleeves and cape hang down in waterfall-like folds. The real dress, on display at Ellen's former home of Smallhythe Place in Kent, is more green than blue, sewn all over with the naturally-shed wings of thousands of jewel beetles, stitched together. When it underwent a period of restoration in 2009-11, it cost £50,000 and took 13,000 hours to restore to its former glory.[25] In her autobiography, Ellen referred to the dress as 'one of Mrs Nettle's greatest triumphs'.[26]

Edna Waugh, later Edna Clarke-Hall, then a teenaged friend of Ida's from the Slade School of Art, found Ada 'formidable and awe-inspiring' and warmed instead to Ida's more welcoming father. Edna particularly enjoyed looking round John's studio, 'enraptured' and 'marvelling' at the detail in his work, whilst he put her at ease, laughing at her informality and taking her hand when she felt unsure of herself. He was 'bald headed, grey bearded and with a nose like an opera glass'; details confirmed by Max Beerbohm's sketch. He 'never said very much' but was always smiling with 'warm brown eyes ... full of laughter and good humour' and most flattering of all, he 'minded' what she said. Visiting regularly, she sensed a darker side to his moods, as he recalled Rossetti's disparaging comments, but usually he was 'delighted' with the impression his work made upon her.[27]

Visiting at the same time as Edna was Nettleship's future son-in-law, the artist Augustus John. His account gives further insight into the painter's character by explaining the presence of the 'giant bowl', or jorum, which Edna Waugh had laughed about on a previous visit. Some years back, a fall from a horse had left Nettleship with a broken arm that did not heal well. He initially self-medicated with whisky but after developing an addiction, underwent a residential cure. It left him with the constant need to sip liquid; tea, coffee or chocolate and, for this purpose, he used a dish which was eight inches wide by eight inches deep. Often appearing barefoot, Nettleship sometimes embarrassed Augustus during his early visits, although he agreed with the commonly held view that his rather eccentric host was the 'salt of the earth'.[28] Nettleship's opinion of Aubrey Beardsley's women as 'damned ugly' suggests how much the family were still essentially mid-Victorian in outlook in the late 1890s, deeply entrenched in the culture and morality of a dying era; an environment which shaped the values of their eldest daughter.

Ida's parents made an unusual couple; the sensitive animal artist, nostalgic for a lost pre-Raphaelite world and a strong-minded businesswoman who relished the status and independence of catering for the upper classes. Ida appears to have inherited many of her father's characteristics, especially the dreamy, poetic nature and absorption in art, which became in her a type of prolonged childhood of sentimentality and romantic, archaic gestures. Among the atmosphere of creative dedication and the smell of oil paints and varnish, it is little surprise that the young Ida displayed an early enthusiasm for drawing, carrying her sketchbook out on countryside walks or trips to London's parks. Supposedly her mother's favourite child, she displayed in her late teens something of that formidable woman's focus and dedication to her chosen path. The family unit appears secure and strong despite the differing natures of the parents; indeed these complementary opposites may have contributed to its success.

In her early teens, or perhaps as young as eleven or twelve, Ida was sent to Grassington Ladies College at 112 Furness Road, Eastbourne.[29] Ethel may have gone at the same time, or else joined her there soon after. An imposing, quirky building with large windows and a projecting entrance porch, the property they would have known was demolished in 1986 and replaced by the present block of flats known as Pennell House. A surviving photograph from 1935 shows girls crowded into the little balcony over the doorway, under an ogee-style archway. Another image shows the extent of the building, which stands at least four storeys high, behind stone walls, with mature trees in the grounds behind. The school was a family concern, run by headmistress Mary Deacon, aged sixty-two, and her three sisters; Ellen, who was Mary's twin, Grace aged fifty and Catherine, aged forty-eight. The 1891 census records that Mary's nieces Alice M Deacon, aged twenty-two and Mary, aged twenty, were teachers at the school, and that the seven-year-old Harold, her nephew, was resident there too. Ten ladies were listed as teachers and there was an additional staff of eleven, including cooks and kitchen maids, housemaids, general helps and parlour maids. The fourteen-year-old Ida and her twelve-year-old sister Ethel would have had their meals prepared by Elizabeth Daniel and Rose Teppett, and their rooms cleaned by Ellen, Ann, Sarah, Lena or Emma. There were twenty-six pupils listed at the school in 1891, their ages ranging between eleven and eighteen, though one was aged only eight. The girls came mostly from the home counties, some further afield within England, but Isabel M Searle, aged fifteen, had been sent over from Madras, India, perhaps a member of the prolific military family from Kanara.[30] As in Frances Hodgson Burnett's 1905 novel *The Little Princess*, Isabel might have regaled her friends with tales of life in the Raj.

At the time of the 1891 census, none of the Nettleship girls was living with their parents. Ursula, aged five, was living near Wooburn Common, in Wycombe, Buckinghamshire. Described as a 'boarder' she was in the house of a Joseph Tyrell, aged sixty-two, and his three daughters, Annie, Katee and Pattie, in their twenties and early thirties. This might indicate that Ursula had been unwell and was sent out of London into the countryside to recuperate. By this time, her parents were living in Wigmore Street, along with a German cook named Sophie Rust, a housemaid Charlotte and three other dressmakers, Mary, Elizabeth and Kate. Right next door at number sixty-two was the Cock and Lion Inn, which still does business today.

Growing up, Ida's main occupations were drawing, often on rambles into the countryside and reading poetry; her favourites were Swinburne, Browning and Christina Rossetti. She also took up the fiddle in order to maintain her concentration and stave off unspecified temptations, later telling a friend to aim 'for the highest you know'. She invented nicknames for her friends and wrote them long, creative letters that were sometimes illustrated; the girls wove their own imaginative world of real and make-believe characters. The impression emerges of a much-loved daughter of two strong figures, protected and indulged, whose created environment of security and poetry allowed Ida to retain her sense of fantasy and play long after many of her contemporaries. Later, some friends found her fey and childish, referring to her and her group as 'the nursery', for behaving in a way they deemed 'younger' than their years. Holroyd's suggestion that Ida was 'worshipped and perhaps a little spoiled'[31] seems accurate, even when we take into account the frequently documented over-protection of nineteenth-century girlhood and Ida emerges, aged fifteen, as naïve, innocent and immature – but delightfully so. In comparison with the loveless upbringings of Sophie Brzeska and Fernande Olivier, Ida's early life was blessed.

3

Fernande

Fernande Olivier was born in Paris in 1881. Ten years earlier, it had been a broken city, rising from the ashes after a four-month siege by the Prussians and the rejection of the Third Republic by the revolutionary Commune. Barricades had been erected in the streets, hand-to-hand fighting spilled over doorsteps and into the gutters; its palaces and key civic buildings had been captured or burned in the spirit of Delacroix's Marianne (*Liberty Leading the People*), in the pursuit of democratic and social freedom. As many as 10,000 communards had been killed, with a similar number being executed after the government regained control. During the worst periods of privation, restaurant served rat, cat, horse and dog; even the two famous elephants in the city zoo, Castor and Pollux, were slaughtered and eaten.[1] By the time of Fernande's arrival, though, Paris had begun to rebuild itself, emerging as cleaner, brighter and more modern. Visiting in 1873, the American Charles C Fulton wrote that it appeared 'gay and sparkling', describing the 'four handsome clusters of lights in the Place de l'Opéra ... the miles of boulevards planted with sycamore trees', each tree surrounded by an iron grating, 'new squares, gardens and fountains'.[2] In 1875, Haussmann's new boulevards were starting to take shape, along with the completion of the new Paris Opera, the first stone of Montmartre's Sacre Coeur had been laid and Bizet's *Carmen* premiered. The year of Fernande's birth also saw the sixth of the eight Impressionist exhibitions open in the Boulevard des Capucines, featuring Degas' famous bronze of 'The Little Dancer'. It was an exciting time to be born into a city which was in the vanguard of modern art.

'Fernande' was not the name she was born with, but it was one she would choose for herself, by which she is remembered. When she arrived, at eleven o'clock on the morning of 6 June, 1881,[3] it was as Amélie Lang, the result of an affair between a Clara Lang and a married man, a fact that she later reflected in the subtitle she chose for her diary, 'an unwanted child'. Almost at once, Clara handed the baby over to a woman named Maman Aubert, who cared for her during her early days and was responsible for having the girl baptised at the age of ten months. Clara Lang never lived with Fernande, or raised her, surely as the result of economic or marital circumstances, but she did reappear at intervals during the girl's childhood, suggesting that she remained close by and maintained contact with other family members. Very little else is known about the woman whose kisses her daughter recalled as 'distant' and whose infrequent visits to the girl interrupted her schooling. Clara was certainly still alive by the time of Fernande's fifteenth birthday, even though the girl referred to her mother as being dead, but this underscores an emotional truth that Clara was as good as dead to her, as Fernande believed she 'felt nothing' for her child. [4]

The identity of Fernande's father was deliberately withheld from her but in a foreword to her diary Marilyn McCully suggests he bore the name Bellevallé or Belvalet, which Fernande briefly adopted in 1907, when seeking a new identity. It is a gallicisation of the Jewish name Schoental or Schoenfield, suggesting that, through him, she had Jewish origins. Fernande later exotically described her heritage as 'middle Eastern', which might suggest some knowledge of her paternal roots, although some of her friends believed there to have been an element of dramatic licence in that claim. Her father had disappeared around the time of his daughter's second birthday and she could only recall a tall man in a top hat, buying her a rubber doll from a toy shop. In adolescence, she was to enquire about her background to no avail, writing in her diary that 'no one will say a word, they avoid me with their eyes, their faces become stern and I'm told not to ask ridiculous questions.'[5]

When still very young, Fernande went to live with her father's half-sister Alice and remained with her until she reached the age of eighteen. The move from Maman Aubert was prompted by Alice's marriage, which must have occurred around the time of Fernande's first birthday, given the age of her cousin Marguerite, who was born about a year later. There was an additional family connection, though, as Fernande described Maman Aubert as the aunt of Alice's new husband, Charles. Alice had been educated at an Augustinian convent and is referred to by her niece as the 'aristocrat' of the family, perhaps indicating that her father also had upper class roots.[6] Along with her new husband Charles Petot and baby Marguerite, Alice lived at 55, Rue Reaumur in Paris, the adjoining street to which was photographed by Eugène Atget in 1907, off the Rue Saint-Denis in the heart of Paris' garment district. Uncle Charles ran a small business called 'Pradines et Petot', manufacturing silk flowers, plants and feathers, and Fernande's detailed diary descriptions of their life are reminiscent of Zola's cramped business and domestic quarters in 'The Ladies' Paradise' (*Au Bonheur des Dames*). Home for Fernande was a tall tenement building, with a poorly lit staircase which people had to feel their way up, so that customers and guests regularly tripped on the journey. The family owned two apartments on the fourth floor, knocked through and divided between living and working space, the latter comprising workrooms, stockroom, shop and office. The domestic half of their property contained three bedrooms, a dining room, kitchen and small formal living room, with the best items of furniture draped in green cloths for special occasions.[7] This intimate proximity but clear demarcation between business and domestic life is similar to the household arrangement of the Nettleships, although the Petot family had to share their building with other tenants, a situation that was to arouse Fernande's curiosity as she negotiated her teenage years.

Fernande says she began writing what she calls her 'diary' early on the morning of her fifteenth birthday. Published in 2001, *Loving Picasso* includes material from her teenaged writings and her two subsequent memoirs *Picasso et ses Amis* (1933) and *Souvenirs Intimes*, written in the 1950s and published in 1988. The text has caused some controversy, raising questions about when exactly the sections covering her early years were written. Rosalind Krauss, author of the 1998 *The Picasso Papers* has seen the diary as the cynical exercise of Fernande as an older woman, 'the document of a mind nurtured on pulp romance', a 'Bovaryism,' employing all the literary clichés of the cheap magazines she devoured. Krauss goes so far as to call the diary 'fraudulent,' and 'clearly no diary ... filled not only with "biographical" details surely modelled on years of romance reading but with embarrassing attempts that constantly fall back into purple prose'. Krauss paints the work as an act of self-validation by the seventy-four-year-old Fernande, in which 'the prostitute-indolent, gluttonous, lesbian (is) able to rise in society and be made whole again by the intervention of the artist.' Regardless of when her text was constructed, this a harsh, unsympathetic judgement of Fernande. The diary's editor, Marilyn McCully, accepted the text as genuine three years after Krauss's allegations and identifies that there has been a process of editing, so the exact truth of its construction may be difficult to recover. The voice of Fernande's diary is fresh and young in tone and focus, it captures incidental details, speech, locations and timings that might have receded over time, giving it a plausible immediacy. Even if this 'teenager' is the cynical product of Fernande's maturity, it is still her voice and certainly proves her gifts as an author. For the purposes of this biography, the McCully edition of Fernande's diary will be accepted as it is presented, as a genuine text, until such time that further evidence emerges to the contrary.

Fernande claims she began writing on 6 June 1896. In an intimate and fluent style, she recorded her morning in a 'little pocket notebook' that she slipped under her bolster for privacy. While her aunt called for her to get up, she scribbled down a few of her hopes for the future, wondering whether happiness was in store for her and lamenting Alice's constant grumbling and the lack of peace. She also admitted that she copied into the book lines from her favourite classic poems and some that she had composed herself. 'I'm sentimental,' she wrote, 'too sentimental and I have to write down everything my heart dictates because I can't talk about my feelings.' There was 'no celebration' that day for her birthday, 'only a little sermon' and the surreptitious gift of a coin from her uncle. As she had now turned fifteen, her allowance was increased from one franc to two.[8]

Fernande did not have a good relationship with her aunt. She continues her diary with 'I don't like my aunt and she certainly doesn't like me either' and refers to past occasions of neglect, saying that now she was older she didn't 'suffer like the little creature I was then'. Fernande had 'spent (her) early childhood with a full heart, always looking for a kind gesture, for some tenderness' and wished her uncle had 'taken (her) away ... so that he had no one to love but (her)'. She found consolation in reading, borrowing books from Charles' library and reading them in secret. Her favourite authors were Eugène Sue and Victor Hugo. In her dreams, she travelled 'through wonderful lands where everyone loves me and I love everyone'.[9]

To the twenty-first century eye, some of Alice's child-rearing techniques may seem harsh, especially the occasion when she forced her niece to swallow the vermicelli and milk soup she loathed and which she immediately vomited straight back up, or the onions that gave her heartburn. In response, her uncle 'angrily warned' his wife that 'he would take me to eat in a restaurant if she insisted on making me eat things that made me ill', causing her aunt to 'sulk for a long time after his act of defiance'.[10] Alice would also regularly search the bedroom that the girls shared while Fernande slept, in particular her school bag, exercise books and pens, 'stealthily as a cat ... embarrassed by the indiscretions she can't help committing'. Fernande preferred the company of their housemaids, but if she 'got attached to one of them' the girl was dismissed by Alice, who was always finding fault with her staff, calling them 'greedy, dirty, thieving, emancipated', the final word being Alice's favourite insult, which she repeatedly fired at Fernande.[11] Her diary betrays her feelings of rejection:

> She seems to relish humiliating me. I've never understood why...
>
> I'm not jealous or envious, but I still feel miserable, although I'm fifteen, being treated like a stranger and I really don't understand why...
>
> I don't know why my aunt doesn't love me; after all if I'm not part of the family, it's not my fault...
>
> And yet I would have really loved my aunt if only she could have responded by caressing me once in a while.[12]

Initially craving her affection, Fernande was hurt by her aunt's boasts to friends of how she'd raised her niece out of 'goodness and charity ... to save her from public welfare'. Fernande reminded her of financial assistance given by her absent father. When the girl felt compelled to return the invitations she had received from school friends, Alice chastised her for 'taking the liberty' of asking them round, telling her, 'you know perfectly well that this isn't your own home. You are raised here out of charity ... I dread to think how you'll end up and where.'[13] Later, Fernande elaborated on her aunt's criticisms:

> I believed, as I was repeatedly told, that I'd end up on the scaffold, that I'd turn out badly, that I'd be sent to a reformatory, that I'd never get married because I was ugly and bad-mannered, that I'd never succeed at anything because I was lazy, that I was heartless and would end up in the straw where I had been born, a bastard.[14]

There were occasions when Fernande was able to judge her aunt more dispassionately. Whilst describing Alice as an anxious woman 'full of old fashioned prejudices' and 'afraid of everything', Fernande acknowledged her to be a good housekeeper who fed them well, made her dresses and sent her off to the hairdresser to look her best on prize-giving days, even if she disliked the outfits and styles that Alice favoured. Proud of her niece's academic achievements, Alice boasted to friends, wanting to show Fernande off and asking her to call her by her given name, not as Aunt, which made her 'seem old' and 'less like a friend'. Fernande pertinently noted that her aunt was not her friend.[15]

Uncle Charles had a warmer relationship with his young charge, based on a sense of mutual protection. On one occasion where Alice unjustly raised the girl's parentage, he 'told her coolly to be quiet as she was going to go on and on' and sheltered Fernande from the storm in his office or library. Charles Petot was a man of simple pleasures: clay pipe, daily cards and absinthe in a café after work, with a 'tall physique, good looks and masculine bearing ... deep melodious voice ... and big hands'. There was a clear a bond of affection between him and his niece, prompting Alice to complain he loved Fernande 'better than his own daughter'.[16] He gave her money on her birthday, took her to see shows and exhibitions, defended her and praised her looks. In turn, she was keen to please him and respected his quiet strength and endurance, casting him as an ally in her struggle against her aunt.

Fernande resented the infirmity that led to her cousin Marguerite's constant pampering and the weak lungs which necessitated family holidays to the seaside at Berck. Situated on the north coast, the resort was popular as a destination for those suffering from tuberculosis, with a special Maritime hospital opened in 1869. Posters for the resort advertise it as being only three hours from Paris by train and a postcard from 1911 shows a crowd dressed in their summer whites, watching as the approaching engine wreathes them in smoke. The Petot family would rent a 'little chalet' in the Rue des Oyats, but the girls were not allowed to enjoy the beach due to Alice's fears of shifting sands and waterholes and the incoming tide. Fernande describes children being ridden around in large carriages drawn by donkeys and how she spent her time looking for shells and digging up cockles. The teenager's dislike and envy of her cousin is palpable in her diary; Marguerite was always given the best of everything. As an invalid, she had the fattest meat and largest portions, the nicest clothes to wear and best quality fabrics, as well as a kiss goodnight. Intelligence was one advantage Fernande felt proud to have, even though this meant she was required to help tutor her cousin when she failed to gain the school certificate.

Fernande's talents appear to have been academic and broad: her range of school prizes encouraged her aunt and teachers to push her towards a teaching career. She read widely, often as a form of escapism at home, locking herself away in the bathroom with books taken from her uncle's library when she was supposed to be sewing. Reading was rarely allowed as it conflicted with Alice's moral principles and introduced excessive leisure and unsavoury influences.

Charles Petot colluded with his niece's passion for the latest novels, which he said 'ought to prepare (her) for life', although Fernande's conclusion that 'if life's really like that, it doesn't look as if it will be very pleasant when I'm thrown out into the world'[17] was to be uncannily prophetic. Genuine intellectual interest and affection for her teachers inspired Fernande's selective hard work and she was pleased to return to her lessons after the long summer break. Aged sixteen, she achieved first prizes in history, recitation, reading, English and French composition, while a second prize for drawing surprised her because she usually spent art lessons eating the charcoal in the belief that it would make her teeth white.

The working section of the apartment at Rue Reaumur was usually out of bounds to the girls but, in the summer of 1897, Fernande's assistance was required whilst Charles Petot was away on a business trip. Her main function was to support the solitary accountant, Maurice Dufour, a 'meticulous old boy' of twenty-eight, who worked part-time, twice a week from three until five in the afternoon. Fernande's assessment of him was balanced but harsh: he was slow, finicky and 'would have made a good teacher' but had been nursing a sick mother for the past eight years, a 'noble act' for which she thought he 'deserved a medal', although she didn't feel much sympathy for him. Nor was he good at copying the letters; with the unforgiving exactitude of a teenager, she found his writing too regular, precise and slow and, in particular, disliked the way her aunt praised his 'oily manners' as an example to her. Possibly Aunt Petot was already contemplating the marriage she tried to arrange between them a year later, as Fernande believed 'to get rid of me'.[18] To her, the idea was out of the question; marriage to Dufour might have brought a secure personal and social identity but the potential bride was romantic and idealistic, in pursuit of nothing less than love. Apart from the presence of Dufour, the young Fernande seems to have enjoyed helping in the office, sorting the flowers and feathers in the high drawers, wrapping them in tissue paper and arranging them in boxes for delivery in France and abroad.

The diary also mentions a godmother from Saint-Cloud, a governess of German origins whose visits to Fernande led the girl to conclude she 'must have known my mother but she never tells me about her.' This unidentified ally visited monthly and treated her to hot chocolate and raspberry and cinnamon tarts in a teashop near the Gare Saint-Lazare, followed by two large pears before she left. This godmother displayed genuinely kind impulses, taking Fernande on holiday and bringing her hand-me-down clothes from her pupil, but there were limits. The girl commented that 'she never asks me questions and I sense that she wouldn't put up with any complaints from me,'[19] closing off another avenue of information about her past. The consistent silence concerning Fernande's origins maintained by all the significant adults in her life was a typical contemporary reaction to the stain of illegitimacy in an era when maintaining a respectable social façade was of far greater importance than individual happiness. This was certainly the case with the family of Parisian Impressionist Edouard Manet, whose illegitimate son Léon Koella continued to be described in public as his wife Suzanne's younger 'brother', even after their marriage provided an opportunity for his legitimisation. Fernande's true origins remain an enigma to the present day.

This godmother also took Fernande for an annual holiday, for two weeks at Rubécourt (Rubécourt-et-Lamecourt) in the Ardennes, with a relative of her mother's, a man whom she called uncle. He was a gamekeeper, living with his 'half rustic, half urban' family in 'a large lodge in the middle of the forest'. Around 250 kilometres to the north-east of Paris, on the edge of the Ardennes Regional Nature Park, the village was then a small one of mostly two-storey dwellings lining the road, but the lodge may have been in the grounds of the sixteenth-century Chateau Lamecourt. Ever the sensualist, Fernande enjoyed their food, the 'mushrooms, fresh vegetables, little meat and, thank goodness, though I don't know why, no dairy produce'. She was particularly fond of the thick cabbage soup and soggy bread. She was something of a curiosity to people there, finding that they looked at her 'as if there's some mystery they want to solve.'[20]

The trip to Rubécourt was often coupled with a stay at Méru, on the river Oise, with Fernande's Uncle Labrosse and his family. This uncle was a retired pork butcher, 'very old, at least seventy, and he's rich.' The Labrosse house was pretty, 'standing right by the drinking trough, with a flower border in front and a long kitchen garden and orchard behind', which climbed steeply to the main road. Fernande loved the old walnut trees lining the street, regretting that she always left the town before they were ripe to pick. Although grateful for their kindness, Fernande preferred Labrosse's brother, Charles, who lived in the nearby village of Lardière, a small gathering of houses with green shuttered windows, 'smothered in Virginia creeper, honeysuckle and wisterias'. Charles made dominoes and allowed Fernande to help him, putting 'the drop of black varnish in each hole' with a very thin brush. He made her a set of small mother-of-pearl dominoes 'as a reward for helping him with his work'.[21]

Fernande felt welcome in the countryside, going on long walks and attending her cousin's wedding. She slept in a little attic room and enjoyed escaping into the surrounding countryside, particularly the little brook in Méru that crosses the town, the banks of which reminded her of a 'fairy-tale'. The town specialised in items made from bone, ivory and mother of pearl, and the residue was thrown into the brook so that everything was 'iridescent ... like walking on a carpet of moonlight ... (and) when the sun strikes it, it looks as if you're on a rainbow'. As a little girl, she would 'run away down to the brook ... sit on the ground, my pinafore full of fragments of pearl'. She especially loved the pink ones and would 'sort them and try to grade them by colour, but a ray of light would make them change hue.' The specks of pearl used to become 'encrusted' in her 'lovely hair the colour of horse chestnuts, which (was) curly' and caught anything that brushed against it, so that it 'glistened with a thousand lights'.[22] Everything was so different from Paris that it sent Fernande into raptures of appreciation:

> I love all the fruits I can gather or pick in the country. I love green sour apples and the acid plums and wild cherries and blackberries. I like the little maggoty windfall pears and redcurrants and blackcurrants. I like the strawberries that are moist and often spattered with mud when it rains. I like the radishes that I dig up, the sorrel leaves which set your teeth on edge. Like a typical Parisian I love almost everything that country children despise. I love it when I get caught in a summer rainstorm that turns me into a streaming creature with hair dripping down my neck, and to feel the water seeping between my underclothes and my skin ... and to feel my face varnished by the rain, water in my eyes, my ears, my neck and then, when the rain stops and a rainbow shines across the newly washed blue sky ... how I love this country in all its moods.[23]

There was far more of a routine at the home of Uncle Labrosse than that there was at his brother Charles' place. They were up at six, to get some 'fresh air' and pick flowers in the countryside, returning at eight for a breakfast of hot chocolate and thick, buttered bread. After that, they washed, then helped the maid to pick and peel the vegetables, before heading off for another walk. In the early evening, they watered the plants, then dined at seven, followed by games of lotto or cards. Bedtime was at nine. There were no books in the scrupulously clean house and Fernande longed to sleep later in the morning.

During her visit of August 1897, at the age of sixteen, the tone of her diary entries suddenly changes. One morning, after the others were out, Fernande's uncle appeared in her room, watching over her as she woke, and progressing to ask suggestive questions. When he tried to caress her hair, she asked him to leave her alone, but he returned the next day, even though she had attempted to barricade the door shut. She repelled his efforts to kiss her and resolved not to lie in bed again but to go out walking with the others. However, the following morning, he assaulted her, leaving her in a 'dreadful state of terror ... sick and trembling'.[24] Saying she was unwell, Fernande was nursed by her aunt, with lime blossom tea, before convincing her uncle Charles to let her stay with him in Lardière for the remainder of her visit.

Fernande's diary is steeped in her warmth of character and desire for love. In spite of all the neglect and cruelty she received at the hands of her aunt, she still remained 'sensitive and affectionate' and, at the age of sixteen, summed up her passionate nature and aesthetic sensibilities:

> I want to love and be loved, to love people, animals, flowers, nature. I love true stories, beautiful poems which make me cry, music which enchants me in a strange way that I can't explain. I'm greedy, I like ripe fruit, as much for the pleasure of looking at it, of touching it, as of eating it. I want to love everything, and when the sun shines I feel in love with the sun. I love the rain which makes me feel melancholy and makes me dream of all kinds of tender things. I think I just love life and what it promises me.[25]

At the age of sixteen, on the verge of womanhood, Fernande's good looks and warmth would soon begin to attract more attention, some welcome, some unwelcome. Her later teenage years would illustrate just how difficult the transition from girlhood to womanhood could prove.

4

The Widening World

Victorian ladies' magazines brimmed with the romance of society marriages: the dresses, jewellery, flower arrangements, the gifts, guest list and photography. *Home Notes* and *Home Chat*, launched in the 1890s, explored practical questions of wedding etiquette, while *Sweethearts* and *Wedding Bells* informed young women how to flatter men into engagements and prepare for their big day. The fashionable tone had been set by the marital history of the elegant Mary of Teck whose first match, to Prince Albert 'Eddy', the queen's grandson, had been planned for 1892. Mary had been planning a lily of the valley dress designed by the famous art nouveau Silver Studios, before the groom died unexpectedly in a flu epidemic that January. Mary laid her orange-blossom bouquet upon Albert's grave and consented to marry his brother George instead, whose wife she became in July 1893. Thirteen carriages had conveyed the guests under streaming garlands and flags, through pillars dressed up to resemble marble, to see the bride in her satin gown, an S-shaped corset, cascades of lace, flowers and feathers. Her picture was reproduced in newspapers, magazines and postcards, inspiring young women of the era to follow suit.

Marrying early in 1895, Millicent Vaughan's big day was hosted by her aunt Julia, mother of the young Virginia Woolf, in their Hyde Park Gate home. The house, Virginia recorded, was thrown into chaos, with doors taken off their hinges, 'multitudes' of lamps and flowers, new carpets, a 'magnificent feast', a detective to guard the presents, pretty bridesmaids and rose petal confetti.[1] When Virginia's half-sister Stella was married two years later, it gave the fifteen-year-old fledgling author her 'first vision ... of love between man and woman ... like a ruby ... glowing, red, clear, intense ... a sense that nothing in the world is so lyrical, so musical.'[2] The family ordered their wedding clothes from Bond Street and Oxford Street, the cake from the famous Gunter's, they experimented with hairstyles in a Kensington salon and purchased their gifts. The wedding favours combined flowers and ribbons, there was lace underwear and red tulips in the church. It took almost three hours for the bride to unwrap her presents, before treating her guests to a 'scrumptious Charbonnel tea, with iced coffee'.[3] This was the ideal, but the times were changing.

Not all late Victorian women were falling over themselves to catch a husband. As they reached their late teens, Sophie, Ida and Fernande found themselves poised on the verge of adulthood at a unique historical moment, when new ambitions called old values into question and women were embracing educational opportunities as a way of redefining their lives. Many girls received only rudimentary schooling before leaving for employment at the age of ten. The Elementary Education Act of 1888 was amended in 1893, raising the school leaving age to eleven and again in 1899, to twelve. Girton, the first all-female college at Cambridge, had been founded in 1869, followed by the London School of Medicine in 1874, Oxford's Lady Margaret Hall in 1878, Somerville in 1879 and St Hilda's in 1893. Ida's aunt Lucy rejected marriage in favour of a career. She attended lectures at Queen's College, Cork, but was not permitted to take a degree; instead she trained as a pharmacist, lectured at the London School of Medicine and was elected as the first female fellow of the Institute of Chemistry in 1894. 'It was a strange time,' wrote novelist and activist Charlotte Despard, 'unsatisfactory, full of ungratified aspirations. I longed ardently to be of some use in the world, but as we were girls with a little money and born into a particular social position, it was not thought necessary that we should do anything but amuse ourselves until the time and the opportunity of marriage came along ... The woman of the well-to-do classes was made to understand early that the only door open to a life at once easy and respectable was that of marriage.'[4]

In 1894, the English-born journalist Sarah Grand coined the phrase 'the New Woman,' in an essay in the *North American Review*. Having submitted to marriage at an early age in spite of her considerable ambition, Grand identified the emergence of a new female sensibility; an individual who desired education, emancipation, independence, including sexual liberation. Amid much satire, this new trope appeared in plays by Henrik Ibsen and George Bernard Shaw and novels by Henry James and H. G. Wells, as well as through popular culture. Part heroine, part devil, the 'new woman' offered a tempting alternative for Sophie, Ida, Fernande and their contemporaries. The Fabian and social campaigner Clementina Black summed up the mood of many women when she wrote that the institution of marriage needed to evolve with the times:

> Marriage, like all other human institutions, is not permanent and inalterable in form, but necessarily changes shape with the changes of social development. The forms of marriage are transitional, like the societies in which they exist. Each age keeps getting ahead of the law, yet there are always some laggards of whom the law for the time being is ahead. The main tendency of our own age is towards greater freedom and equality, and the law is slowly modifying to match ... At present the strict letter of the law denies to a married woman the freedom of action which more and more women are coming to regard not only as their just but also as their dearest treasure; and this naturally causes a certain unwillingness on the part of the thoughtful women to marry.[5]

In Poland and France, Sophie and Fernande came under pressure from their families to accept unwanted marriage proposals. Initially, neither of them was opposed to marriage as a concept, in fact the lack of affection they shared made them both actively long for romance and love. And this warmth was tantalisingly within reach, encountered in the streets, on social occasions and among the extended family. Yet their efforts to connect with sympathetic men were thwarted by financial and moral questions. Their courtship histories expose just how little real control they had over their lives in the face of parental pressure and male desire. Both were acutely aware of the loss of freedom such a union would entail, as well as the dangers of sex, to their reputations and their health, in the event of pregnancy and childbirth. The stigma of illegitimacy haunted Fernande, while Sophie had observed the misery of marital unhappiness. As intelligent young women, they were aware that marriage was not their only option, with Sophie longing to write and Fernande's teachers keen to enter her for an exam that would qualify her for the teaching profession. A life as a teacher or governess provided a viable alternative to marriage, allowing an intelligent girl to escape an unhappy family situation and acquire a degree of independence.

Having passed through puberty, Sophie was considered less of a burden to her family and more as a valuable marital commodity. Nor was she unattractive, as H. S. Ede's description of her in her late thirties proves, accentuating her diminutive height, pointed chin, thin lips, tilted nose, sensitive nostrils, large eyelids, and wide staring eyes.[6] A sultry blue and orange oriental style pastel drawing of a reclining woman survives in the Tate collection: dark hair coiled up, arched eyebrows, aristocratic nose, prominent lips, indigo shadows under her cheek bones. This was Sophie aged forty. Writing around the same time, Brodsky described her as 'proud without being haughty ... sweet and charming', with an 'artistic temperament ... erratic and volcanic in nature ... amiable and jolly despite her background of misery and depression'. Physically he saw her as beautiful but short, with an 'unattractive carriage', although she had a 'finely formed head set on a small body'. In later life, she 'did not follow fashion but (was) attractively clothed' with merry and sparkling eyes which 'radiated intelligence'.[7] Gaudier's colourful pastels seemed to support this.

The world of adult sexuality and marriage negotiations that Sophie entered at the age of sixteen was fraught with family jealousies. Keen to benefit from the possible financial benefits, her mother initiated discussions with Jewish intermediaries, the traditional matchmakers, to find a wealthy husband for the 'lively ... exuberant ... idealistic'[8] Sophie. They found a willing young man to whom Sophie refers in her autobiography as 'X,' a 'stupid ... ridiculous ... pot-bellied young man' who would make her a laughing stock. Sophie did not hide her disdain, showing her 'huge aversion to the gentleman ... very strongly and to his face' but her mother threatened to make her life a 'complete misery ... and impossible' [9] unless she consented to an engagement. Faced with this reality, Sophie complied. Rings were exchanged and the matter went so far as for the banns to be read out in church but the bride was making herself ill. Sophie was 'wasting away with nobody taking pity'[10] and planned to commit suicide at the last moment, as the only escape she could imagine. It was often a stance she adopted when under pressure, although she never seems to have made any serious attempt on her life: it was more the expression of desperation from a completely powerless child. To Sophie's immense relief though, the threat was suddenly removed without the need for action on her part. Her rapacious parents took offence as soon as the bridegroom's family demanded a dowry. The Brzeskis' high social status is again suggested by her father's anger at the 'obscure' young man's failure to be 'sufficiently honoured' by the offer of his daughter's hand. He was insulted by their request for money, having hoped to send her 'like Cinderella with nothing, not even a trousseau'. In 'transports of joy,' Sophie returned her ring.[11]

Although she had disliked her parents' first choice of husband, Sophie was not averse to the idea of marriage, especially considering the comparative freedom it could bring. An opportunity to escape her 'hell' presented itself when she went to stay at the home of her cousins. Her sympathetic male cousin 'pretended to fall violently in love' with her, even though she did not really like him and was 'suspicious of his transports and heated declarations'. At this point, Sophie hints that she had actually fallen in love with someone else; she had 'given my heart to a young man whom seemed to me to be good and noble' – who had married someone else because Sophie was too poor. It was in the wake of this, in her 'despair' and not wishing to 'fall under the venomous teeth' of her mother again, that she consented to become engaged to her ardent cousin. The action went 'against (her) heart' but stemmed from a desperate need to 'feel sympathy for a human creature' and her fiancé's feelings for her had provoked an 'affectionate friendship'.[12] Once again, the question of money arose, leading to a fierce quarrel over a game of cards, and the young man was sent packing. Still respecting her parents' decisions, docile and unquestioning as her upbringing 'deep in the country' had made her, Sophie accepted their behaviour and learned to loathe her former fiancé and then to forget him.

At the age of nineteen or twenty, Sophie managed to escape home again by staying with another group of cousins. The concentration of families to the north and east of Krakow in the 1890s bearing the name

Brzeski tallies with her information, suggesting a sizeable network of relatives – and potential partners. On this occasion, she developed a more genuine romantic attachment, finding a sympathetic friend who was kind and affectionate, but not particularly good-looking. In *Matka* she refers to him as 'Y'. 'Everyone takes pity on him,' Sophie recorded, because he was 'without position' and had neither beauty nor brains.[13] He was a distant cousin, as his mother was the sister of Sophie's cousin's husband, although this mother also claimed descent from a German line, so they were related by marriage rather than blood. Sophie appreciated his kindness and his obvious affection for her, judging that looks were nothing in comparison. They exchanged promises and, during their 'intimacies' he attempted to persuade her to relinquish her virginity, to take her 'into the dangerous paths of love'. Yet the notion of purity had been instilled in her, along with the belief that 'only the legitimate wife ... had the right to enjoy love completely,' so at first she rejected him 'in spite of passion'. However, Sophie hints that she may have given in and slept with her admirer, as after she explains her scruple in *Matka*, she adds that 'then I overcame it.'[14] This may have been a confession about the new level of their physical intimacy, although it is rather ambiguous.

Yet the problem of her father's imminent bankruptcy proved to be decisive for a third time. His 'brute of a materialistic mother,' who was 'rich enough, very miserly, squalid (and) greedy' opposed the match because of the lack of dowry and created an 'inferno of intrigue' in the house. The lovers were forbidden to meet, despite exchanging letters professing undying affection and, although Sophie continued to cherish hopes, she later heard of his attempts to make a more 'profitable' marriage.[15]

After this string of romantic disappointments, Sophie decided that she would try to further her education as best she could. The life she had known was crumbling as her father's years of regular debauchery in Krakow finally caught up with him and he was declared bankrupt. Sophie begged her parents to give her the means to earn her own living, to let her go to town 'for a year or two so that (she) could learn a trade' but she was told she should find a husband, despite being too poor, too ugly and 'too dangerous for a faithful wife having too much temperament'. Instead, Sophie saved 'hundreds of francs on (her) clothes and went to town to study'.[16]

Exactly what she meant by 'town' is difficult to know; whether it was the nearest large urban centre, or Krakow. She may have enrolled in the university there or one of the private gymnasiums that were increasingly prepared to accept women. It is also possible that she followed the study pattern she would later adopt in Paris; attending free lectures, museums and reading in public libraries, driven by intellectual curiosity. Following the advice of a sympathetic aunt, Sophie took courses on French, German, English and book-keeping, for which she felt little aptitude and toiled unhappily, even 'frantically' for six months.[17] She may have lodged cheaply in a city boarding house, or stayed with relatives and, for the first time, experienced the sort of freedom and independence that gave her a taste for study and travel. Perhaps she attended the newly built baroque-style Municipal Theatre (later the Juliusz Slowacki Theatre), with its new electric lighting or viewed the National Museum's impressive collection of Polish works of art, to celebrate the threatened national identity. Miles from the neglect of her mother and constant teasing of her brothers, Sophie's horizons expanded considerably. Education could provide the ticket to employment and freedom. If she acquired enough learning, she could take on that notorious role of mixed blessings, the governess, which would give her a glimmer of social standing and protection.

Then, in 1899, Sophie received news that her father Mieczyslaw had died at the age of fifty-eight or fifty-nine. One of her many cousins bought the estate and her mother had been left as administrator. Sophie assisted her, helping with everything whilst still pursuing her studies and hoping to find a teaching job abroad 'in order to perfect (her) languages'. But instead of appreciating the support, her mother chased her out of the house, telling her 'I don't care where you go – go and work in a shop, it's all the same to me, get out!' Her attitude was quite different towards two of Sophie's brothers who remained at home, aged twenty-one and twenty-four, who were 'looked after and fed', supported while they studied. Sophie concluded that her mother 'hoped to be maintained by them later', or even that, at the age of fifty-three, she was hoping to remarry.[18] Sophie returned to Krakow, where she accepted 'a small mean job as a provincial housekeeper'. She 'starved' in the job and was 'extremely weak physically and morally', suffering from the chronic stomach catarrh that her father had experienced.[19] However, she had formulated a plan to join an uncle in Paris and began to put aside a little money to pay for her journey.

*

On the streets of Paris, sexuality was more difficult to avoid than among the extended families of Sophie's Polish countryside. Four years before Fernande's birth, the prolific novelist Emile Zola had created Nana, one of the most famous courtesans of French literature, who debuted as an eighteen-year-old in *L'Assommoir* before becoming the heroine of her own story in 1880. The brothels and 'maisons de tolerance' of the Pigalle and Montmartre were being brilliantly recreated by Henri de Toulouse-Lautrec, in sympathetic works like the 1894 'In the Salon at the Rue des Moulins' and 'The Sofa'. It was the era of the Moulin Rouge, where the double-jointed dancer La Goulue invented the Can Can, Yvette Guibert and Jane Avril sang and the champagne flowed all the way from the cabaret to the brothel. The law insisted that such establishments were discreet in appearance, regulated and run by women but, apart from that, there was no intervention, from the high-class Le Chabanais, frequented by the Prince of Wales, to the small-scale establishments such as that on the ground floor of the Petot family tenement in the Rue de Réamur.

At sixteen, Fernande was only vaguely aware of the establishment three floors below them, which she described as a 'shop'. She and her cousin were forbidden by Aunt Alice to look at it, but look at it was precisely what the curious young girl did, thinking it 'enormous fun' and wondering 'what harm there can be?'[20] The shop front was painted green with strange red and yellow figures, with the door set back behind a green trellis and the glass in the front windows opaque for privacy. It was owned by a fat woman with red, dishevelled hair, and when she appeared in the street, haloed by the brilliant light behind, Fernande could hear music playing in the room. The girl saw this madame in something of a romantic light, describing her amid all the darkness as 'a luminous or supernatural apparition' and the women inside as wearing 'fancy-dress', venturing out only on public holidays, to dance in the street.[21] Charles Petot referred to the brothel in hushed terms as the 'convent', fuelling Fernande's fear of being locked up there as a punishment and pitying the women inside. Too naïve to comprehend its true nature, Fernande instinctively understood that the 'shop' represented something illicit and raised questions about it in her diary that were destined to go unanswered. This establishment, literally on her doorstep, represented the dangerous Parisian proximity of innocence and experience, which, along with the family's refusal to discuss Fernande's parentage, made the young girl aware of a thin veneer of respectability under which the taboo of sexuality lurked.

With her thick, wavy chestnut hair, Fernande was an attractive girl, as the earliest photographs of her show. She was critical of her looks, though, acknowledging that while others might appreciate her, she didn't 'like (her) type of beauty'. Her breasts were like 'two half apples stuck onto a chest' that protruded too much, her eyes were too small and her hair too curly. As a younger girl, she had used to 'cry in front of the mirror' because of the unfavourable comparisons her aunt used to draw between Fernande and her cousin, whose eyes were 'big as doorways' and who had lovely plump hands instead of the fingers of 'a monkey or midwife'.[22] In an effort to improve her appearance, Alice sent Fernande to the hairdresser, where the girl was forced to submit to 'ridiculous' styles, 'like a monument' or wear stiff ringlets when she preferred her hair loose or plaited. Alice also made Fernande's clothes herself, which were 'too short' and 'hideous' in colours she disliked and ostrich feathers in her hat, not the parrot feathers she thought were so pretty.[23] In spite of her aunt's best efforts, though, she was already attracting attention.

At the age of sixteen Fernande mentions her first admirer, knowing 'perfectly well' that she had 'made an impression' upon the tall, dark-haired boy who worked for her uncle. There were others, too, of whose gaze she was aware, youths who had 'never spoken to (her) but who come out into the street or stand by the window when they see (her.)'[24] Whilst staying with the Labrosse family at Méru that summer, the local coachbuilder asked for her hand in marriage after having glimpsed her as she passed his house. He was the 'richest fellow for ten leagues around' but she was considered too young at the time.[25] Then, the night before she was due to leave for home, Fernande attended a dance at the local inn, where she was approached by the grocer's son, who said he would like to marry her if she could wait three years until he had completed his national service. Back in Paris, she was admired by the shirt maker who lived opposite, college boys on the walk to school, a young man named Albert, others named Pierre and Gaston, and, at Berck, a boy in the next chalet. Mostly, it was shy glances and smiles but there were also compliments and letters exchanged on street corners.

Fernande was appreciative of the beauty of her friend Antoinette Seller, who showed her breasts in the bedroom when the girls were alone together and when Fernande stayed the night, they lay together 'right up close,' cuddling, and falling asleep 'entwined'. Fernande commented that it was 'very sweet' and that she felt like crying at the thought of returning home.[26] The possibility of being a lesbian did not enter Fernande's mind any more than a real understanding of the mechanics of heterosexual intercourse. While homosexuality was castigated in France at the time, with Zola refusing to publish the memoirs of a gay Italian aristocrat, same-sex relations between women was considered a 'chic urban vice' amongst the upper classes. Julien Chevalier's 1893 *Inversion Sexuelle* helped make it a fashionable 'neurosis' among leisured women, a bohemianism fuelled by the works of Toulouse-Lautrec and racy novels by Catulle Mèndes and Maurice de Souillac. In 1889, the erotic lesbian novel *Ze Boïm*, with its suggestive cover, was censored and its author and publisher fined and briefly imprisoned.[27] Fernande would not have associated her activities with Antoinette as comparable; they speak more of experimentation and the desire for affection.

Over the next year, Fernande attracted many admirers, who increasingly absorbed her attention and raised her previously low sense of self-worth. Almost any young man of sufficient good looks was fair game, yet there is a childishness and restraint about these flirtations; some are labelled 'boyfriends' or 'admirers' after fleeting eye contact in the street; one who was bold enough to write a love letter and follow her home was immediately promoted to the status of 'lover' and the subject of marriage fantasies. Insecurity and the fear of discovery prevented many fledgling relationships developing beyond an initial connection: 'but I can't make a date with him, he's crazy! What if we met someone!' The seventeen-year-old Fernande's raptures smack of innocent flattery and a craving for affection; 'yet I must hear him say such nice things to me, I'm not used to it. All of a sudden I need this as much as I need air to breathe.'[28] Most suitors were acquired in the street, on the walk to school, or on holidays or public occasions.

The boys themselves are shadowy and two-dimensional, rapidly replaced and soon forgotten; consistently, though, they are the instigators, surprising Fernande with their interest. There seems to have been little opportunity for courtship or developing an understanding of the opposite sex; only polarities of experience were available; the distant, courtly-love style crush or the impromptu engagement, often offered by a man she did not know. Men emerge in the diaries as one of two extremes; bashful boys or urgent men seeking to legitimise their sexual impulses. They seem to arise as a danger, a threat to the academic path her teachers were keen to set out for her.

Increasingly, young women in France were seeking the opportunities offered by work. For various reasons, the French suffrage movement advanced at a different rate to its English counterpart but, gradually, more women joined the workforce: after the introduction of free primary education in 1881, girls who previously would have begun unskilled, low-paid jobs at a young age, could now gain qualifications leading to a position that included a degree of upward social mobility. Contemporary French statistics show that in 1913 the post office employed 13,000 women nationally, while 8 per cent of pharmacists were female, as were 3 per cent of doctors, and there was a fifteen per cent rise in the proportion of women in banking between 1866 and 1911. By the time that Fernande was faced with decisions about her educational future, the Sorbonne was already accepting women students, who comprised 11% of their intake in 1897, which rose to 22% in 1906.[29]

To her aunt's surprise, Fernande was proving a success at school. In July 1897, at the age of sixteen, she won first prizes in French composition, history, recitation, reading and English, with a second in drawing. One of her prizes was a book about mythology, in which she saw a likeness of herself in an illustration of Minerva, although she would have preferred to be Diana. Another was an atlas about half a metre long, which was difficult to hold under the arm. Far from being proud though, she was embarrassed, feeling her prizes a burden, longing to go home and showing more interest in a visit to a café on the way home. In her diary, she claimed that the 'idiotic' formal clothes and hairstyle imposed by her aunt spoiled the occasion for her but these may have been masking her true discomfort. Expressing frequent surprise at having done so well and confessing to lacking faith in her own abilities, Fernande preferred not to dwell on success because 'whatever I win I'll still be criticised.'[30]

Increasingly, her attitude became mixed, even apathetic. She admitted she 'would often get top grades' but also that her results 'came too easily' and agreed with her teachers that with harder work, her results would be even better: criticised in later life for her self-confessed laziness, she already knew 'I only like work that amuses or interests me.'[31] One experience that engaged her enthusiasm was a production of *Pour la Couronne* Uncle Charles took her to see at the Odéon Theatre, after which she determined to become a tragic actress and study at the Conservatoire. Aunt Alice's reaction was to predict the complete disgrace by association she had always been certain of, by alluding to her illegitimacy: 'Mind you, it doesn't surprise me, blood will tell.' As the number of Fernande's admirers increased, writing her diary and reading love letters began to take precedence over homework, causing her school work to slide. 'This morning in class, I didn't know my lessons. I did everything the wrong way round and failed to do a simple equation.'[32]

The following year, at seventeen, Fernande prepared for her diploma. The pressure made her ill beforehand, inducing a 'sort of black out', which was unsatisfactorily explained by the doctor's suggestion of a 'weak heart'. She was advised not to work too hard but sat the exam regardless a few days later and 'would have done exceedingly well'[33] if her maths mark hadn't brought the average down. She was awarded fifth prize, gaining entry to the Sophie Germain School at 9, Rue de Jouy. The establishment had been set up in 1882, with sixty-five pupils. It adopted the mathematician and philosopher Germain as its patron six years later, and as a symbol of the female struggle for equal education. By 1900, 425 girls were enrolled in the majestic building in the Marais, known as the Hotel de Fourcy, built around a cobbled courtyard hidden behind plain double doors onto the street. A family dinner was held in celebration of the news, at which Fernande was guest of honour but this still did not prevent her aunt from serving her last at table. Receiving her final awards at the high school ceremony, again paralysed by the 'huge construction of hair' on which Alice insisted, Fernande was presented with her prizes by the local mayor: Michelet's *Natural History* and a volume on stoic women from Sparta to the French Revolution. Her academic future looked secure but Fernande herself was uncertain. Even when about to enter her new school in the late summer of 1898, she suffered doubts, framed within her conflict with her aunt. 'Why this determination to make me a teacher?' she asked her diary. 'Since I hate the idea, this provides my aunt with a great opportunity to thwart me. I'd so much like to go on the stage. I recite verses to myself, I learn long speeches from the classics and my aunt insists that I perform them at every dinner party she gives or that we go to. And at weddings too!'[34]

Confusingly though, given Fernande's recent academic success, Aunt Alice now proposed she disrupt her education in order to take up a post as a teacher in England. She took her niece to be interviewed at an employment agency run by a Monsieur Lortat and arranged to collect her birth certificate for the necessary paperwork. Perhaps she had decided Fernande was old enough to earn her own living or believed her duty to the girl was nearing its end. Almost eighteen, Fernande was lucky to have remained in education so long and must have been aware of the financial demands continuing her studies would place on her uncle. The Petot family had been in regular receipt of financial assistance from Fernande's natural father but, after supporting and resenting someone else's illegitimate child, Aunt Alice was keen to seize the opportunity of a teaching career for her niece, as well as expanding her skills to include the English language. Whatever her motives, Alice Petot accompanied Fernande to Monsieur Lortat, intending to give her the means to earn a respectable living. It was not to be a viable avenue for her cousin Marguerite who, at fourteen, had still failed to achieve her primary certificate. Fernande did not appreciate her advantages or her aunt's efforts, wishing instead for a more traditional solution: 'How I'd love to be married so as never to have to see her again.'[35] Although she showed great academic promise and her passion for reading would continue throughout her life, Fernande's self-confessed apathy and emerging interest in boys led her away from the type of intellectual escapism relished by Sophie Brzeska.

In the late summer of 1898, a series of events occurred which would change Fernande's life irrevocably.

5

Art School Ingénue

In 1860, the all-male Admissions board of Royal Academicians gathered inside the grey, Palladian mansion of Burlington House. Under the presidency of the historical painter Charles Lock Eastlake, they included such luminaries as Edwin Landseer, Thomas Heatherley and W. P. Frith, whose iconic works had defined artistic style in the early-Victorian era. On this occasion, they were so impressed by the technical skill displayed in a submission of drawings that an offer was made to an 'L. Herford, esquire,' to take up a place as a student of the Academy. Having resisted pressure to admit female students for the last two decades, the Academy was thrown into disarray when the new student appeared, named Laura, and dressed in crinoline and bonnet; by then it was too late to withdraw the offer. In the following years, a gradual trickle of talented women infiltrated the system, but each subsequent battle was hard-won. Forbidden from drawing life models, the women petitioned for equality in 1878, 1880 and 1883-4, but were not successful until 1893, when women artists were finally permitted to draw partially draped bodies.

At the end of the nineteenth century, Ida's generation was still struggling with their parents for permission to enjoy the same opportunities offered to their brothers. In Hyde Park Gate, the young Virginia and Vanessa Stephen were given lessons in languages, drawing and dancing, while their brothers were sent away to preparatory schools as a prelude to Cambridge. Gwen Darwin was fortunate that her parents took her artistic talents seriously and engaged Graham Greene's aunt to guide her drawing. In Wales, Gwen John had to fight to persuade her father to let her join her younger brother, Augustus, at art school and her fellow alumni, Gwen Salmond and Ursula Tyrwhitt, joined them against the loud protestations of their families. The struggle was complicated by the fact that some well-heeled 'artistic' parents considered a few years spent drawing as an alternative 'finishing school' for their daughters, as a prelude to marriage. As late as 1910, Slade School Professor Frederick Brown told Dorothy Brett, 'We don't like people from your class. They usually come only for amusement or because they are bored at home. They take the place of a girl or boy who needs a scholarship,'[1] yet he was forced to admit her after her portfolio revealed her talent. Other eminent Victorians allowed their daughters to pursue art once it was a proven passion: Leslie Stephen arranged for Vanessa's tutelage with a Mr Cope in South Kensington and later at the Royal Academy; Charles Darwin's granddaughter Gwen's prowess convinced her parents to let her attend the Slade; Dora Carrington's mother stipulated she might only attend if she lodged in an all-female boarding house nearby. Lord Esher had resisted for almost a decade until friends intervened to release his daughter Dorothy, who entered the Slade Art School at the age of twenty-seven.

Founded in 1871 by philanthropist Felix Slade as part of University College London, the Slade Art School had been opened with the express purpose of offering an artistic education to men and women. Other art schools did admit women, especially Kensington and Heatherley but the courses there could be 'tedious and some of the pupils of rather humble origin' so it was 'to be expected' that middle and upper-class young ladies would opt for the Slade, under the leadership of its first Professor, the distinguished pre-Raphaelite painter Edward Poynter.[2] Among its early intake were Evelyn de Morgan (née Mary Pickering) in 1873, who overcame parental disapproval to win a scholarship, Mary Sargeant-Florence, whose daughter Alix Strachey would translate Freud, Emily Kemp, who was a graduate of Somerville College, portraitist Beatrice Offor and Clare Atwood, who achieved notoriety for living in a lesbian ménage à trois, which included Edith, the daughter of actress Ellen Terry, the client of Ada Nettleship. The sculptresses Ellen Mary Rope and

Rosamund Praegar were also recent graduates, embarking on the next stage of their careers by exhibiting at the Royal Academy and studying in Paris respectively. The Slade had secured its reputation with such pupils, and by 1892, when Ida applied to study there, was dominated by three teachers, Professor Fred Brown, ex-surgeon Henry Tonks and English Impressionist P. Wilson Steer.

The 1890s represented a period later Slade students looked back upon as a golden era, the first of two that Professor Henry Tonks referred to as a 'crisis of brilliance'. Augustus John explained this as being due to the presence of so many 'talented and highly ornamental girl students: the men cut a shabbier figure and seemed far less gifted' in comparison.[3] Also enrolling in 1892 was Emily Beatrice Bland, then in her late twenties, who had already studied at Lincoln Art School, and was soon followed by the talented Edna Waugh, one of the youngest pupils at the age of fourteen, Ethel Hatch, who was Lewis Carroll's much-photographed 'Alice', the educated and experienced Ethel Walker, the Welsh Gwen John, Australian Dora Meeson and sculptor Katharine Maltwood.

The Nettleships were well able to afford the fifteen guineas annual fee for Ida to attend the Slade yet, at first, her relative youth prevented her from studying full time. The usual age of their first-year students was sixteen to eighteen on commencing a three-year course, so she enrolled part-time in 1892 at the age of fifteen, attending three days a week in order to practise her drawing technique in preparation for full-time study later. The decision to allow her to pursue art as a career in the 1890s was not revolutionary but did represent some forward thinking on the part of John and Ada. Nettleship was also following a Bedford Park tradition. Jack B Yeats' talented son, six years Ida's senior, had been taught at Westminster School by a Professor Frederick Brown, who was about to transfer to the Slade.

Arriving in the morning, Ida would sign the attendance register; ladies on the left-hand page and gentlemen on the right. For most of her first year she was forbidden to speak to the model or any young men she might happen to meet on the stairs. The masters insisted that the Slade was not to become a 'dating agency', although some actually believed that the sexes would benefit from being taught together, so long as the promising young women were not seduced by offers of marriage.[4] In the 1890s, the student body comprised two-thirds men and one-third women and the surviving floor plan shows that the women were located mainly in the basement.[5] Student Wyn George was advised by one of the female Slade teachers that

Man and woman are equal ... (but) a woman cannot compete with a man on his ground ... there has never been any very great woman painter, which goes to show that man has a greater creative, more imaginative force than a woman, and the woman has more intuitiveness of refinement, grace and beauty in drawing. So many women go onto men's line and it is hopeless ... woman must find out her ... groove in art and never attempt to do things as a man.[6]

The fear of seeming masculine did not stop competition between the sexes; in 1896, Ida would write to her sister that she was smoking a cigarette, usually an exclusively male pleasure, before beginning to sketch, as tobacco was thought to stimulate creativity.[7]

Since its inaugural lecture, Slade teaching methods favoured the French emphasis on realistic sketching, producing swift, clear and accurate lines. At that time it was essentially a drawing school, and many pupils supplemented their training by attending artists' studios after hours. All students began in the Antique room, where 'casts of Classical and Renaissance sculpture were scattered everywhere, around the walls, on plinths, on trestle-tables or simply lying on the floor; heads, busts, torsos, complete figures; here and there an odd foot. Among these and various overhanging plants, the students worked, most of them seated astride wooden donkeys.'[8] Contemporary photographs show the women, seated on these wooden trestles with their hair scooped up and their clothes covered with voluminous white aprons. Their sketches are pinned to boards resting on half-easels as they contemplate the Greek heads in white marble.

After rigorous training, Ida progressed to life drawing, which for the women took place in a small room on the first floor, governed by yet more strict rules. The female students and professors were not permitted, on grounds of decency, to be together in the room at the same time with the morally 'dubious' nude models. This meant the girls had to file out and wait, whilst comments were written on the bottom of their work, then file back in for the next session. The environment was very different in the men's large room in the basement, which 'smelt like a chapel and extended upwards through two stories', full of tobacco smoke, heated by the coke stove and the hot water pipes. However, their drawing methods as described by student Adrian Allinson, were the same as for the girls: '...a chorus of voices sang out "Change." Whereupon to my surprise, the model took up an entirely new pose ... this was life drawing with a vengeance ... the last hour of the day was devoted to short poses, the drawings of which should train the eye to quick reactions.'[9]

The greatest initial influence upon Ida was the drawing master Henry Tonks, who had trained as a surgeon and used his precise anatomical knowledge to set a new standard in the Antique room. His teaching emphasised draughtsmanship and the emulation of old masters such as Rembrandt, Ingres, Rubens, Watteau and Michelangelo; but his methods became the stuff of Slade legend, especially the criticism reserved for female students, regularly reduced to tears by the cutting comments that they would be better off at home, sewing or knitting. The best response to this was made by Barbara Baegnal, who earned his respect with the prompt reply that she had made every stitch of clothing on her body, but he succeeded in scaring away Vanessa Stephen (later Bell), who only managed to endure him for a few weeks and defected instead to the Royal Academy School. Usually, though, students knew they broke his strict rules at their peril: according to John, they were allowed only paper, charcoal and a 'chunk of bread for rubbing out'.[10] Tonks was known to throw erasers out of the window in a rage. His reputation was still fearsome by the time of Gwen Darwin's arrival in 1908 and his criticism was unsubtle. 'After staring at a piece of work with his heavy lidded-eyes, he could demolish it with a pithy phrase,' such as 'what is it? Horrible! Is it an insect?' Gwen's contemporary Paul Nash summed up the teacher's influence: 'Tonks was the Slade and the Slade was Tonks and some students took up the chant, "I am the Lord thy God, thou shalt have no other Tonks but me."'[11]

Ida reached the Slade a year before Henry Tonks but his later influence over her was immense; during her second and third year she and fellow student Edna Waugh shared the sole purpose of trying to please him and both achieved a degree of success; Edna even became one of his favourites and attended his famous 'at home' teas. Often working together or sitting for each other in dramatic poses, the girls literally tied themselves in knots to please him in their biblically and mythically inspired pieces. Tied to the bedstead by Ida, for her 'Stoning of Nabob', Edna had to plead to be released from ropes which had cut into her flesh: all in the name of Tonks. Despite his fearsome exterior, their teacher was committed to the equal education of his female students once they had proved their skill and intentions. He demanded their full attention and raged about promising girl students who had deserted their studies in order to marry. He inspired the girls, as well as later students, to be as dedicated and fanatical about art as himself; firing them with his belief that 'in art, nothing short of the best would do and everything must be sacrificed to achieve it,'[12] a total commitment which Ida and Edna's later lives made it difficult for them to fulfil.

Ida must have pleased her teachers, for in 1895 she won a three-year scholarship and was able to enrol that autumn as a full-time student, from ten o'clock until five each day. Being a full-time student also enabled her to maintain and develop the friendships she had made. Aged eighteen, lacking significant male friends outside the home, she was still childlike and fey in her friendships and outlook, keeping herself aloof from the students who referred to her circle as 'the nursery'. Delighted by the recent publication of Kipling's *The Jungle Book*, Ida renamed herself 'Mowgli' giving her friends animal pet names and rapidly developing a clique who encouraged each other's work and indulged in intense, sentimental Victorian friendships. The girls regularly exchanged letters of passionate devotion and small tokens of their affection such as rosaries, pin cushions and flowers. To Dorothy Salaman she concluded one letter; 'Bless you with jungle joy. Your bad little man-cub, Mistress Mowgli Nettleship.'[13] In a similar vein, two fellow students, Logic Whiteway and Dolly Jeffrey, later produced a book of caricatures of friends and tutors, called the 'Slade Animal Land', where the Tonk was a 'voracious bird which lives on the tears of silly girls'. Ursula was the Peewit, Ida the Nettlebug, Gwen John the Gwengion.[14] John's biographer, Michael Holroyd refers to this as a 'golden world of Victorian emotionalism, a timeless place with the prospect of being girls eternal', stressing the cosy safety net of these relationships when the prospect of imminent marriage and its ensuing dangers became increasingly difficult to deny.

Of all her companions, Ida's closest friend was Edna Waugh, with whom she drew, read poetry and roamed the countryside with sketchbooks, often around the Waugh's family home in St. Albans. Their friendship continued in the same intense vein established by the language of the Kiplingesque animal menagerie. Her letters to Edna – 'my willow,' 'my darling,' 'my wondrous lady of the flowers' – reveal a passionate, sentimental vocabulary of wooing in the vein of her favourite poets; she was Edna's 'slave' and 'servant', with 'a great bosom of longing for thee' and recalling their walks under 'those whispering trees that ever wave an adieu.'[15] Such emotions were commonplace in single or mixed gender Victorian and Edwardian friendships; contemporaneous letters from offspring of the pre-Raphaelite group and their circle employ similar images and passions; sentimental friendships were tolerated, even encouraged as a desirable outlet for passion.

Into the girl's close friendship now came the first real threat to their youthful innocence, even though both were too naïve to see it for what it was. Often on their country walks, Ida and Edna were accompanied by William Clarke Hall, a barrister in his late twenties, who had known Edna since before her Slade days and would become her husband in 1898. Before Clarke Hall's unexpected declaration to Edna, the girls never questioned his motives or their perception of his innocence and 'Willie' became the first significant male friend Ida made independently of her parents; she and Clarke Hall began a correspondence based mostly upon their country rambles and mutual admiration of their friend.

Other young men began to infringe upon the close female group. When fellow student Dorothy 'Baloo' Salaman, introduced Ida to her brothers, the young men were immediately impressed by her looks. Aged nineteen, Ida had blossomed into 'a very sexually attractive girl, with slanted oriental eyes, a sensuous mouth, dark curly hair and a dark complexion' but even more appealing was her

'untamed … smouldering … enigmatic' quality.[16] Early sketches
of Ida, made by Augustus John in the coming years, wearing a
wide brimmed hat and sultry expression, capture an alluring blend
of youthful provocation; the full lips and penetrating eyes are
particularly remarkable in each, as is the well-developed, womanly
figure. Her character was one of mystery too, with Arthur Symons
describing her as 'as wild as a Maenad in a wood pursued by Pan …
intractable, a creature of uncertain moods and passions. One never
knew what she was going to say or do … the almost terrible
fascination of the wild beast … something almost witch-like in her.'

The Salamans were a large wealthy Jewish family living at 20,
Pembridge Crescent, Kensington. Their father, Myer, then in his
fifties, was a merchant dealing in ostrich feathers, and their mother
Sarah, had borne eleven surviving children, then living at their
Kensington address. The census of 1891 records that Clement
was the eldest at twenty-three, a student-at-law, while his brothers
Elkin and Euston, aged twenty and nineteen, were feather buyers
for the family business. The other brothers, still at school, were
Redcliffe, Harry, Michel and Archibold, who was only five. Of the
four girls, Bessie was slightly older than Ida, while Louisa shared
her birth year of 1877; Dorothy was then nine and Brenda seven.[17]
Earlier census records indicate that there were four older children
who had left home, including a son, Isaac. In 1891, the family had
six live-in servants – a cook, housemaids, general servants and a
nurse. Today, the house stands solid and double-fronted, detached
and four-storeys high, with a wide set of steps leading up to the
front door inside a pillared portico. The remnants of a front garden
remain behind the low brick wall, which would formerly have been
topped with iron railings, obscuring the view to the cellar windows.

The Salamans could afford to send at least four siblings to the
Slade during this period; their money had been 'raised from ostrich
hunting' and was now sometimes used in the more traditionally
English pursuit of foxes. The son of a feather dealer, Myer had built
up the family business in Lamb's Conduit Street.

He died in 1896, just after Ida had come to know him, but the
business was continued by Isaac, with premises on the corner of
Falcon Square and Monkwell Street. All the Salaman children were
red-headed and conventionally good looking. Art student Michel was

already a particular friend of the young Augustus John, accompanying him on home visits to Wales. The older Clement, born in 1868, was training to be a barrister and considered by the Nettleships to be a suitable catch. Ida wrote to Edna that she and Clement were the two people she cared about most, but she also confessed she did not love him, not yet. This did not prevent her from indulging in a little mild courtship and kissing, responding crossly to her sister Ethel when she discovered them together, claiming such activity should not be laughed at because it was 'holy'. A sketch of Clement made in 1909 shows a solid, well-modelled face, with intense eyes, pronounced nose and sensitive mouth, while one surviving photograph from 1929 captures a tall, white-haired distinguished-looking man.

Clement's affections were much stronger than Ida's. He had serious intentions and became more ardent in his wooing. Although she had confessed the nature of her lukewarm feelings to Edna, Ida was deeply entrenched in social convention and dreams of romance. When Clement proposed in February 1897, she accepted, more to please his sister and her parents than out of real desire. She saw marriage as an inevitability, although did not feel herself prepared for it and tried to keep the reality at a distance. When William Clarke Hall shocked the naïve Edna with his declaration of love, it was to Ida, then holidaying at Aldeburgh in Suffolk, that she turned for advice. Quite possibly drawing from her own lack of feeling for her fiancé, Ida wrote that Edna should wait and be patient; 'she would know' when she grew to love Willie. In the meantime, she should throw herself back into her work and not get distracted: 'walk down that road and don't go looking at the sky.' To Willie, Ida tried to be reassuring whilst conveying the enormity of the step he wanted Edna to take; 'for the present, it is a child's love that Edna bears for you,'[18] hoping he would allow her time to adapt to his expectations of her as a woman. To other girls contemplating marriage, she urged dedication to their work despite outside pressure, 'keep a brave, true heart' and always 'strive high'. To school girls, she advised the best ways to avoid temptations and 'affections' were to take walks and play tennis.[19] It sounds as if she was prepared to be patient while her 'childish' affection for Clement developed into the love that would please her family and secure her social position.

The Slade's female students of the 1890s faced far more of a tug between convention and career than the women of even a decade later, when the 'crop heads' Dora Carrington, Barbara Baegnal and Dorothy Brett chopped off their long hair, donned riding breeches and defied social expectation more openly. The question of women's abilities to combine roles as a successful artist and mother was crucial for Ida's generation, as the slightest defiance of contemporary gender expectations could lead not just to social rejection but the far more damning artistic compromise. In 1924, Edna Waugh (by then, Edna Clarke Hall) found her comeback show marred by patronising male critics wondering what she might have achieved had she not been absent for years raising her children. The *Daily Express* ran the headline 'Woman Painter's Romance: Art sacrificed to Motherhood,' pointing to Edna's choice to stop using acid in her etchings in case they injured her young son, claiming she had 'sacrificed herself on the altar of motherhood'.[20] It wasn't until 1929, more than two decades after Ida's death, that Virginia Woolf summed up most eloquently in *A Room of One's Own* woman's relation to the world and new possibilities: 'then the opportunity will come and the dead poet who was Shakespeare's sister will put on the body which she has so often laid down.'[21]

Other Slade girls of the 1890s were rejecting marriage proposals, or experimenting with alternative living arrangements, in the attempt to preserve their artistic autonomy. Fellow art student Kate Saunders turned down two proposals from Walter Sickert, believing it was not in a woman's interests to marry another artist, as she would 'inevitably relegate her own artistic needs below those of her husband'. Gwen John stated she would prefer to inspire Rodin's art than produce his children, explaining that 'beautiful monuments were erected to artists who produced great works (but) nobody ever erected a great monument to anyone for having children.' Another close friend of Ida's, Ursula Tyrwhitt, had only been allowed to attend the Slade after her family's matchmaking had failed to yield results. Ida's advice to her friends and her own tepid engagement suggests a suspicion that marriage could interfere with, or even end, a young woman's artistic career. It was not until she fell passionately in love that she began to experience this dilemma more keenly.

During the 1890s, the Slade School of Fine Art became synonymous with a particular kind of bohemianism, drawing its influence from the left bank of Paris, from the world into which Fernande was emerging. As early as 1845 Henry Murger had published *Scenes of Bohemian Life*, a collection of stories, thematically linked, set in the Latin Quarter. Three years later, they were dramatised by Théodore Barrière and enjoyed such a successful run at the Théâtre de Variétés that Murger reworked them into a novel in 1851. This would form the basis of Puccini's opera *La Bohème*, which was first produced in 1896. Ida's time at the Slade was also concurrent with the publication of George du Maurier's *Trilby*, presenting the 'alternative' lifestyles of three English artists in Paris, and their models. One art school student, Wyn George, recorded in her diary for 1896-7 that Gwen John had asked her if her name was Trilby, prior to sketching her. Gathering in the Café Royal, which was patronised in the early 1890s by Oscar Wilde and his set, the students experimented with flamboyant, shabby clothing that had the touch of the gypsy; wide-brimmed hats, long hair and earrings, flowing scarves, wide sleeves and loose dresses without corsets. Wyn George noted that 'the girl students are all very nice looking, artistic, most of them very tall and fine, after Venus of Milos types, big waists and figures, hair done very untidily.' Edna Waugh recalled wearing 'a belted overall of Holland, three rows of coral about my throat'.[22] Out of this colourful bohemianism emerged a man who seemed its personification: Augustus Edwin John.

6

New Found Land

It was 1897 or 1898 when Sophie Brzeska travelled the 1,500 kilometres from Krakow to Paris. Far from being the battered city in which Fernande had arrived, it was now in the grip of the Belle Époque, fed by the profits and culture of a flourishing empire, recently host to the World's Fair. Sophie may have stared up at the new Eiffel Tower or strolled in one of the fountain-filled parks, as Fernande and her school friends hurried past. Perhaps she sat beside the girl and her uncle Charles when they went to see the new film *Caligula* at the Odéon or maybe Sophie read the serialised novel *La Porteuse de Pain* in the newspaper, which Charles Petot read aloud to his family each evening after dinner. Crossing the street, drawn by the smell of the boulangerie that Fernande loved, Sophie may have witnessed the girl leaving her school prize-giving, with her elaborate hair-style crowned by a wreath of silver laurel leaves. Perhaps she saw Aunt Alice stop to purchase a little bunch of violets to pin to Fernande's jacket as they made their way to see Monsieur Lortat.[1] Within months, Ida Nettleship would also make her first trip to Paris, bringing all three women within reach of each other for the first and only time in their lives.

Sophie had gone to Paris on the promise of assistance from her uncle. He was a man of forty-four, recently married 'to a French girl who was almost a child,' and the father of a new baby. Only one Brzeski is listed as resident in the city during this period and, if this was a paternal uncle, it is likely to have been Philemon Brzeski and his wife Jeanne Ordo. However, the connection does not directly link back to Sophie's parents and may have been a Witski, or another man related to Sophie, whom she considered an uncle. Whoever it was, Sophie was unhappy under his roof.

She helped with the child and it gave her a place to stay, but increasingly Sophie found her hosts a disappointment, as their home was 'a hovel' and their habits were 'dirty'. Her aristocratic sensibilities were offended, as she described them as living like 'petty country squires' and was forced to be patient, to persevere, while she looked for another position. In the meantime, her aunt joined her husband in being 'indignant at (Sophie's) outmoded ideas of women's virtue and honour', to mock her bad accent and to 'exploit' her.[2]

Desperate to escape, Sophie took a job as a nursemaid for a few months, looking after the children of a Parisian family. However, this was hardly more amenable, as the other domestic staff 'made fun of' her and neither her employers nor her charges were good or kind. Her 'pride suffered atrociously' and she resigned her post. Determined not to return to her uncle's 'hovel' she went to an employment agency, an 'abominable place', who gave her the address of a 'German house', which may have been a refuge or a boarding house.[3] Sophie reached rock bottom, moving from one job to another every couple of weeks, taking any situation that was offered to her, 'just to stay alive.'[4] After a period of time, she could not sustain the uncertainty and the change. She fell ill through exhaustion.

Sophie's diary doesn't state whether or not she visited a doctor. It is quite likely that, in her position, she was unable to afford it. The diagnosis of the era would have been 'neurasthenia', or weak nerves, first identified in a psychopathological context in 1869, to cover a variety of symptoms in women including exhaustion, headache, depression, palpitations and high blood pressure. It was an illness particularly associated with late nineteenth-century urbanisation, linked to the pace of living in cities, a competitive environment and sedentary work. Patients were usually recommended a rest cure, or to attend one of the private clinics where pills, electrotherapy, enforced invalidity and bland diets were followed. Undoubtedly it was financial necessity, even desperation, that had brought Sophie emotionally and physically so low but then she heard of a vacancy for a governess in the family of a steel magnate[5] bound for America. She was invited to accompany the family to Philadelphia, in charge of their sixteen-year-old daughter and ten-year-old son.

Working backwards from New York, it is possible to trace Sophie's route from Paris. Between 1892 and 1924, all immigrant arrivals in New York were processed at Ellis Island, just off the tip of Manhattan's Battery Park. Sophie joined the queues inside the main building at the receiving station. Penned in by railings, they underwent eye and basic health examinations before being registered at an inspector's desk. Interpreters were on hand but, given Sophie's two references to taunts for her accent, it would come as no surprise to find her surname recorded phonetically. One candidate emerges: a Sofia Bujaroska, with the substitution of the j for z reminding us of the Polish pronunciation of 'Brzeska'. This Sophie arrived in New York on 17 August 1900, a single woman, with no accompanying party of the same surname. Her age is listed as twenty-three, which might have been a guess, or else perhaps Sophie decided to take the opportunity to make herself appear younger. No other similar name appears in the Ellis Island Records during this time period. Further mystery is created when Sophie's record tells us that she departed from the port of Hamburg and her last residence was at 'Caine'.

Hamburg to New York was a major immigrant line from its establishment in 1847, carrying Eastern Europeans to a new life. Their passenger database includes a Sofia Bojarksa, again a phonetic recording of her name, who boarded the ship from the northern French port of Boulogne-sur-Mer. So although Sophie was recorded at Ellis Island as having disembarked from the Hamburg ship, she had, in fact, joined it en route, before it headed to Plymouth, then out across the Atlantic. Her employers either made the trip north to Boulogne directly from Paris, or else they had stayed for the early summer months on the coast at Caen (Caine) before travelling to join the boat around 10-11 August. The Ellis Island record also contains the name of that boat, the SS *Fürst Bismark*, an ocean liner commissioned in 1890 specifically for this route. It had been built by the Vulcan Shipbuilding Company at Stettin, in Poland, with five decks and three funnels; 502 feet long and weighing 8430 tonnes, it usually made the crossing in five or six days. The first and second class rooms were in the middle of the ship, with separate areas for men and women.[6] The deck plans indicate the music room and ladies' saloon on the promenade deck, a confectionary, doctor, pantry and barber on the upper deck and ladies' baths and toilets on the main deck.[7]

And yet, the ends do not quite tie up. There appears to have been a mistake somewhere. Further searching of the Hamburg-American line archive reveals that the *Fürst Bismark* set sail from Hamburg on Thursday 9 August, under the captaincy of H. Barends. This timescale would tie in perfectly with Sophie being processed through Ellis Island on 17 August. Yet no Sophie appears on this list and the ship called at the port of Cherbourg, not Boulogne, on this occasion. Presumably the lists were drawn up in advance, or at least at the point of embarkation and, while the names of the forty-five passengers disembarking at Cherbourg are included, there is no mention of the passengers who replaced them boarding ship at Cherbourg for America. The Caen connection would make more sense if they went from Cherbourg, as it is just over an hour's ride, placing them far nearer the port. It may be that amid the notorious bustle at Ellis Island, the wrong French port was recorded. But then there is a second passenger list dating from that October, from a sister ship of the *Fürst Bismark*, the *Patricia*, captained by H. Leithaüser. The *Patricia* left Hamburg on Sunday 7 October and did call at Boulogne. Interestingly, this list includes a '*Scholastika* (teacher) Bascynska', another phonetic approximation of Sophie's surname. Was this the 'teacher' Brzeska, reflecting her new title and the fluidity with which she shaped her identity? If so, the family with whom she was in service could have been Mr and Mrs Edmund Brown with their children Philipp and Ethel, or Mr and Mrs Alfred Boy, with Oskar and Beatrice, or Dr and Mrs A. Cuny, with master 'A' an Miss 'H'. The date of this voyage sits uncomfortably with that recorded at Ellis Island but stranger mistakes were recorded there, of timing, names, nationality and personal details.[8] The *Patricia* also carried the passengers J. Durand-Ruel and his wife, the son (Joseph) and daughter-in-law of the famous Parisian art dealer Paul Durand-Ruel, along with their children Paul and Marie. Joseph and his two brothers ran the family gallery in New York where many of the Impressionists first made their transatlantic debut, so it is fairly plausible that this voyage saw works by Monet and Renoir loaded on board.

Passengers on the 7 October voyage of the *Patricia* were told that breakfast was served at 8am, lunch between 12 and 2, dinner at half past six and tea at 9. Menus survive from the Hamburg-America line from around the time of Sophie's voyage.

The breakfast fare served in February 1902 included buckwheat pancakes and baked apple dumplings, hominy and oatmeal, potato pancake with cranberries, fish balls, rump steak in herb butter, Vienna sausages, calf's liver, omelette with parmesan, ox-tongue, smoked eel, all kinds of cheeses, tea, coffee and chocolate. A lunch menu from 1905 included beef, potato or kidney bean soup, lamb curry, ducklings and olives, roast beef, roast chicken, veal, mutton, spinach and eggs, six different kinds of potatoes, fruit compote, vanilla pudding, lemon tarts, salads, fruit and cheese.[9]

Passengers were also advised that steamer chairs could be rented from the High Steward, for the duration of the voyage at a cost of one dollar. The baths contained sea-water and could be used at no additional charge, either hot or cold. Smoking was not permitted anywhere on the ship save for the deck and the designated smoking room, where the lights would be extinguished at midnight. An 'experienced physician' was attached to every ship and there was no additional charge for sickness contracted on board, or for medicines, although this implies that passengers might pay a fee for help with existing complaints. The company fixed the tariff for the barber's services, so any relevant medical costs were also likely to have been regulated. Sophie might have used the library of English, French and German books, or the writing paper available from the Saloon steward. In total there were 330 cabin passengers and 15 senior officers and staff to run the ship, assisted by a number of domestic and general staff.[10] Providing she was travelling in at least second class, paid for by her employers, Sophie is likely to have had a pleasant voyage. However, there is a chance that they travelled in different classes, and that as a 'servant' or employee of the family she was placed in a different category. Below decks, the third class and steerage passengers were far more crowded, with simpler facilities and few of these services available. Photographs dating from around 1900 show them crowding onto their portion of the decks, where they slept in hot weather, and queuing endlessly to be processed amid their belongings.

The prospect of America cannot have failed to excite Sophie as a land of opportunity and freedom, a Mecca for immigrants keen to benefit from the rapid commercial and industrial advances made there in recent years. After going through Ellis Island, she would have joined the shuttle boat ferrying the processed passengers to the tip of the

Battery, in south Manhattan. Riding the waves, her first impressions of the city may have been similar to those described by immigrant authors Mary Antin, Anzia Yezierska, Abraham Cahan or, here, Henry Roth:

> ...before them, rising on her high pedestal, from the scaling swarmy brilliance of water to the west, Liberty ... The ship curved around in a long arc towards Manhattan, her bow sweeping past Brooklyn and the bridges whose cables and pillars ... spanned the East river ... the grimy cupolas and towering square walls of the city loomed up. Above the jagged roof tops, the white smoke ... this was that vast incredible land, the land of freedom, of immense opportunity, that Golden Land.[11]

The noise and bustle of Manhattan, economically well in advance of anything Sophie had experienced in Europe, must have been fascinating and terrifying, although on this first visit there was little time to explore. From New York, the steel magnate's family travelled around a hundred miles south-west to Philadelphia. They probably used the Congressional Limited Express, established between the two cities in 1885, bringing them into a city that had recently witnessed a huge expansion in population and industry. Sophie would also have found many other immigrants from Eastern Europe, with 5,000 Jews in the city in 1881, rising to 100,000 by 1905. There was also a considerable number of African-Americans in the city, making for an ethnic diversity that Sophie would not have encountered before. The dominant industry was textiles, engaging around 35% of the population, although oil, sugar and cigar production were also strong. Sophie may have become familiar with the city's leading department stores along Market Street or visited one of the nine swimming baths that made the city unusual. The census of 1900, compiled shortly before Sophie's arrival shows that there were other Polish immigrants resident in Ward 21 of the city by the name of Brzozoski, perhaps a corruption of Brzeski, or derived from a similar root. Four children, Wladyclaw, Boleslaws, Felixy and Theodora, aged between ten and three, were living together, although there was no mention of their parents, Anthony Brzozoski and Sophie's near-namesake, Sophia Brzozoski, who may have been deceased or elsewhere on the day of the record.

Settling into her new job, Sophie became deeply attached to the 10-year-old boy in her care, and grief-stricken when he suddenly died a few weeks after their arrival. From that point, things began to go wrong for her. The family's daughter, aged sixteen, repeatedly asked Sophie to recount indecent stories and complained to her mother of her dullness when she refused. She stated that she knew none and had no desire to 'ruin her morals'. In *Matka*, she describes the girl as 'corrupt to the marrow' and far more knowledgeable about life than her governess. Giving credence to her daughter's protested innocence, the magnate's wife urged Sophie to try harder to 'entertain' the girl, but her invented scandals about Parisian actresses were overheard by the parents, who decided she could not stay. Sophie suggests lesbianism as the true cause: the daughter was 'in love with me in a forbidden way' and 'too attached'.

Her employees were sympathetic though; the mother accompanied her back to New York, helped her find a situation and lodgings in a 'Home Français', a house run by French nuns. Many similar charitable boarding houses were run by women for women in the city, providing bed and board with strictly high moral conduct of the lodgers a prerequisite. A search of the contemporary benevolent institutions in New York reveals that Sophie is most likely to have gone to the Jeanne d'Arc Home for Friendless French Girls. It had been opened by the Sisters of Divine Providence in 1898, and was situated at 251-253 West Twenty-Fourth Street. Statistics collected in 1904 show that throughout that year they had admitted 788 individuals and that there were an average of 50 in residence per night.[12] The establishment is still there today, occupying an old brownstone mansion, as a 'private and temporary residence for women who are seeking to improve their lives by working or attending school in New York City'. Today, the rooms retain something of their original grandeur with large rooms, pillars and big windows; there is a kitchen, library, roof garden, laundry and beautiful chapel with stained glass windows, which looks much as it would have done during Sophie's stay. The cell-like bedrooms are long and thin, with a dormer window at the end, a bed and dressing table or cupboard.[13]

This period was not a happy one for Sophie. Central New York at the time was a city of paradoxes: in the Jamesian brownstone town houses of Fifth Avenue and north to Central Park, the rich lived in privilege only a few blocks away from the crippling poverty of the immigrant tenements. The 1900 census listed nearly three and a half million people living in the Manhattan district, in an era when the city was approaching the apogee of its self-confidence, a vibrant cultural mix enhanced by expansion outwards and upwards. Sophie, arriving in the dying years of the nineteenth century, must have met fellow Poles: between 1880 and 1920, two million Jews from Russia, Poland, Austria-Hungary and the Balkans established their own ghettoes in the tenements on the lower East side. These slums were among the poorest districts in the city, unhealthy, overcrowded and unsafe, although efforts were being made to bring the plight of their inhabitants to public attention, especially in the lectures, photographs and writings of Danish immigrant Jacob Riis. Legislation in 1879, 1887 and 1895 had attempted to improve standards but the ever increasing population, coupled with inflation and low wages, meant more and more people were crammed into unsanitary conditions. Manhattan's 42,000 tenement blocks listed in 1900 housed over a million and a half people. Towards the more affluent west side, Sophie's Jeanne d'Arc home was in the borough of Chelsea, although the notorious Hell's Kitchen bordered it to the north, and the garment district to the south. She records that she dreamed of a quiet life and became friendly with the women around her, even though they often repaid her with 'ingratitude'.[14]

In *Matka*, Sophie described this period in her life as a 'martyrdom' when she frequently changed jobs and suffered from bad treatment by 'terrible' children and employers 'without heart and judgement'. This made her more 'messed up and nervous' and she looked for ways to improve her situation through learning. If her Paris schedule is anything to go by, she may have pursued her own education on an enthusiastic but informal level when she could afford it, attending lectures, concerts and museums. A few blocks West from where the infamous Bowery crossed Broadway, New York University stood on Washington Square, so it is possible she took advantage of this establishment or the charitable Settlement houses or Missions modelled on London's East End's Toynbee Hall. The Metropolitan Museum of Art in Central Park had opened in 1880; cheap theatres, music halls and the 1895 Public Library were also close. In 1906, she may have heard of the Metropolitan's appointment of English artist Roger Fry, as curator and advisor to the paintings department; a man who provides a social and artistic connection between all three men loved by Sophie, Ida and Fernande.

Alongside the city's crippling poverty were the dazzling developments in industry and commerce; electric street cars, elevated railways and subways carried citizens quickly and efficiently to places of employment and entertainment. For those in the fast lane, life was a heady race of activity and competition, for the fastest Atlantic crossing or the tallest building; Sophie probably saw the iconic Flatiron building go up in 1902 and, with her superstitious tendencies, may have been among those too fearful to pass by in case of a strong gust of wind.

Pleasure seekers travelled out to Coney Island to eat frankfurters and ride the big dippers, on Saturday nights they attended theatre and vaudeville shows, or the new moving pictures, accelerating far in advance of anything Ida or Fernande would have seen at the time. Such entertainments of course cost money.

As the years passed, one of two scenarios seems to have been likely for Sophie; either she managed to secure a long-term situation as governess in a family, with whom she lived and gained a degree of social access, or her life was more as it had been lived in Paris, with intermittent employment and the resultant fluctuating finances. The second appears more likely; her later claims of having been forced to fend off unwanted attentions from her pupils' fathers suggests transient employment. She was aware that there were 'many men and honest fathers of families who would have paid me in a few weeks more than I had earned in four years' degrading work, if I had wanted to be friendly and obliging to them.' Describing herself as pure, honest and proud, she maintained her intention to only 'give myself for love'. Made clear in New York's contemporary literature by authors as diverse as Stephen Crane, Theodore Dreiser, Edith Wharton and Edgar Fawcett, sex was a fast route to social if not spiritual damnation; for a girl of Sophie's disadvantages it would spell the end of any teaching career. Nor is the literature over-romanticising or simplifying the situation, as Russian author Maxim Gorky found to his cost, on visiting New York in 1906. Fêted upon arrival, Gorky was ostracised overnight when it was discovered that his female companion was not his wife, as had been assumed. In an interesting connection, Fernande would later name as her heroine Evelyn Nesbit, the mistress of architect Stanton White, whose dramatic rooftop murder by Nesbit's husband in 1906 led to what was known as the trial of the century. Yet this equation of love and sex on a higher plane than a bourgeois arrangement, as something distinct from marriage, is another defining feature of bohemianism.

Later, Sophie hinted to Katherine Mansfield of a period of intense lesbian attachments, more prolonged and passionate than the innocent admiration and affection of Fernande and her friend Antoinette. Perhaps she hoped such sentiments would elicit sympathy from Mansfield, given her own close relationship with compatriot Ida Baker but, physically repulsed by Sophie, Katherine 'shuddered and retreated into Beauchamp gentility'.[15] Ever complex, neurotic and obsessively secretive, Katherine's own unconventional love life was kept from her conventional New Zealand family; it was clearly not a topic she wished to discuss with Sophie. Still subject to the disapproval and disbelief that led, in 1885, to Queen Victoria's famous denial, lesbianism was not subject to the same degree of harsh moral censure of male homosexuality that had led to the infamous Wilde trial of 1895–7. In certain artistic circles it became increasingly overt, even fashionable; Americans in Paris, such as Gertrude Stein, Djuna Barnes, Natalie Barney and Romaine Brook were in the vanguard but, increasingly, bisexuality became less of a secret, with several high-profile English women's female friendships becoming sexual, including those of Virginia Woolf, Vita Sackville West, Violet Trefusis, Dora Carrington, Sylvia Townsend Warner, Mary Campbell and others. No matter how successful some were at shedding their sexual limitations, the jealousy suffered by supposedly socially 'enlightened' husbands, including Havelock Ellis, John Nash and Stephen Spender, mixed personal betrayal with patriarchal disapproval.

In *Matka*, Sophie records that during the last year of her stay in the States, her elder brother wrote to her, hoping to immigrate to New York. He was 'the best of my brothers' she stated, 'a noble soul' whom her parents had treated 'with the cruellest and most agonising savagery from childhood', which had quite 'broken his will'. Unable to complete his studies, they had 'pushed him about from one trade to another'. He did not speak English, which Sophie recognised would be a difficulty, but she could not refuse his pleas and sent

him the money for his voyage. Sophie refers to him in *Matka* as 'B',
which certainly was the initial of his surname, although records list
the elder Brzeski boy as being named Michael Georgius.[16] However,
in his biography of Henri,[17] Roger Cole adds that this elder brother
changed him name to Joseph Bresser and cites a section of a letter
that Sophie reputedly wrote to him in 1911:

> There is no wonder our days are dragging so unhappily, we
> cannot shake hands as victims of our mother's tender endeavours,
> she can be proud of our lot, which she so deliberately prepared ...
> I am a bundle of nerves, torn like strings on a clavichord. Leaving
> Cracow in great dejection and irritation, I was decided on death.[18]

Brother and sister were reunited in New York. Sophie would have
travelled down to Battery Park to greet him, to help him find
lodgings or take him to one of the immigrant Christian missionary
houses for men, like her French residence in Chelsea. Sophie
describes him as kind and intelligent, but a 'poor shy boy' who
could find no work in spite of her efforts. She had to 'maintain'
him, which is likely to have been emotionally as well as financially
draining; this added to her concern that, 'desperate, he might
commit suicide', a pressure which 'drove (her) to madness'. After
five months, he found a job, but it was 'the most sordid' – washing
saucepans. Disgusted and defeated, he blamed his sister for making
him come to America, sulked and stopped coming to see her. At
this point, Sophie was also finding it difficult to find a position
and longed to return to Paris, but with no diploma or education
certificates to show for her efforts, she feared the only people who
would hire her would exploit her. Thus, after 'a lot of humiliation
and suffering' she felt she had little choice but to return home to
Poland. She would have bought her ticket from the American office
at 9–11, Broadway, overlooking Bowling Green, just up from
Battery Park, within sight of Ellis Island and the State of Liberty. It
was a Palladian-style tall grey building with ornate carving, pillars
and portico over the doors. At some point in 1908, Sophie left
behind her American adventure and set sail across the Atlantic.

7

Sex

It only took a few short days in 1899 for Fernande's life to unravel. She had grown close to one of the shop girls, the 'easy going' Hélène who had been charged by Aunt Alice to accompany her on the walk to school. In the early autumn of 1898, Hélène spoke to Fernande in secret, confiding that her brother-in-law, Paul Percheron, an older man of twenty-eight, had seen Fernande and could now think 'of nothing else' but her. Just past her seventeenth birthday, Fernande was 'not particularly anxious to get to know him' and had heard gossip among the other staff that Hélène was 'a wicked girl who lives with a man without being married to him'. Although Fernande was aware that this was enough for Alice Petot to dismiss the girl, she did not see what was wrong with her situation. It seemed as if Fernande had avoided the situation, although this admirer had not forgotten her and the following May Hélène passed on a letter and little presents, with the man's pleas that Fernande 'do the impossible' and meet him, so he might speak with her. She was flattered, admitting it was 'touching to receive attention from someone so serious' but she had not yet seen him and had no idea what he looked like. However, an opportunity arose when she had to go to collect her birth certificate from Saint-Sulpice so, in the last days of May, she agreed to meet her admirer.[1] After this, Fernande's diary goes quiet. She filled in what happened retrospectively.

Paul Percheron proved to be a disappointment. The man Fernande met was on the short side, with regular features 'but a strange look'. He had large black eyes which looked 'misplaced and seem(ed) to diverge,' a dull complexion, a thick mouth, short chin, thickset, rather heavy, long arms, blunt hands and black curly hair, which Fernande adds that she hated in a man. He was already waiting for her and, although she found him repellent, she did not have the courage to reject him, so allowed him to take her in a taxi to the Mairie at Saint-Sulpice. In the back of the cab, he looked at her in a frightening way, covered her hands in kisses and only refrained from kissing her because she cried out. He confessed that he loved her, 'that he'd been driven crazy' ever since he first set eyes on her and that she was 'the only thing he could think about'. Starved of affection and unskilled in the ways of men, Fernande admitted that this attention was 'quite nice'. Instead of dropping off her certificate at the Sophie Germain School, she agreed to drink some hot chocolate in the Bois du Boulogne, providing that she was home by six.[2] She wasn't.

In the carriage, driving under the trees, Fernande felt a 'sense of (her) own importance'[3] for the first time, basking in Paul's happiness and pride. The Bois de Boulogne was some seven kilometres away from the Rue Réaumur, an ancient hunting ground that had been turned into a pleasure garden in the 1850s, drawing visitors of all classes to its park, grotto, woods, lawns and lake. Van Gogh painted 'Strollers in the Bois de Boulogne' in 1886, with figures walking under a smudgy autumn canopy of red and brown, while an 1897 illustration from *Vanity Fair* captured one of the latest crazes to dominate the park, as crowds of both genders took to their bicycles. In 1899, the most obvious destination for Paul and Fernande was La Grande Cascade restaurant, with its splendid interiors preserved from a Napoleonic hunting lodge and its outdoor terrace and petal-shaped canopy and glass walls. The following year it would become the official restaurant when Paris hosted the World's Fair. However, Paul may have had something smaller and more intimate in mind. Fernande describes the place they went to as a 'chalet' suggesting that they went instead to Le Chalet des Isles, on Lake Inferior, which was reached by boat. Photographs of the time show couples sitting before its wooden façade at iron tables covered in white cloth, drinking wine. Paul ordered tea for them both, plus cakes and sweets for Fernande, so that she quite forgot the time.

At a quarter to seven, Fernande began to panic. Horrified, she did not 'dare' go home, certain that she would be sent to the convent or the reformatory. Paul's solution was that she should not return, but go home with him instead and, in the morning, he would ask her uncle for her hand in marriage. Fernande was crying as they walked down one of the woodland paths. Paul 'dragged (her) roughly under the trees, took (her) by the waist and glued his mouth to (hers).' His kisses were 'disgusting', almost 'suffocating' her and his insistence that 'there's a lot I'm going to have to teach you now that you're my wife,' repelled and horrified her. Fernande felt she had no choice but to go with him, an opinion that he reinforced: 'I couldn't go back to my aunt's after my misbehaviour, Paul made that perfectly plain to me.' Instead, he took her in another cab to a restaurant, where her predicament did not stop Fernande from listing the food they ordered; consommé, chicken casserole, foie gras, salad, ice-cream, wine and cherry-brandy, which made her 'feel better'. From there he took her to a café-concert, then back to his home, a 'tiny apartment on the sixth floor of a modern house opposite the Parc Montsouris',[4] six kilometres south of her uncle and aunt.

This uncomfortable narrative raises the question of just how far Fernande was a willing participant in her own 'abduction'. The hearty enjoyment of her food reminds the reader of her innocence, of just how child-like she still was, to be wooed by ice-cream and treats. Yet it points to the darker truth of her yearning for affection, the lack of love at the heart of her life that led her to seek admiration, even in dangerous places. The earlier responses she makes in her diary, to the question of the brothel downstairs, the advances of M. Lortat and her reaction to Hélène's unorthodox situation imply a naivety about sex that her aunt had done little to inform. The issue is further complicated by Krauss' suggestion that the diaries were constructed retrospectively, with Fernande recasting herself as the virginal victim, who had never enjoyed sexual passion until she met Picasso.[5] Yet Fernande's words, her accusations of abuse, must be allowed to stand. She was guilty of an error of judgement by agreeing to meet a strange man but, in Paul Percheron, she found a Svengali-like figure, persuasive and experienced, who knew exactly how to exploit her innocence and unworldliness. The awakening that followed was brutal and distressing. Later. Fernande confided to her diary that she was overwhelmed with 'horror, terror and disgust. Only a few hours earlier I had been a child, how could I bear the hateful revelations of that night.' She was 'paying dearly for this sudden impulse, which is going to scar my life for ever'.[6]

The following day, still at Percheron's apartment, she hoped that a search party would be sent out for her, and the unavoidable subtext is that she needed rescuing. However, these hopes vanished with the arrival of Hélène, who reported that Alice Petot was wearing a 'funereal look' and there was 'whispering in every corner'. Paul had gone out to buy her more cakes, candy and fruit that she had 'ever seen in (her) whole life' as well as some new underwear. Fernande was 'made to smoke', which she found unpleasant and was 'ill, miserable, unhappy, sick to death'. A casual comment from Hélène, who appeared oblivious to her distress, reveals that Paul had not just taken her virginity but had initiated sex with Fernande seven times the previous night, a fact upon which Hélène congratulated her. The only sympathy came from Paul's brother, Henri, who called her a 'poor little child' and promised he had not known about the 'irresponsible' scheme. Henri threatened to inform Fernande's family, which prompted an argument between him and Paul, but Henri insisted that Fernande be put to bed with hot water bottles and that both men would sleep on the couch while the women shared the bed. Clearly, Fernande was suffering physical and emotional trauma, as she recorded her fear alongside the pain: 'my bones and my flesh were hurting.'[7]

Henri and Hélène stayed in the apartment for four days, but after that there was nothing to protect Fernande from Percheron's 'bestial frenzy'. He spent the nights 'loving her' leaving her alone all day, unable to eat, returning at six to find her 'dazed, dishevelled and with (her) clothes in a mess'. It was obvious, she wrote, that he was 'not pleased, but he (kept) his anger under control.' Paul found Fernande unresponsive, finding no pleasure in sex, like a 'beautiful marble statue that nothing could ever bring to life' but her fear forced her to 'let him do what he wants'. She had not 'heard a thing' from home and when a complaint was made by the former policeman who acted as concierge to the apartments, Paul bought his silence. 'Sometimes he hurts me,' she wrote, 'and

I'm covered with red marks that turn blue.' He called her 'his little virgin' and took pleasure in hurting her. After a week of her 'living hell' Fernande was longing to escape, but she was afraid to leave the place. Eventually, her family involved the police, who interrogated Hélène and discovered the details of her situation and Paul's address. Fernande feared her arrival, knowing that she would be treated like a leper and not permitted to return home in case she 'might contaminate the lily-white purity' of her cousin,[8] who, she added, had explained the facts of life to Fernande when she was eleven.

> I was so happy, she wrote in her diary, life seemed so glorious, so sweet, so pure, so full of hope. Must I give up the happy future that I was looking forward to only two weeks ago? Is everything so ugly, so low, so hateful? Is it a woman's lot to submit to this disgusting behaviour from men? ... I don't want to marry Paul. I'd like to go a long, long way away, so that he could never find me.[9]

Paul certainly feared she would run away, as he hid her hat and shoes.

Eventually, Alice Petot arrived at the address, along with Fernande's godmother and a policeman. Her first act was to slap Fernande and treat her with 'disgust and amazement', even though the godmother urged her to be gentle as Fernande was 'still a little girl'. Fernande fainted at the approach of the policeman, who she believed was about to arrest her, only to find that he was offering to arrest Percheron. 'As for the child,' he said to Alice, 'you can decide what to do with her, she seems to be innocent but the man is a real bastard.' Aunt Alice then insisted that Fernande marry Paul as soon as possible to punish her 'depravity', in spite of her complaints of his abuse and pleas not to be left alone with him. The only alternative was a reformatory. She was not permitted to return home. Fernande had no choice but to agree to marriage. After her aunt's visit, she became seriously ill with a fever, hallucination, dizziness and vomiting. A doctor was called, who diagnosed her with the 'after effects of shock' and persuaded Paul to spend a few nights away from the apartment. His return prompted her to think of ways she might get rid of him, 'pushing him out of the window, making him drink poison' but she was 'too frightened of the guilt'. Her fear of him was like a phobia, 'like my fear of snakes ... I go cold all over and feel faint.' She even cried out, during sex with him, that she wanted to die.[10] But on Tuesday 8 August 1899, at the Mairie in the 14th arrondissement, Fernande and Paul Emile Auguste Percheron were married.

Fernande's intimate account of her abduction and rape by Percheron makes for very difficult reading. Yet without evidence to the contrary, it can be accepted as a genuine account. The responsibility for it must lie between Percheron himself and Alice Petot, whose strict and loveless regime instilled such fear into Fernande that she believed that going home with Paul was preferable to returning late to her aunt's apartment. When faced with the opportunity to rescue her niece from a man who had imprisoned her and was sexually, emotionally and physically abusive, Alice chose to preserve the social codes rather than listen to Fernande's distressed pleas. The godmother present at the interview did not intervene with Alice on her decision, even though the policeman assessed the situation more accurately and offered to arrest the 'bastard'.[11] Once the wedding had taken place, with tears in the eyes of the bride, Alice sent Fernande a trunk full of her possessions, with a grey dress and shoes to be married in, plus 500 francs and an additional 500 from her godmother. After the service, they dined at a restaurant in the suburb of Robinson, where Fernande was made to drink champagne, which she disliked and which made her nauseous on the train home. Hélène correctly deduced from this that Fernande was pregnant.[12]

*

Sophie Brzeska did not receive a warm welcome on her return to Poland. Her family had been forced to sell their former home but Sophie does not say where they were now living. Her mother's mercenary approach involved counting every sou spent upon her food, although Sophie offered to hand over her entire thousand francs of savings in order to purchase a 'plot of land' on which the old woman might live. This suggestion was met with 'biting sarcasm' as her mother saw it as reducing her to the life of a peasant. Worse was to come when she discovered that an elderly uncle, on whom she had always looked as a surrogate father, had been spreading malicious rumours in her absence. After the death of his wife, this uncle had been giving out reports that his niece Sophie had been his mistress and her absence enforced as a result of an illegitimate, incestuous pregnancy. Sophie was deeply hurt by the betrayal and 'almost died from this blow'.[13] The specific cruelty of this story was compounded by her more immediate family, who laughed at her notions of virtue and the correctness of behaviour she prided herself upon. In addition, her former fiancé 'Y' had engaged himself to a young heiress and, despite Sophie's epistolary pleas for their last chance at happiness, he declined her coldly and politely. Perhaps he believed her uncle's rumours. Having stayed for only two weeks, Sophie found it intolerable to remain and left her mother again.

Sophie accepted the position of a governess in the Polish countryside, although in *Matka* she does not specify where this was. It soon proved 'bad' and she took a second, which rapidly appeared 'worse' until she settled with a third family of German descent, raising their daughter. The family was 'not wicked' but 'too selfish' and repaid her 'devotion badly'[14] so when they planned to leave the country for life in the city, she declined to accompany them. Sophie's experiences of New York made her yearn for a quieter life and her pupil had exhausted her, so she decided to put her savings to better use by seeking out a rest cure. On the way, Sophie visited her married brother, whose kind wife paid for her to have more comfortable transport and her mother, who advised her to sleep with a man in order to entrap him into marriage and assure herself of a 'tranquil independent life'.[15] With her high morals, this suggestion was initially repulsive to Sophie but now, in her late thirties, her decision to act on it was a measure of her increasing desperation and unhappiness.

Sophie sought a cure in the 'picturesque and pleasant' Austrian spa town of Baden, more formally Baden bei Wien. Not to be confused with Baden Baden on the German-French border, the town lies sixteen kilometres south of Vienna (Wien), close to the thirteen hot springs of the Vienna woods. Rebuilt after a fire in 1812, it was an example of the Beidermeier style, fashionable with the Imperial family and frequented by Beethoven, and more accessible to all after the establishment of a tram line. This is probably how Sophie arrived, making the long train journey from Cracow to Vienna before changing onto a tram in the city centre, for the final hour-long ride into the hills. The town was clustered along a main street, overlooked by the villas in the hills.

Old postcards show tree-lined roads winding upwards, the river running under the bridge, domed churches, restful benches overlooking sublime views and the central square, dominated by a similar plague monument to that found in Vienna. There was also the *Dolbhoffpark*, a central 'English park,' open to the public, featuring a Rosarium, castle and a swimming pool in summer that doubled as an ice rink in the winter.

While Sophie was recuperating, an acquaintance introduced her to a wealthy manufacturer from a noble family, known only as Monsieur 'M'. At fifty-three, he was almost twenty years her senior, kind, caring, amusing, intelligent and provided a sympathetic ear, quickly understanding the causes of her unhappiness. The anonymity, intensity and protective holiday atmosphere temporarily sheltered them from the outside world, allowing for the development of a greater degree of intimacy. Her cynical confession in *Matka* that she had decided to follow her sister-in-law's advice and 'entrap' him into marriage belies the fact that she fell 'violently, passionately' in love and, in return, was assured of his love. But 'M' made no promise to marry her, hinting at a past, unhappy connection, although his words were enough to make her hope. When the holiday came to an end, they wrote to each other and arranged to meet again 'in a strange distant town'. 'Totally flooded with passion' Sophie 'gave' herself to him, although through an excess of 'gentlemanly' behaviour, 'M' 'satisfied his need' without 'exposing her to danger'.[16] This might have been to avoid pregnancy, or because he was aware of carrying an untreated sexually transmitted disease. Considering his later confession to her, of fathering a child outside wedlock, it is likely to have been the former.

Once again they parted and exchanged letters. Passion enveloping her 'like a dangerous element', Sophie waited for a proposal that did not materialise. Their next meeting took place on New Year's Eve, a year after they had met. She travelled to the town where he lived, where they were again intimate without full satisfaction; his 'trembling' prevented him from 'relieving' his need 'over my poor tormented body'. Later she realised that privacy was a problem: he was unable to 'relieve' himself at any place which was not 'intimate'.[17] Finding secret locations for sexual liaisons between an unmarried couple proved difficult and caused arguments, as Sophie refused to spend the night with him in a hotel. It was on this occasion that Sophie realised Monsieur 'M' had no plans to make her his wife. She was now thirty-six or seven. After a traumatic and dreadful scene, which H. S. Ede describes as nearly resulting in 'the death of both', her lover confessed the existence of an illegitimate son, to whose mother he had promised always to remain free; his one ambition was to make a home with her and the give the boy his name. The disappointment proved too much for Sophie. She lunged at a revolver hanging above the bed, although her lover intervened and took it from her. Begging him to end her life, she wept desperately and lost control; 'my brain was disturbed for some time' and saw 'madness waiting for me'. 'M's' regret, apologies and finally anger, did little to calm her own anger and sense of betrayal. They met once more after this but he looked 'careworn' and received her with 'bad grace'[18] offering to pay for her to undertake a cure for her nerves but continually rejecting her proposals to spend the summer together. Eventually he persuaded her to go to the Tatra mountains to recover her health.

Located at the southern tip of modern Poland, the Tatra mountain range is the highest part of the Carpathians and forms a natural border with Slovakia. In the nineteenth century, the mountains were used for mining and sheep grazing but the beauty and varied flora increasingly attracted tourists and scientists. Sophie enjoyed the greenery and pines, which she likened to 'young gods' and felt that nature was having a calming influence upon her body and soul. She remained there for two months, walking and growing stronger, building a new 'exuberance' and confidence. On her return, still clinging to hope, she met with 'M' a few more times but it was clear the affair was over. His coldness, rejections and silence were only exacerbated by her increasing desperation and jealous demands. Their last meeting took place in a park, where they discussed the possibility of living together somewhere, anonymously, in some large town, but he told her they would not be happy as she was too jealous and imagined 'impossible things'. When he confessed to no longer loving her, she was tempted to warn him not to 'play with fire' but instead gave an 'icy au revoir' and 'was gone like a bomb'.[19]

Still entertaining hopes of a reunion, Sophie returned once again to her mother, who now seems to have been living with her son and daughter-in-law. There, she lay on a sofa for hours, despairing and absorbed by her misfortune, trying to decide how best to kill herself. She wrote in *Matka* that not a single soul would mourn her loss, that she was 'passing through life as a brute, as an imbecile, without leaving Mankind a trace of my passage, all the while burning with the fire of creativity'. It was unfortunate that Sophie's intense and sensitive responses often elicited the opposite reaction in those whom she most wished to provoke love. Despite her undeniable suffering, she did not make it easy for friends or family to offer the warmth she wanted; her later acquaintance, Enid Bagnold, found her 'treacherous, suspicious, easily affronted, violently hurt' and witnessed Sophie 'clawing' at Katherine Mansfield, who found her neurotic and disturbing. At home in Poland, Sophie's violent outbursts were directed at a sympathetic aunt who told her it was a shame she hadn't accepted the neighbour when she was sixteen, as he had been stupid but possessed a kind nature. In response, Sophie shrieked with rage and stamped her feet, flinging insults at her aunt, while her mother stood by smiling, saying 'you see what a toad she is, what a scorpion, didn't I tell you? But you would never believe it and now you can see it for yourself.'[20]

Sophie was determined to commit suicide but found the thought of worms eating her body repellent. Thus, she decided to leave Poland, where she would have received a traditional burial, and enact her plan in Paris, where cremation was available. At some point late in 1909 or early in 1910, she made the journey back to France and found lodgings. It was a morbid way to return, alone, unloved and bent on suicide.

As would often happen at times of emotional stress, the strain of the last year's disappointments made Sophie ill again. This time, though, the physical symptoms included an 'abominable illness of the sexual organs that I had not known existed … a filthy thing gets hold of my weak body, disgusting, abominable.'[21] There has been speculation among Henri Gaudier's biographers about the nature of the illness Sophie suffered from. Her heavy discharge, pain and irritation were symptomatic of cystitis and general poor health, or the parasite Trichomonas Vaginalis suggested by writer Paul O'Keeffe.[22] But the publication of *Matka* casts doubt upon former theories of a sexually transmitted disease, possibly gonorrhoea or syphilis contracted from 'M'. If her retrospective account is taken at face value, Sophie appears to have genuinely not experienced full intercourse. Racing to a specialist, she naively believed she had contracted syphilis by infection, due to the poor condition of her rented rooms. The doctor reassured her it was due to her weakness, asking in astonishment: 'How could you get syphilis having never had intercourse?' and recommended a series of injections.[23]

Sophie was relieved not to have been suffering from syphilis. The curse of the incurable illness in an unmarried woman was experienced by the writer and suffragette Violet Hunt. Brought up in the pre-Raphaelite circle, and reputedly the recipient of a proposal by Oscar Wilde, Violet fashioned herself as a 'female rake' rejecting eligible husbands on principle.[24] Her lovers included H. G. Wells and Somerset Maugham, although her most significant affair was with Ford Madox Ford. In 1905 she was diagnosed with syphilis, which led to her social ostracism, even though she attempted to deny the truth for years: it was the tell-tale spots on her skin which marked her entry into the second stage of the illness and advertised her suffering to all.

Sophie did not find death in Paris, as she had planned; instead she found a renewed hope in life, and in love. It was probably in a communal lodging house or home similar to the one run by the New York nuns that Sophie found herself 'in a circle of women' of French, English and Russian backgrounds, who were keen to study and educate themselves. Their dedication and their praise of her intelligence inspired Sophie to reject her morbid plans and attack life afresh. She wrote to one of her brothers whom she had helped financially during his studies, and to whom she refers as 'B', asking him to lend her some money to stave off her hunger. She also wrote to 'MS' inviting him to come and live with her in a platonic way, so that she might 'care for him as a devoted sister' but he rejected her offer, saying that he had retreated into his shell. The affair was definitely over but she vowed to move on. Determined to improve her lot, Sophie began to attend lectures at the Sorbonne, to take notes and spend her evenings studying in the St Geneviève Library. It was there, in the majestic glass and iron reading room, that 'the best and at the same time the unhappiest time of (her) life' was to begin.[25]

*

Ida Nettleship had been studying at the Slade School of Art for two years before Augustus John first signed his name in the register. Busy with her dedication to Henry Tonks, art and the fantasy world she was weaving with Edna, it is quite likely at first that Ida barely noticed her future husband, who had yet to develop his distinctive, imposing style. The quiet, shy seventeen-year-old boy from Wales, who arrived in 1894, dutifully studied and copied the old masters. Born in 1878 and raised by his father in Haverfordwest and Tenby, John had made a quiet start to his Slade studies, developing his skills of draughtsmanship and visiting the National Gallery or British Museum on the advice of Tonks, one of the few teachers he found could sustain his awe and respect. He was suitably impressed, however, on the occasion Whistler appeared in the life room at the Slade: 'An electric shock seemed to galvanise the class: there was a respectful demonstration; the master bowed genially and retired.'[26] Initially, John found London overwhelming and his early shyness was not aided by poverty, but his situation began to improve when he made friends among the other students; Benjamin Evans, Ambrose McEvoy and Michel Salaman, brother of Ida's fiancé Clement, friends with whom he would attend the theatre, galleries or clubs, or anywhere they could sit and sketch. He progressed steadily and, at the end of his second year, was named on the prize list for figure drawing, advanced antique drawing and awarded a two-year scholarship.

In 1895, Augustus John went through a transformation. Spending the summer at his father's home, he dived from Giltar Point into the sea, hitting his head on submerged rocks. This appeared to trigger a dramatic character change, emerging from the waves, so he claimed, as 'a bloody genius'. When he finally arrived back at the Slade, after a long spell of recovery, he was a changed man. Whether the result of his injuries, or a more self-conscious reinvention, John's new appearance surprised his old companions; the once clean-shaven student was sporting a tufty red beard and his usually tidy clothes were now scruffy and dishevelled. The embroidered smoking cap his father had given him to conceal his scar became an essential part of his new look and with it came increased confidence and, apparently, talent. Where his drawings had previously been merely 'methodical', according to Tonks, they were now 'remarkable' and were passed around in awe, whilst other students rushed to pluck his rejects out of the waste bin. Fellow-artist Wyndham Lewis recalled his first sight of the new John: '… a tall bearded figure with an enormous black Paris hat, large gold ear-rings decorating his ears, with a carriage of the utmost arrogance, strode in and the whisper "John" went round the class … this redoubtable personage … John left as abruptly as he had arrived. We watched in silence this mythical figure depart.'[27]

This change had perhaps greater significance for his friends and mythmakers than John himself, who would later prove dismissive of this event's 'undue importance'. In his memoirs, *Finishing Touches*, John observed that his lengthy absence and unusual headgear 'caused a sensation … and thus was born the myth of (his) genius, due, it seemed, solely to the bang on the head … it was all nonsense of course.' Although he did speculate as to whether his 'fitful industry with its incessant setbacks … squandering of time, my emotional ups and downs and general inconsequence can be charitably imputed to that mishap.'[28] Whatever the truth, John began to make his mark on the Slade.

Augustus had been joined in London by his sisters. Gwen was a year older, at nineteen, and the younger Winifred was a student of music. Together they took a flat on the first floor of 21 Fitzroy Street which was to become a significant meeting place. The house was owned by the eccentric Augusta Everett, who late in life was to enrol herself at the Slade. Calling herself Aunt Aurelia, she invited the students to her Sunday teas, filled with hymn singing and holy talk, taking an interest in their material and spiritual wellbeing. A painting by Gwen John made in 1897 or 1898, depicts an inviting, cosy looking room with floral wallpaper and large window: a hatted Augustus stands in the background and a flamboyant looking Rosa Waugh, sister of Edna, floats in towards the seated figures of Winifred and Michel Salaman; Gwen herself is glimpsed as a shadowy figure walking outside the window. A contemporaneous John study shows a dreamy looking Ida, Gwen and his then girlfriend Ursula Tyrwhitt together on the same page, although the poses suggest three separate angles or sittings. At the time of these portraits, John's circle of friends was widening to include William Orpen, who lived in the basement at Fitzroy Street, Albert Rutherston and music student Grace Westray, who took a flat on the fourth floor, further mingling the hitherto segregated sexes.

Although it is unclear exactly when Ida and Augustus first met, their friendship groups had merged by 1897, marking a new maturity that also yielded artistic benefits. Together, they formed a formidable, dedicated group, serious about their art, sitting regularly for each other and taking their sketchbooks with them wherever they went, even when they paid a shilling for a box at Old Sadler's Wells or in the pit of the Empire. In later life, John nostalgically recalled those days of passionate devotion, doubting whether 'present-day art students bring their sketch books with them to the cinema' or to anarchist meetings to sketch 'characters'.[29] Edna Waugh recalled calling on the Johns with Ida after having been to a show in Drury Lane, and an occasion when they dressed up and rechristened Augustus prior to sketching him. In these first months of their acquaintance, John was deeply attracted to Ida but, through his friendship with Michel Salaman, he was aware of her engagement to Clement and kept a respectful distance. Never one to pine over a woman, he was soon involved in a love affair with an older girl in their circle, Ursula Tyrwhitt. But the growing attraction between John and Ida could not be ignored.

Even before John's personality change, Ida had begun to suspect her feelings for him were stronger than those she had for Clement Salaman. She confided in Edna that her fiancé often assumed a distasteful superiority over her and was dismayed when he flicked his cane at some boisterous children near them in the park. In comparison, she was aware of Augustus' strong feelings for her and hoped he would be able to offer understanding of her artistic endeavours and be sympathetic to her ambitions, as well as acknowledging her growing attraction to him, which soon deepened into love. John was the only man Ida ever fell in love with: certain of her feelings, yet fearing her parents' disapproval, she tried to throw herself into her work, as she had advised Edna. But John was not easy to ignore: charismatic, over six foot tall, with his imposing red beard and flamboyant but quickly tattered clothes, as well as an increasingly awe-struck Slade following with devotees referring to him as a Christ-like figure, Ida's feelings only grew stronger.

Early in 1897, when the method of hard work had proved unsuccessful and the problem had not resolved itself despite John's involvement with Ursula among others, she invited Edna and Gwen Salmond to spend a few days with her in Aldeburgh, Suffolk, to consider her options. Edna later remembered Ida's wild desire one night to walk by the sea, which would never have been permitted by their landlady, so the three of them climbed out of the window and walked by the turbulent waves until daybreak.[30] Something about this night acted as a catalyst. Upon their return to London, Ida ended her engagement, to the disappointment of her parents and William Clarke Hall, who wrote to her with accusations of fickleness and falsity.

Almost immediately afterwards, Ida travelled to Italy on a scholarship. It may seem surprising to a modern reader that a young, unmarried woman of nineteen should be permitted to travel alone to a foreign country at the turn of the twentieth century. But as well as living in a period of great social change, the Nettleships would have seen this as an essential extension of their daughter's artistic training, as well as a much needed escape from the situation with Clement; they may also have been aware of Edna's successful visit to Florence six months before with the Clarke Halls, the family of her fiancé. Their decision to allow her to travel was a risk and a mark of trust, possibly fought for by Ida, who wrote with constant reassurances to her mother; 'I do assure you, there's nothing to fear.'[31] Yet concealed from Ada was the swarm of admirers who sent Ida flowers and wooed her ardently: poets, Americans and a musician named Knight, about whom she wrote to her sister Ethel that he was 'constant and kind' but miserable and 'cribs other people's ideas on art'. Her virtue, firm morality and dedication to art prevented any misadventure with these suitors; as at the Slade, her attentions were focused more on the other girls, Italian lessons and her drawing, which attracted crowds, who must think her 'either a fool or a genius'. Despite spending six or seven hours daily sketching outdoors and being enthused by her surroundings – 'Italy has claimed me for one of her lovers' – her work was not transformed, as she warned her mother. 'Don't expect great things … it's no easier to do in Italy than in England.'[32]

After the delicious warmth and beauty of Italy, Ida felt flat upon her return to London losing, for the first time, some of her enthusiasm and drive, suffering from what she gave the Sickertian diagnosis of 'eternal ennui'. Soon she was organising another painting trip, this time to New Quay in Cardiganshire. Ada travelled with her, Edna and Gwen Salmond staying just long enough to check the suitability of their lodgings before leaving them alone to their work and returning home. Unbeknown to her, the girls had arranged for the presence of a male model, who would sit for them daily, satisfying Ida's desire to paint the tones of sun on flesh. It did not take too long, though, for the model to become too familiar and a sly remark made them aware he had been a witness to their early morning bathing sessions. The only honourable option was to send him back to London, and he was replaced by Edna's sister Rosa. When Ida returned, it was to begin her final year of study at the Slade and to her and John's mutual recognition that they were falling in love.

Ida's parents did not consider Augustus John a suitable partner for their daughter. Although the accounts of Wyndham Lewis, Mark Gertler and his contemporaries make plain John's charisma and status within the Slade school milieu, the Nettleships failed to understand the attraction. Ada in particular was horrified by his appearance: '… a lanky, unwashed youth, shifty-eyed and uncouth to the point of rudeness, with a scraggy, reddish beard, long hair and scruffy clothes'.[33] She hoped Ida's infatuation would not last. Less vociferous in his incomprehension, Jack wished his daughter's suitor would at least clean his shoes. On a more serious note, he knew from experience what financial hardship a life dedicated to art could bring. Augustus' visits to Wigmore Street became increasingly uncomfortable; their visits coinciding, Max Beerbohm described him sitting in the window seat looking pale and sinister, 'like Lucifer'. Also, Ida had to go through the difficult process of breaking off her engagement with Clement, whom her parents had considered a good match, telling him she hoped it would lead to a 'great friendship'. Clement was still unmarried according to the 1901 census, practising as a barrister and living in Hendon. However, soon afterwards he married a woman named Dora, who appears in the 1911 census with their four children, the eldest of whom was eight. The family were then living in Wootton, Somerset. He died there at the age of sixty-seven in September 1935.

The main problem existing between Ida and Augustus was what the Edwardians would soon be calling 'the blue beast' – sexual passion. Ida was torn between him and her parents. She was steadfast in her refusal to submit to his advances and sleep with him, despite John's protestations that he was suffering 'torture'; and she was equally unwilling to defy her parents by consenting to what she knew would be an unwelcome engagement. Throughout 1899, which was their final year at the Slade, John continued to pursue Ida with a typically paradoxical inconstancy and passion, hoping to wear down her resistance and diverting himself with other women when it became clear that he could not. Work was still her main focus, although after six years at the Slade and reaching the landmark of her twenty-first birthday, she could not help but be aware that an uncertain future awaited her at the end of her formal training. She did not wish to exemplify Henry Tonks' perennial disappointment about the fate of his female students: 'They improve rapidly from sixteen to twenty-one. But then the genius that you have discovered goes off and they begin to take marriage seriously.'[34] On the other hand, though, a union with John appeared to offer Ida the way to combine marriage with work; they were serious about their art together, visiting galleries and working side by side, which seemed to offer hope that he would support her future as a committed artist in a way that other men might not.

There was also no denying the social cachet attached to being John's muse and whilst Ida's impulses and motives appear genuine, she could not help but be affected by the universal admiration that caused fellow students to stand up when he entered a room. At the end of their final year, John won the summer figure composition prize and Edna Waugh's rose decorations on behalf of the leavers prompted Tonks to enquire whether an empty pedestal had been left for John.[35] The sexual tension between Ida and John built to a peak during that final Slade summer, at Edna Waugh's birthday party in St Albans. Never one for abstinence or patience and growing accustomed to easy conquests, John urged Ida to become his mistress and live with him; an action which would have represented a rejection of her religious and moral values. She had been hoping that given time, her parents would come to accept, even like him, and did not wish to disappoint them. At first, her denials served to inflame John; he became convinced 'his happiness seemed to depend upon the secret of her beauty ... upon his possessing it.'[36] Soon though, Ida came to recognise she desired John as much as he did her.

The summer of 1898 was a last long, glorious period of girlhood for many of the Slade students; for Ida and Edna in particular, it ended the innocent enjoyment of each other's company before issues of sexuality and duty began to alter the direction of their lives. There is a childlike, humorous joy about John pursuing both girls up to the top of a haystack, launching himself off dramatically after Ida's rejection and being saved only by them holding onto his trousers. Likewise, the final dinner in London, an 'evening full of delight' and Ida and John sitting back to back on the way home after a picnic, wreathed in roses and trying to bite cherries hanging on each other's ears. It was time to put aside the carefree student days and take their place in the adult world.

8

Liberation

In September 1899, Paul and Fernande moved to Fontenay-sous-Bois, a suburb to the east of Paris, where they rented a ground floor flat with a small garden. A doctor had confirmed Fernande's pregnancy and she suffered constantly with nausea, as well as the loneliness of her location and her continuing dislike of her husband. Paul did not welcome fatherhood. He told his wife 'I love you alone, a child would get in our way and would cost too much' and proposed that, in a month, he would take her 'to see a woman he knows who'll do something so that the child won't be born.'[1] At the end of October, Fernande slipped on the five icy steps in the garden, landed on her stomach and miscarried. The concierge wrapped her in hot towels and summoned the doctor, but it was too late. Fernande was put to bed for five days. She felt weak, but not in any pain, except for a sharp stab when she breathed deeply. A few days later she reported 'that episode's over with' and she was back to her 'monotonous' life.[2]

Shortly after this, Fernande went to visit her uncle and aunt. Going into the bedroom she used to share with Marguerite, Fernande lay down on the bed and tried to imagine herself back, before the abduction had taken place, when she was 'still a child'. Her cousin told her that she had behaved badly and her uncle was cold and told her she had ruined her life. As she left, Charles Petot gave her twenty francs, which she spent on some handkerchiefs and a bottle of carnation scent. Back home in Fontenay, Paul smelled the new perfume and lost his temper, as she had not had his permission to go and had not told him that she had been given money. For the first time, Fernande argued back, shouting that she was bored and wished to go out, and that she would leave the door open and hope that all their furniture, which she hated, would be stolen. Her diary makes clear how the situation escalated horrifically:

> Then he started to beat me again like the first time, and like the first time, I was incapable of reacting, not screaming or crying although he was hurting me quite badly. Afterwards he took me in his arms and carried me to the bed saying the worst and most horrible things, so obscene that I felt ashamed, and he took me in his usual way, and in my usual way, I submitted disgusted, lifeless, cold. This is my life.[3]

Hélène, who had colluded in Fernande's abduction and rape, and was her only female companion, now started to ask questions about her feelings, realising that Fernande still loathed Percheron. Hélène was seeing another man whilst still being engaged to Paul's brother Henri. She explained to Fernande that becoming the mistress of a man she didn't love was acceptable, 'because he gives me money' and wanted to enlist Fernande as her partner. After expressing initial horror at this suggestion and fear of her husband's response, Fernande decided to accompany Hélène regardless. Perhaps she saw it as an opportunity to regain some control over her life, or to explore an outlet that was hers alone. Virtually a prisoner, a slave to her husband's violent mood swings and sexual battery, any outlet may have appeared welcome. Hélène and Fernande met two men for lunch in an 'elegant bachelor flat' and drank liqueurs; but the initial advances of 'L.G.', a manager of a big café on the Boulevard Saint-Denis, caused Fernande to flee screaming, in anticipation of the brutality she was used to at the hands of her husband.[4] However, she consented to return for another visit, and accompanied 'L.G.' to lunch, after which his gentle caresses began to relax her and she took an increasing degree of pleasure in his lovemaking. The transition to adultery was easily made; clearly Fernande felt her husband's behaviour had obviated any loyalty and that perhaps this offered her a potential escape route. If nothing else, it was a way of getting back at Percheron.

However, it was a new and unexpected sexual experience that offered Fernande her first true sensual pleasure, inspiring a 'wonderful secret ... (of) ... heavenly sensation'. One day, after lunch, Hélène lay down beside her on the couch and kissed her. Fernande 'felt strange', aroused, just as she had with 'L.G.', but then Hélène sat down at her feet and proceeded to caress her in the same way that he had, suggesting oral sex or perhaps stimulation or penetration by Hélène's fingers, which made Fernande tremble. Hélène told her not to tell Henri, but Fernande had no intention of doing so, being thrilled by their 'wonderful secret' and the 'heavenly sensation'. Less to her taste were the advances made to her by Paul's father, who tried to kiss her 'in dark corners' and whose basic gestures were suggestive and revolting.[5] Her husband objected and spoke to his father, which made Percheron senior turn sulky; but at least he then left Fernande alone. In contrast, she found Paul's mother very sweet but she was relieved when the Percherons' visit was over.

In April 1900, on another visit to the Rue Réaumur, Fernande made a desperate appeal to her uncle, Charles Petot, explaining her unhappiness and inability to cope. Instead of sympathy, she met with a stern call for resignation. 'Get used to it, poor child,' she was told, 'you're married, that's the end of it.' In addition, she was ridiculed and insulted by Margeurite, who told her 'you were a desperate case without money or morals. Look what became of you. Without Maman, who forced you to get married, you'd be living with the fallen women.' To her credit, Fernande expressed only pity for her cousin's 'petty morality ... and her meanness of spirit'.[6] However, Uncle Charles was not as hard-hearted as he pretended. He was the only person who attempted to intervene to improve her conditions, speaking to Percheron regarding Fernande's unhappiness, but little changed and the continuing escalation of violence made her realise that she would never be happy with Paul.

Undoubtedly, Hélène, as a friend and lover, significantly altered the direction of Fernande's life by introducing her to Percheron, and followed it with experiments in adultery and lesbianism. Fernande's sexual awakening had been brutal and sudden, her suffering at the hands of a violent rapist constituted an horrific and protracted ordeal, which was recognised as a crime by the policeman who attended her in the company of Alice Petot. It is difficult to assess objectively whether Fernande's new attitude of sexual experimentation was liberating in a personal sense, or an extension of the manipulation she had already experienced. In one way, though, it did serve as the catalyst for her regaining control of her life. Percheron did not find out about her activities at first and this period of discoveries afforded Fernande a new perspective on the relations between the sexes, which gave her sufficient confidence to leave him. The denouement occurred soon after their visit to the Petots. Responding to his criticisms of her frigidity, Fernande told him that she found sex with him 'obscene' and 'hateful' because he disgusted her. 'What have you ever tried to awake in me that's clean or beautiful?' she asked him. She was 'disgusted by ugliness' and everything about Percheron was ugly, 'the expression in (his) eyes, (his) gestures, (his) pleasures', which she had come to realise as 'the way all women live who have loveless marriages to insensitive men.' In response, his face changed to that of a 'madman' and he brutally raped her, making further threats to kill her. It was this incident that made Fernande determined to leave. As she tried to go, he hit her with a carafe so hard that she had a 'gash in (her) shoulder where a splinter of glass penetrated a centimetre into (her) flesh.' He raped her again, as she was pulling a piece of her dress free from the wound, which would not stop bleeding.[7]

The following morning, as soon as he left the house, Fernande gathered her papers, her clothes and few possessions and boarded the ten o'clock train. Half an hour later she arrived at Bastille Station in Paris. It was a spontaneous act. She had nowhere to go and headed immediately for an employment agency for office workers, sales girls and teachers, where she left her documents and received the optimistic promise that work could be found for her. She was instructed to return at four but she never went back. Just as with Percheron and her former schooling, the attentions of men got between Fernande and her career; within hours of roaming the Parisian streets, she had met the young artist who was to become her next lover.

Starting that day, Fernande embarked upon a promiscuous lifestyle of casual sexual relations among the artistic quarters of Montmartre, modelling at renowned studios for well-known artists and basking in the attention her beauty received. Her account of the four years following her escape reveals the same desire for affection and protection, the fleeting connections and sudden declarations from admirers, as she described in her school days; but although this was consistent with the past, the personal and social circumstances of her new relationships were drastically altered. No longer cushioned by her aunt and uncle, her life was hard and spent in primitive living conditions, although Fernande derived pleasure from her friendships, associations with art students and developing her own painting. The ease with which she made the transition between lovers and sustained multiple sexual relationships suggests a level of freedom unthinkable if Fernande had continued her life with the Petot family; she rapidly became the embodiment of her aunt's worst fears but she side-stepped the moral and social censure Alice represented. Instead, Fernande revelled in the attention she received from men and conducted her sexual relations with an attitude more redolent of late twentieth-century sexual freedom, undoubtedly assisted by the alternative 'bohemian' lifestyles of her new friends. She never obtained a formal divorce from Paul Percheron.

Fernande arrived in Paris, in April 1900, at ten-thirty in the morning. After the employment agency, she did not know what to do, concerned that she might run into a member of her family or friend of her uncle. She sat and read a book in a square, walked about and became hungry, but all she had was one franc and fifteen centimes and her return ticket. It seems significant that she bought and retained a return, so that she had the means to go back to Fontenay. Had events not transpired as they did, had she found herself as friendless at dusk as she had upon arrival, perhaps she would have weakened and returned to Paul, if only for the roof over her head. But, as she was standing outside a patisserie, gazing longingly at the cakes on display, she felt an arm slip through hers and she was led to a table inside. A 'bearded man, young and smiling' ordered her hot chocolate and 'several warm golden brioches' that brought her to her senses. She passed from 'despair to gaiety, from despondency to confidence … restored and full of optimism'.[8]

In her diary, Fernande refers to the young man as Laurent Debienne, although he also went by the name of Gaston de Labaume, or de la Baume, a sculptor of twenty-nine. With his 'large black eyes … sombre face marked by wrinkles … scrawny cheeks … jutting out Adam's apple … thin neck and small skinny body'[9] he was never her physical ideal, but hope and romantic ideals kept her in place. 'When I was a young girl, I'd dreamed of knowing artists,' she admitted. 'They seemed to me to inhabit an enchanted world.' She sensed this young sculptor might be her introduction. Although dependent on his father and based in the western suburb of Neuilly, Debinenne worked every day in his Montparnasse studio between nine and six. He offered to take Fernande back there after he had pointed out the practical difficulties of her situation and she had confessed that she did not wish to work in an office. In return, she was to pose for him, so that he might sculpt her in marble. Debienne took her back with him to the Avenue de Maine, cutting through the heart of the fourteenth arrondissement alongside the Cimetière du Montparnasse. There, he made her comfortable in his 'pleasant enough' studio, leaving her overnight with supplies of food, to sleep naked rolled in an animal hide. There was a grey velvet couch with red cushions, a bed in a small closet room, a piano, bookcases, furnished alcove and an enormous stove. She found tea, sugar, chocolate and coffee in the cupboard and washed in the little 'lean-to' that served as a washroom and toilet. When she woke in the morning, Fernande made herself tea, found a copy of Goethe's *Sorrows of Young Werther* and sat down to await her host.[10]

The following day, Fernande sat for Debienne. In return, he brought her bedding, slices of roast beef, biscuits, a bottle of Eau de Cologne, curling irons and rice papers for her face. Over the coming days, she stayed put, reluctant to go out for fear of being seen, posing during the day and resting at night. When she mentioned that she liked drawing, he supplied her with paper and pencils, offering to give her some guidance if she required it. Laurent also arranged the sale of small items of her jewellery, including her wedding ring, and she used the money to purchase underwear, stockings and a nightgown. After a while, she was brave enough to explore the neighbourhood, appreciating the street vendors, although the haberdashers' windows were a disappointment. One evening Laurent did not return to Neuilly but took her on a tour of the city and for ice-cream at the Café de Versailles. Afterwards he kissed her gently and told her she didn't 'know about sensuality yet' but that it would come, and he was patient. He made the decision to return to his father's house only to dine, and would now sleep in the studio. Fernande recorded that she felt 'gratitude towards him' but was not in love with him.

Soon, Laurent suggested that Fernande might model for other artists, in order to earn a bit of money. She sat for an old Italian sculptor in Neuilly in the mornings, then for a Montparnasse artist who had seen her in the communal courtyard and wished to paint her as Eve. In the evening, she posed for Debienne, who wished to depict her in a series of figurines, in different dance moves. More offers for her to pose were flooding in than she had time for, but they encouraged her to see that she might make an independent living for herself one day. She earned ten francs a day, which she put away in a box, but the work was exhausting, making her lose weight and feel tired all the time. An argument occurred when Fernande vehemently rejected Laurent's request for her to assist the cleaning woman. 'I work quite hard enough as it is. He's too selfish,' and another when she went to buy herself some clothes and found he had spent her money on modelling clay. 'Why didn't he think of leaving some money for me? What an egoist!' Fernande resolved that she would leave and live on her own as soon as she was sure of regular work.[11]

In the autumn of 1900, they moved into a studio in the 'Bateau-Lavoir', a rambling, ramshackle complex facing onto the Rue Ravignan, towards the top of the butte of Montmartre. Fernande found it a nicer district than Montparnasse and it was more convenient for her, as she was posing for many artists living on the nearby Boulevard de Clichy, also home to the area's most notorious nightclubs, the Moulin Rouge, Le Chat Noir, Le Ciel and L'Enfer. Away from Haussmann's drastic redevelopment, surrounded by countryside and topped by wooden windmills, Montmartre had attracted artists with low rents and a moral freedom that created a unique environment. As Roland Dorgeles wrote, 'Once past Rue Lepic, normal behaviour was thrown overboard. Everyone did just as they pleased, not giving a damn. Besides, when it came to the way people dressed, outlandish garb was almost the norm.'[12] The building had been a piano factory, then a locksmith's workshop before being converted into studios, originally taken over by anarchists before a police raid made way for the artists, sculptors and poets that were to give it its creative reputation. The Spaniard Paco Durrio, sculptor, ceramist and jeweller, was one of the first to move in, counting Gauguin among his visitors between 1893 and 1895 and drawing in fellow Spaniards Ricard Canals and Joachim Sunyer as residents, as well as the Dutch artist Kees van Dongen and his family, most of whom were to become significant friends for Fernande.

The Bateau-Lavoir was divided into a number of sections, little more than connected shacks, progressing shakily down the hillside to the Rue Garreau, three storeys below. The accommodation was basic. There was a single tap serving thirty studios and a lone, unlockable toilet, whose door banged in the breeze; no gas or electricity served the building, the walls oozed moisture, it was freezing in winter and boiling in summer; there was little privacy and the paper-thin walls meant every sound could be heard; 'laughter, tears, you can hear everything. Everything echoes around the building and no one has any inhibitions.'[13] The studio was smaller than their one in Montparnasse but the back bedroom was flooded with sunlight and Fernande was pleased to have moved, and although she was critical of Laurent's efforts to make shelves, and even of his work, she was keen to meet more artists, an opportunity which their new location offered. Initially, Laurent and Fernande rented the third of four studios in the ground floor brick part of the building, on the Rue d'Orchamps, where their immediate neighbours were sculptors: Laurence Deschamps and his nightclub singer mistress and the elderly Pozzi. The fourth studio was empty.

By spring the following year, they had moved to a larger studio, still within the Bateau-Lavoir, but on the ground floor of the Place Ravignan. Soon after, Fernande was becoming dissatisfied with Laurent's behaviour, 'which some might find amusing, but I found it disgusting.' Sticking to her regular modelling routine, rising at seven and leaving the house at eight, she returned early one day when the artist she was posing for was ill, only to find Laurent had returned to bed. It was the concierge who explained his secret habits. 'It's a pity to see a girl like you wearing yourself out for a man who sleeps all morning and spends his money in the afternoon on the sluts who pose for him ... don't be so trusting; open your eyes if you care about your sculptor and your health ... these artists are all the same. The woman goes out to work to help them make ends meet, so they can be free to work at their art.'[14] It was a harsh lesson for Fernande, and the concierge's warning that artists usually squandered their money on 'the sluts who pose for them' was confirmed when Fernande returned early home again to find him 'in bed with a girl of twelve or thirteen years old he had been using as a model.' 'Furious, ashamed and sickened' at the girl's age, Fernande was also indignant that she had had to pose for three days in order to pay for the girl's sitting and found Laurent's excuses patronising and demeaning: 'You're not capable of understanding an artist like me. I find your narrow-mindedness so upsetting, I don't even want to bother to explain. I could have created a masterpiece, but you stifle me completely.'[15]

After this incident, Fernande decided she was justified in seeking affection elsewhere. She had previously avoided the attentions of other artists who had made their admiration clear, but now she confided in Jacques, a Montmartre singer thirty years her senior, whom she encouraged to visit her whenever Laurent was out. They became close, as he provided a sympathetic ear and company, but when they became intimate, she was repelled by him at the point of consummation and the affair dwindled into a friendship. By the autumn of 1901, her relationship with Laurent had become violent, triggered by her self-confessed unwillingness to do housework and this brought back bad memories of her marriage. Montmartre, for all its artistic freedom and excitement, exposed her to more overt, aggressively sexual conduct: friends of Laurent propositioned her regularly; a weekend recuperating in Berck became an ordeal when she was forced to share a room with illicit lovers; nor had the scars inflicted by Percheron healed.

I'm always on the defensive with a man. I can't let myself go and be confident, even with those I might like … instinctively I recoil physically and this makes me recoil emotionally too … I long to love and be loved in return … I'm frightened when I remember my husband's wild eyes … I'm struck with such a vivid image of this whenever a man wants me.[16]

Disillusioned with Laurent, she craved a close friend in whom to confide:

I've stored up so much tenderness in my heart … building up since my childhood, which I haven't been able to give anyone.

I've buried it so deep inside me, I'm sure nobody has any idea just how tender and loving I could be ... how could I open out my heart? This is such a weight to bear and so troubling, I'd like to unburden myself. I'm not really the woman I seem to be, but who can I reveal myself to?[17]

Whilst modelling for Léon Bonnat, Fernande met artists Raoul Dufy and Orthon Friesz, currently Bonnat's students at the Ecole des Beaux-Arts. Friesz was twenty-three, a student who had rejected his fine art training in favour of the looser brush work and vibrant colours of the Fauves. His friend Dufy was then twenty-five, 'very sweet and rather shy ... fair-haired, tall and has lovely soft blue eyes which are artless and knowing at the same time.' Fernande appears to have taken a particular liking to him. As rapidly as all her relations were formed, she was already wondering 'is he going to be the one I fall in love with?' shortly after meeting the gentle, Dufy and deciding she was ready 'to be married, have children and a husband I could trust and respect.'[18] This impulse may have sprung from desires for stability as her emotional life was becoming increasingly complicated: she and Laurent were still living together, even though he only slept at home two or three times a week, the singer Jacques was a constant companion, as was his son Marcel, and two other men named Roland and Jean, while all the time she was still legally married to Paul Percheron. On one occasion, the young painter called Jean flew into a jealous rage in the studio and attacked a head of her that Laurent had been making. She also embarked upon an affair with the Catalan artist Joaquin Sunyer, also resident at the Bateau-Lavoir, painting his soft, neo-impressionist portraits and landscapes. Yet all these emotional connections, this search for one man with whom she could fall in love, was exhausting. Fernande wrote that she was 'tired of all this' and longed for stability. The artist Fernand Cormon, whose favourite model she became, advised her to 'marry a young man who's rich. Think of your future. Don't get sucked into this Bohemia.'[19]

Then, in 1903, 'the one thing (she) dreaded more than anything else in the world happened.' As she was leaving the house of an artist on the Boulevard Saint-Germain, at around noon, heading for a tram, Fernande ran into Paul Percheron. She was immediately 'seized with a sort of panic', trembling inside, fearing her legs would give way under her and feeling her heart stop beating. However, she 'managed to put on a brave face'. He had changed, looking 'thin, pale and hollow-cheeked', his clothes 'hanging from his skeletal body' although his eyes still burned with 'that strange fire'. Her diary provides the details of their exchange:

'It's you,' he said 'I've been waiting so long to find you, and here you are at last!'

I didn't reply and he went on. 'You're going to come back, aren't you? You have nothing to fear. I'm living in Paris, near the Parc Montsouris.' His voice was soft and not angry.

Then I answered, 'I'd really like to, but not right now. I'm on my way to work, I'm due there now. Would you like me to meet you tonight?'

'That's fine. Tonight. Promise me, won't you? Right here at seven o'clock.'

I agreed eagerly, squeezed his hand, jumped onto my tram ... and he'd disappeared into the distance before I got over my amazement at his letting me escape like this.[20]

Needless to say, Fernande did not go back. For a while she avoided the Left Bank, where they had met, not feeling able to return until the following year. She confided to her diary that she felt 'even more frightened and (couldn't) control a sense of panic at the thought of him'.[21] Although she did not know it at the time, Percheron would not reappear in her life again and, after this point, he disappears from the records.

Around this time in 1904, Fernande began painting. A few of her works survive, including a Cezanne-style still life of fruit and a vibrant vase of flowers, executed in loose brush strokes.[22] In an intensely descriptive diary entry she gives an insight into her art, her appearance and her passions at this point, just as she was about to meet the most significant man of her life:

I've started painting. I seem to have an eye for colour, but I don't have the patience to draw well. I only enjoy putting in shading and bright colours. I'd work harder if I had more time. I wonder if I ought to continue my boring career as a model ... It's not that I want a lot of fashionable clothes, or at least I only want certain things. I like white collars, lace at my throat, hats, handkerchiefs and underwear. I adore perfume and I stick to rose or sandalwood ... As for my clothes I like dark suits and brightly coloured blouses. Oh yes, and veils, I'm crazy about veils. I have quite a collection of them, and I wear them halfway down my face to my nose. They lend mystery to my eyes, which aren't big, beautiful and wide but are elongated slits shaped like almonds which slant towards my temples. This way I think I look more glamorous, or at least I make more of an impression ... I'm a bit too tall, and a bit too heavy ... but my face is young and fresh, though only my mouth, forehead and colouring are really striking, and I have luxuriant hair, the colour of very ripe chestnuts, with big natural waves ... I'm pining for a kindred spirit ... I'd like to be an artist myself, independent, a bit of a tomboy, like a few I've met. But I'm ruled too much by my heart, and my need to love and be loved soon overrides all my ambition to live alone by my mind.[23]

Later, Fernande reflected on this period as an artists' model and the nature of the work for which she posed. Several representations of her survive, including Walter MacEwen's 1903 *Study of a Redheaded Woman*, Francois Sicard's 1905 statue *Algerian Woman with a Basket of Fruits*, Fernard Cormon's tapestry *Jean Duc de Berry Buying Works of Art*, for which Fernande posed as the Duchess of Berry. Yet, in retrospect, she was critical of the figurative style of 'academic painters' such as Cormon, Axilette, Henner, Boldini, Rochegrosse, Deyrolles, Dubuffe and others who were still chasing approval from the Academy. Their art, she wrote, had very little to do with 'the revelation of their subject' and included no brushstrokes inspired by imagination. For them, 'the eye was law.' They favoured 'accurate, exact copying' and did not understand that 'the essence of painting is to deceive the eye ... so that personality is really the only thing that counts in art.'[24] By the time Fernande was editing her diary, in the 1930s, the artistic revolution of these years had been embedded for decades. The Academy had dominated the art world for years, until the arrival of the Impressionists, who established the Salon des Refusés to showcase work that was rejected for not following formal lines. While Fernande was modelling, the Impressionist influence had spawned a number of new groups, including the Neo-Impressionists, Pointillists, Post-Impressionists, Symbolists, Primitivists and others, whose art was inspired by the imagination rather than the strictly realistic style that had created the huge set pieces depicting historical and mythological subjects. In 1904, Fernande met a young Spanish artist who was to lead the most innovative artistic changes of the new century.

Pablo Picasso had been making regular trips to Paris since 1900, when he visited the World's Fair. An artistic prodigy who had outstripped all his father could teach him by the age of thirteen, he enrolled in the formal art schools of Madrid and Barcelona and swiftly made his mark. Since then he had been travelling back and forth to Madrid, depressed by the suicide of a close friend, creating the melancholy images of grieving figures and harlequins that would later be known as his blue period. In the spring of 1904, he took over the studio vacated by the artist Paco Durrio and soon proved he could equal Fernande's over-populated love life, with his three mistresses Alice, Margot (Marguerite) and Madeleine in tow in his early years at the Bateau-Lavoir. A photograph of him taken that year by fellow resident, Ricard Canals, shows a young man in a thick corduroy jacket, with a flamboyant scarf knotted at his throat. His thick black hair is parted on his right, above a pair of dark eyes that capture some of the intensity of his personality. Another photograph, showing him outside in the Place Ravignan, captures his compact figure and barrel chest encased in a roll-neck jumper, his hands deep in the pockets of his loose trousers, a half smile playing over his regular features. A self-portrait dating from his blue period also has this feeling, with brooding eyes under a thick mass of hair, and a moustache and beard that he did not keep for long.

Fernande became aware of Picasso soon after he arrived at the Bateau-Lavoir. For a while they skirted around each other, while she felt his 'strangely intense gaze ... sharp but brooding, full of suppressed fire'. In the evenings, Fernande sometimes sat in the square with a book, while Laurent was having dinner with his family and Picasso was often standing in front of the door to the building, talking noisily with a group of other Spanish painters. He was something of an enigma to her, she didn't 'know where to place him on the social scale' and couldn't tell how old he was. In fact, he was three and a half months younger than her. She admired the 'lovely shape' of his mouth, which made him look young, while the 'deep lines from his nose to the corners of his mouth' gave him the appearance of age. She noticed that 'even when his lips are laughing, his eyes remain serious,' with the pupil 'steeped in an inexpressible melancholy'. He 'seemed very much taken' with her but for a while she did not answer his attempts to make conversation, unsure of whether she found him attractive.[25]

However, that August they were thrown together while sheltering from a thunderstorm. Blocking her way in the corridor, holding out a pet kitten, Picasso invited her into his studio and she 'couldn't resist his magnetism'. Impressed by the work she saw there, despite the frugality, Fernande became a frequent visitor, assisted by Laurent's absence on military service. Finally, previous doubts dissolving, she believed she 'may eventually come to love this young man', undoubtedly influenced by his powerful devotion: 'his eyes plead with me and he keeps anything I leave behind as if it were a holy relic ... if I fall asleep, he's beside the bed when I wake up, his eyes anxiously fixed on me ... he's asking me to come and live with him ... I'm very tempted; it's sweet to be loved like this and I like him physically too.'[26]

After an argument with Laurent, Fernande moved into the Bateau-Lavoir studio rented by Spanish artist Ricard Canals, his wife Benedetta and their son. A photograph shows the two women posing together in national costume, draped in lace and shawls, capturing the sense of light-hearted playfulness that marked Fernande's stay. Evenings were spent entertaining friends, including Picasso and Paco Durrio; the day was still devoted to modelling, for Canals, Cormon and others. Away from Laurent, Fernande was much happier. The relationship with Debienne limped along through the autumn of 1904, into the spring and summer of 1905, although Fernande's dissatisfaction was evident. 'Whenever we see each other, which isn't often, we argue ... I'm only living at his place temporarily but I don't know how to economise.' Visiting Picasso in his studio, she confessed 'I think I've grown fond of him this past year' and despite his obvious desire for her, she was impressed by his 'sensitivity to let me leave without asking anything of me'. Here, she had her first experience of smoking opium, which triggered the 'spiritual intensity and sharpening of intellectual awareness' that she admitted finally cemented the new relationship: 'It's probably thanks to opium that I've discovered the true meaning of the word love ... at last I understand Pablo, I sense him better. It seems as if I've been waiting all my twenty-three years for him. Love has risen up in me like a feeling that is suddenly coming into flower ... a curious closeness makes me feel as if he's a part of myself ... how could I have been blind for so long?'[27]

It was only through opium that Fernande was able to feel sufficiently relaxed and secure to fall in love for the first time. Despite her many sexual relationships, she had always been clear about her feelings and, in her mind, these new emotions were closely associated with the drug; 'I love to smoke opium, I love Pablo.' The induced relaxed state allowed her to overcome emotional and physical barriers, finally able to abandon herself in sexual enjoyment; 'I'm happy in Pablo's arms, much more fully happy than I ever was with Sunyer.' She felt in tune with a mentality she was now able to voice:

> The old Bateau-Lavoir defends its bohemians from the approach of undesirables. Wealthy bourgeois, keep out! Keep away from this retreat where artists lead a full, demanding life that you know nothing about. Here, life is preserved by hope, love and intellect. Here the law is made by youth ... make way for artists, the only people with the right to live outside society ... I really have been won over by the madness of the people I'm going to be living with now.[28]

The combination of love and opium gave Fernande the push she needed to justify her rejection of the bourgeois values instilled in her at birth. At last, she felt as if she were playing a part in a significant wider world, where art and morality were being redefined. On 3 September 1905, she took out a trunk Picasso had lent her, 'packed in haste and carried (it) across to his studio even more hastily.'[29]

9

Fin de Siècle Paris

The cultural significance of Paris in the first decade of the twentieth century is difficult to overestimate. Writers and painters flocked to the artistic community at Montmartre from all over Europe in search of greater freedom and opportunity; the Salon des Refusés (actually originally dating to as far back as 1863) and proliferation of dealers and smaller galleries offered a tantalising glimpse of avant-garde success often unthinkable at home. The previous decade had seen the final Impressionist exhibition and the arrival of Gauguin, Van Gogh and Cezanne; new techniques were being explored by Symbolists, Synthetists, Primitivists and Expressionists, with the colourful Fauves exploding on the scene in 1905. There was a sense of liberation between the sexes, too, in personal and professional ways. A few prominent female artists had come to the fore by the turn of the century, with Impressionist Berthe Morisot holding her first solo exhibition in 1892, the former model Suzanne Valadon becoming the first woman to be admitted to the Société Nationale des Beaux-Arts in 1894 and the writer Colette, who was Sophie Brzeska's exact contemporary, publishing her first novel in 1900, although it appeared under the name of her controlling husband.

Artists from overseas were drawn to Paris by depictions of Bohemian life by popular authors such as Henri Mugler, George Du Maurier, Eugene Sue and Emile Zola, as well as by the comparatively low prices of studios and café meals. In London, a spell in one of the Parisian art schools was seen as the best way to develop skills in paint and colour after schools like the Slade and Royal Academy had laid the classical foundations. However strong the lure of Paris as an artistic centre, it was still full of potential dangers and only in the 1890s did it become more popular as a destination for English women, singly and collectively. British art journals had been recommending study in Paris for a decade but increasingly, these adverts were directed at young women of fashion; a 1909 'Woman's Guide to Paris' was published in response to the rise in lone female travellers. The city was to provide the backdrop for Ida, Fernande and Sophie, as a place of employment, love and artistic experience, and all three were to make it their home during a significant time of personal evolution. For all three also, it was a city the brilliance and culture of which was underpinned by currents of threatening sexuality. Fernande steered her course through its new personal and artistic freedoms, Sophie travelled there to embrace death but instead found love and Ida saw it as a representation of a different life, where she could pursue her dreams, before the net of marriage closed in.

Achieving Paris was not always easy. Sophie and Fernande had shaken off parental control but Ida was still sensitive to the wishes of John and Ada, as well as partly dependent upon them to supplement her bursary. Other families were less supportive than the tolerant, liberal Nettleships, and saw their daughters' desires to visit the city as thinly veiled justifications for the pursuit of depravity. The parents of Kathleen Bruce, herself a sculptor who visited the city in 1901, wrote '...to say that a lass perhaps not out of her teens had gone prancing off to Paris to study art was to say that she had gone irretrievably to hell'[1] and the undeniable freedoms encouraged by the relaxed atmosphere of late café hours and concentration of artists often did prove equally as attractive as the opportunity to study at one of the academies. There were understandable fears that the great masters might corrupt their students, leading at best to heartbreak in the case of Gwen John and Auguste Rodin; and at the worst, to ruin.

In September 1898, Ida and Gwen Salmond, a friend from the Slade, set out for Paris, hoping that Augustus' sister, Gwen John, would shortly join them. By studying in the studios of a master, the girls would be following in the footsteps of Slade teachers Brown and Steer, and William Rothenstein, a visitor to the Nettleship home, who had studied at Julian's earlier in the decade, as had many of the Impressionist artists. They stayed in a hotel in Montparnasse before finding lodgings in a 'very old lady style' pension at 226 Boulevard Raspail, close to the Boulevard Montparnasse, 'looking down on a boulevard with rather brown rustling plane trees and cafes[2]' on the 'delightful' side of the river. They were a mere twenty-minute walk from the Avenue de Maine, where Fernande first lived with Laurent Debienne in April 1900. Ida and Gwen headed straight for the Louvre upon arrival, just as did Clive Bell six years later, tracing the footsteps of a multitude of Edwardian visitors. In a letter to Michel Salaman, Gwen showed her awareness of how much the green Slade students had to learn in Paris. 'My four years show me that a sort of technicality is the wall I break myself against.'[3] Eventually, Gwen John wore down her father's resistance and joined Ida and the other Gwen to begin their artistic adventure.

Finally, the girls found what they were looking for on the fifth floor of 12 Rue Froidevaux, a wide leafy avenue in the cheaper Montparnasse district, which they misspelt as Froidveau and mistranslated as 'cold beef'. The ground floor was a café but a separate side door gave them a degree of privacy and quiet, the balcony with 'good views' overlooked the cemetery and the toilet was of the old variety, which required water being thrown down it. The old female concierge was 'very high in character' and strict about visitors; 'les dames, oui, mais les monsieurs? Non! Jamais,'[4] information which Ida was keen to pass on to her mother. It cost 900 francs, but Ida worked out their combined finances, planned for basic living expenses and decided they could afford it for three months. What finally swung them in its favour was its proximity to the Louvre and Julian's. The present-day building, occupying a right angle on the corner of the Rue Froidevaux and Rue Boland, is an eight-storeyed pink-bricked residence, with the café Le Table d'Eulalia on the ground floor and ornate iron balconies at the long windows above. A low, bricked-up door around the side is probably the one the girls used to access their apartment.

Their studio was basic and had clearly seen better days but the girls had great plans. 'Half the wall is covered with brown paper, and when we have spare time and energy we are going to cover the other half,'[5] Ida wrote to her mother, but spare time was lacking amid their busy schedule of gallery visits, sketches and exploring the narrow streets for shops selling artist's supplies. They ate at an 'anarchist' restaurant, some of the waitresses of which became their models; at breakfast they read Shakespeare's history plays and when they were out in the street, they kept an eye on Parisian fashions. Evenings often became dressmaking sessions, based on what they had seen in the department store. Ida collected a series of fashion plates from the 1850s for her mother's theatrical costumes, sending her prints from 'Un Siécle des Modes Feminines,' which the girls wanted to keep as they were 'so pretty' and that Gwen John was copying.[6] One of these works was almost certainly Gwen's 'Interior with Figures' which shows Ida in one of these historically inspired creations, wrapped in a heavy pink shawl and with a full, ruffled skirt. The girls also had visitors from home, Michel Salaman, Augustus and his father Edwin John, who took exception to a dress of Gwen's, modelled on a picture by Manet, in which her father claimed she looked like a prostitute.

The nearby Julian's, run by Benjamin Constant, was the girls' first choice of school but it was very expensive and, with thirty pounds remaining in her budget for fees, Ida considered the cheaper Académies Colarossi or Delécluse. However, the new Académie Carmen had recently opened near the Luxembourg Gardens at 6, Passage Stanislaus, and was run by Carmen Rossi, a model of Whistler, who would be undertaking some of the teaching. Originally Rossi charged the female students twice as much as the men, but Whistler soon discovered this and put a stop to it, although it is not clear whether this was before Ida and the Gwens arrived. At first, only Gwen Salmond, with her sixty pounds for fees, could afford to enrol but she generously paid for Gwen John to attend as an afternoon student, while Ida enrolled at Colarossi's. Writing a pamphlet on Paris' lure in 1902, Clive Holland reflected the popularity of their choices; 'a year or two at Julian's, the Beaux-Arts or Colarossi's is worth a cycle of South Kensington with its "correctness".' By 1900, one in three students of the Beaux-Arts was a foreigner.[7]

The American artist James Whistler was coming to the end of a distinguished career by the time the girls arrived in Paris.

The school rules were strict, even more so than those of the Slade; the sexes were segregated into different studios, there was to be no drawing on the walls, no smoking, no singing, even no talking, which made it very unpopular with male students who soon rebelled against what they considered an unnecessarily draconian regime. A head student, the massièr or massière, was appointed to handle student matters and maintain the list of rules pinned to the wall; during part of 1899, this post was held by an English girl, Inez Bate, who had achieved favour by painting exactly as Whistler taught, but taking orders from a young woman irritated some of the male students further.

Whistler's methods of teaching were somewhat unexpected; 'I do not teach art,' he claimed, 'I teach the scientific application of paint and brushes.'[8] This emphasis on colour and tone meant he would often be looking at the student's palette rather than their canvas, although this tonal method had great implications for the work of Gwen John, as Whistler later asked Augustus. 'Character? What's character? Your sister has a great sense of tone.' Nor did he offer any 'tricks of the trade' that students had hoped to pick up; he wanted instead to take them back to the beginning and build up their skills slowly, with no substitute for persistence and hard work. Like the Slade, these studios were sometimes viewed as a form of finishing school, so Whistler's methods soon weeded out those with only a passing interest in art, or those who felt they had already advanced beyond his restrictive methods. Here, the two Gwens encountered a figure just as imposing and difficult as Henry Tonks, revelling in the role of the master with his band of 'dedicated disciples' and alternating his 'romantic susceptibilities' with 'monocled sarcasms'.[9] The female students responded in the same way many had to Tonks, happy to be presided over as part of his dedicated band; Gwen Salmond explained 'Whistler is worth living for ... a first rate master who knows how to teach,'[10] 'very beautiful and just right' and even Ida rushed to his defence, rebutting attacks on his teaching as 'stupid and unkind'.[11]

The Académie Colarossi had opened in the 1870s, in the bohemian district of Montparnasse, offering cheaper, mixed classes, which could in themselves provide an education. Located at 10, Rue de la Grande Chaumière, it was run by the Italian sculptor

Filippo Colarossi as an alternative to the stuffy formality of the school of Beaux Arts. In a scandalous departure from the usual practice, female students were allowed to draw the male models. Describing her first day in 1901, innocent Kathleen Bruce felt sick at the sight of a string of nude men, who took it in turns to 'jump for a moment on to the model throne, took a pose and jumped down,' as a means of choosing the life model for that day.[12] It is likely that Ida also attended sessions with the two Gwens at the Académie Carmen, even though it was more expensive. Perhaps she enrolled part-time, or modelled in exchange for lessons. In his autobiography, Augustus John relates how he mentioned Ida when he met Whistler in London: 'I mentioned Ida Nettleship, who had been his pupil in Paris, had posed for him and was now my wife. Mr Whistler spoke of her with much sympathy, asking me to send her his compliments.'[13] Influenced by Whistler, Paris and a new-found freedom, that autumn was a 'most promising time,' full of inspiration and hope; in her letter to Ada, Ida describes them as almost intoxicated with the possibilities of art. 'We all go suddenly daft with lovely pictures we can see or imagine and want to do.' [14]

Augustus John was in Paris at the same time as the three girls, working in his own studio and copying the masters in the Louvre. He gives an account of first meeting Whistler, a 'slight, dapper figure' clad in black, who took charge of him and conducted him around the Louvre on an impromptu tour. Later, he visited the artist in his studio on the top floor of 86, Rue Notre Dame des Champs and found him engaged 'on an immense self-portrait', about seven feet high. This was *Brown and Gold*, an almost ethereal depiction of Whistler aged sixty-four, dressed in a long brown coat, which John rightly described as 'a ghostly figure'. It was exhibited to great acclaim in the 1900 *Exposition Universelle*, where one critic summarised it as 'vague like an apparition, but so gripping, so real'.

John also wrote of the pleasures of life in Paris, in almost Baudelairean terms, when 'to go forth upon the boulevard after a day of work is always exhilarating.' Playing the part of the flaneur, he united 'with the crowd,' enjoying it the more for being 'an outsider' wondering who the passing characters were. On the terraces of the Nouvelle Athenes or the Rat Mort, he 'conjured up the ghost of the last enchanted epoch' and 'the forms of Manet, Pissarro, Renoir,

Cezanne, Degas seemed to rise again, to argue, laugh or quarrel across the marble tables.' He described a Montmartre where 'the little Place de Tertre had not at this time been converted into a bad open-air restaurant,' where students paraded 'bogus works of art', where the 'sails of the Moulin Galette revolved as usual' and he sat for hours in the Rue de la Gaîté 'under the spell of an unusually efficient mechanical orchestra'. Camille Pissarro's 1897 *Boulevard Montmartre* presents something of this crowd, with pavements full of strollers and horse-drawn cabs between the avenue of trees and the tall, cream buildings behind. There was also the Eiffel Tower to explore, newly constructed in 1889, the explosion of luxury goods in the vast, colourful department stores, the building of the Metro and the bright, gas-lit streets.

It is unclear exactly when the three women returned home; Michael Holroyd[15] and Sue Roe[16] claim Ida and Gwen John returned to London early in 1899, while Susan Chitty[17] states that the two Gwens returned in February, leaving Ida to continue working in Paris for a month or two more. It seems unlikely that Ida would have failed to attend the wedding of Edna Waugh to William Clarke Hall in December 1898, although this does not rule out a brief visit followed by her return to France in the new year. It had been a glorious interlude, during which Ida had been able to saturate herself in the Parisian atmosphere, smoking cigarettes to fire her creativity, mixing with artists and models, walking in the steps of the masters. She was now aged twenty-two, by which point her mother had been married and borne a child. Yet Ida was determined to pursue her art and not to sacrifice her talent to a domestic life. Whenever she returned from Paris, it was to face the same dilemmas concerning career and marriage as she had left behind the previous autumn.

*

Paris was also to prove a significant location for Sophie Brzeska, who found her zest for life renewed among its libraries, theatres and lecture halls. She studied Nietzsche, Pliny, Plato, Molière, French art, German literature, medieval history, Buddhism, colonisation and Euripides, who proved a favourite, and attended performances of Madame Butterfly and Tosca at the Opéra Comique, various theatre productions of *Chantecler*, *La Barricade* and Sarah Bernhardt in *La Dame aux Camellias*.

Sophie had spent several months enjoying lectures and operas before she noticed the young, dark-haired boy sitting opposite her in the Sainte-Geneviève library. For her, Ida and Fernande, this complex, vibrant city was to become at different times in their lives the paradoxical embodiment of intense suffering and great happiness. After years of loneliness and the rejections she had encountered when seeking affection from both sexes, Sophie's meeting with Henri Gaudier in June 1910, was to mark an important turning point. His significance in her life is to be found in the fact that history now knows them by their hyphenated surname of Gaudier-Brzeska.

Henri had been born on 4 October 1891, making him nineteen years Sophie's junior, young enough to be her son. He arrived in St Jean de Braye, five kilometres east of Orléans, an area which is now absorbed into the suburban overspill of the city. His origins were solidly working class; his father Germain was a carpenter and his mother Alice was the daughter of a wheelwright. Although then little more than a hamlet, the family's wider environment combined the rural beauty and corresponding labour and activity of a 'garden city' with the bustle and trade of the historic metropolis of Orléans. On the South Bank, in the last decades of the nineteenth century, the 'market gardens' produced the best apples and pears, beans and asparagus, to supply Parisian market stalls. Friends visiting the Gaudiers in 1913 were taken by Germain on a long walk through the surrounding countryside, where he pointed out names of flowers and creatures; although on the cusp of the bustling city, the Gaudiers were still very much country folk. Young Henri delighted in exploring the vast forest of Orléans, producing detailed sketches of the animals, birds and plants he saw there. The family also took great satisfaction from the memory of an ancestor who had worked as a mason on Chartres Cathedral, whose family likeness Horace Brodsky later claimed to have spotted in the stone work.[18] The world had changed significantly since Germain was young and he recognised his son's future may lie more profitably in business or industry, rather than carpentry. It was a realistic view, to which Henri initially submitted, although never to the same degree as the delight he took in working with his hands. He enjoyed being a craftsman and 'getting dirty', later dismissing tidily dressed and clean, washed Londoners as the 'bloody bourgeois', a typical bohemian insult.

One of the disciplines in which the young Henri distinguished himself at the Benjamin Franklin school in Orléans was languages; friend and fellow artist Nina Hamnett later claimed he could speak five fluently and temporary work he undertook in adulthood often involved some element of translation. In 1906 he beat a thousand competitors to win a scholarship to study in London and improve his English. Leaving France for the first time, he spent the months of June and July lodging in Bayswater. The success of this first visit and subsequent hard work paid off again soon, for the following year he was awarded a second scholarship, for three thousand francs, an impressive amount, to enable him to study business methods abroad.

Returning to England in September 1907, Gaudier set out for Bristol, this time lodging with friends of his Orléans teacher Monsieur Roux; his host George Smith taught at the Merchant Venturers' College where Henri's studies were based. It was during the academic year 1907–8 that Gaudier finally decided that he would try to make a future from his art; the rest of the time the scholarship allowed him would be useful experience and a good opportunity to travel but it would not lead to a career at the expense of his drawing, which was increasingly becoming the driving force in his life. Producing many more sketches, he was careful to preserve, name and date them, fuelled by a greater sense of their importance as markers along the path of his artistic development. He no longer threw away complete pictures, regarding them as finished, as he had done as a child. The sketchbook he kept at the time had a front page of heraldic devices and versions of his own name, affiliating his artistic talents with the family tradition of skilled artisans.

Already impressed by his academic ability, his hosts the Smith family witnessed the flowering of Gaudier's ability in spite of the limited resources at his disposal: soon after his arrival he was working from a child's box of paints, with only twelve blocks of colour. On frequent forays into the surrounding countryside, he always carried his sketchbook to capture a quick impression, using the ideas they gave him in the more permanent pencil drawings or watercolours he took more time and care over. During this period, he particularly enjoyed sketching local buildings and architectural features in pen and ink, harking back to the prominence of masonry and carpentry in his youth, as well as producing his usual nature studies, where his skills were often shown at their best.

In the summer of 1908, when the academic year drew to a close, Gaudier took the opportunity to travel a little and seek new material for his sketch book. First he went south to Devon and Somerset, before making a brief visit to London. Wales may also have featured on his itinerary at this time, as preparation for his coming spell in Cardiff; in later years it was clear he knew Wales well, telling his friend Horace Brodsky that he had walked all round it and knew its traditions, castles and historical buildings. Particularly fine sketches of Llandaff Cathedral and Caerphilly castle survive, as well as the tale of a local tree that attracted pilgrims by blooming earlier than was usual, until Gaudier explained to the villagers that it was the warmth of the gulf stream causing this miracle and not the hand of God. He was back in Bristol in August, spending a little time with the Smiths, drawing in Bristol Museum and putting his affairs in order for the next stage of his travels and experience of the world of work.

For his year of work experience, Gaudier was placed with the firm of Fifoot, Ching and Company, coal exporters with links to the French government, based in Cardiff Bay. Now lodging in the Roath district, he worked for a nominal wage, learning more English and gaining experience in trade. Fellow employee Alfred Hazell was impressed by Henri Alphonse Seraphim Mari Gaudier, as he was calling himself, recalling him to be an extraordinary youth who 'could not fail to make his mark in the world', who gave the impression of 'mysterious power' within.[19] Easily fulfilling his duties, Henri's spare time was dedicated to his art; his lunch hours were spent down at the docks, whence he would return with sketches of boats or cranes in pen and ink that he would proudly show off. His boss, Mr Ching, generously encouraged his drawing 'because I felt that commerce was not his forte and he was bound to leave it at the first possible chance.'[20] Gaudier was lodging at 29 Claude Road, but according to Ching, was the kind of boy 'to have lived in a garret while he got on with his life's work.' When not at work or sketching at the docks, Henri drew in Victoria Park or copied birds from the Welsh Museum of Natural History, concentrating on the quality of his drawing rather than just realistic interpretation. It was in these depictions of animals and birds that the real energy and vitality of Gaudier's talent begins to show, rather than his previous stiff, Ruskin-style architectural studies.

In April 1909, Henri's contract with Fifoot and Ching came to an end. After a brief visit again to the Smiths in Bristol, he travelled to London, sketching on the train and spending a day drawing in the British Museum. Then he left England, bound for the German city of Nuremburg and the home of Doctor Uhlemayr and his family. Over the next four months, the doctor was to something of a cultural mentor to Henri, discussing civilisation, art, ideas and literature, before the youth departed for a short stay in Munich before returning to Paris, at the age of eighteen, where he rented a room in the Rue Bernard-Palissy. Disappointed at having failed to get work as an illustrator, he took a clerkship with the publishing firm of Armand Colin and spent his evenings in the Sainte Geneviève library. He decided to become a sculptor, modelling himself on Rodin and Michelangelo and considered himself to now be 'in the midst of Bohemia, a queer mystic group but happy enough, there are days when you have nothing to eat, but life is so full of the unexpected that I love it as much as before I used to detest the stupid regular life of employment.'[21]

It was there that he met Sophie Brzeska. She pored over books dedicated to German language and literature, conscious that the glances of other students were drawn her way, indulging in a little flirtation with a nearby Russian, although eluding his attempts to reach 'an understanding' with her. The friendly overtures of the young Frenchman copying the illustrations from a medical textbook, received more encouragement; one day she sat beside him, overlooking the sketchbook where he had recorded rapid impressions of those around. When she asked to see his work, Sophie may have been surprised and flattered to see that he had been sketching her and the unlikely friendship began. Gaudier wrote to Uhlemayr 'she ... has beauty à la Baudelaire ... she is lithe and simple, with a feline carriage and enigmatic face, the fine character of which reflects her most intimate thought.' In the same letter, he described himself as 'in love' with a woman whose 'ideas on the family, society and Western civilisation are the same as ours,' who like him, was 'mad as a hatter'.[22] The first day they spoke in the library, Henri waited for her at the entrance and they walked up and down the Rue Cujas, deep in conversation, until finally reaching her hotel. This 'poor dreamy child', she admitted in *Matka*, had 'taken me by storm by the most tender fibres of the heart'.[23]

An emotional intimacy developed very quickly between Henri and Sophie, although the question of physical desire would prove more difficult to settlel. Attracted to this lively, passionate young man, Sophie's feelings were complicated by the age difference and her maternal feelings, as she confided in her diary that she longed for a son, whom she could have protected and nurtured. Outside her hotel that first night, she told him 'I am too old to be your lover, but I could be your mother if you want to.' He complimented her that she was beautiful, to which she replied that since her childhood she had been told she was ugly. Henri's response was that 'vulgar people don't know true beauty, which consists in delicacy and individual expression' and he saw how she was 'at some moments completely drowned in (her) studies' while 'at others (she) lift(ed) her eyes to the ceiling with a tragic mask on (her) face.' What appears to have created such a quick, deep bond is Sophie's recognition that he was 'without love and without friends', had 'suffered a lot', was not understood by his parents and that he had the same 'illness' which exhausted her. She noticed that his hands sweated, his cheeks were hollow and she supposed 'he did not feed himself enough,'[24] although she did not specify exactly what this illness was.

The thought of a sexual relationship with Henri filled her with foreboding; she had already lied to him about her age and the thought of 'breaking into' his life, when she considered herself ill in mind and body, roused old memories of madness, rage, terror and crises, suicidal impulses and presentiments of evil, convincing her she must not burden the young man. She may still have been suffering from the emotional turmoil of her failed Baden relationship and her suicidal impulse. She explained as much to Gaudier:

Do not fear that I wish to encroach upon your innocence – I have just been through a crisis, from which perhaps it may not be possible to recover, but even apart from that, I am not the sort of woman to corrupt boys of your age ... it is only right to establish some ground rules for our relationship. Would you like me to be a mother to you, an adoptive mother, since your own mother does not understand you?[25]

Henri agreed. They met the following day to visit the Louvre, where the adoptive son endeared himself to Sophie by doffing his hat before the huge *Victory of Samothrace* and soon she was a regular visitor to his room in the Rue Bernard-Palissy, where Gaudier sketched her, entrusted her with his diary, listened to her writing ambitions and where they memorised Shakespeare's sonnets together. As the relationship intensified, Sophie felt the need to repeat her earlier clarification of their roles, telling Gaudier 'I do not love you as a lover, it is quite a different feeling.'[26] Not yet nineteen, he was legally a minor and nineteen years her junior. Henri was disappointed, as he was clearly pressing for them to become more intimate and may have read her early reluctance as prudishness; but when he asked her whether these feelings might change and attempted to kiss her, she dismissed him firmly. 'There are no kisses in our programme.'[27] She favoured him only with a chaste maternal peck on the forehead. Sophie's sexual reticence belied the depth of her feelings for Gaudier; almost from their first visit, they were constant companions, corresponding when apart, sharing their beliefs and aspirations. Poor health, a broken heart and possibly fear of censure were allied to the maternal longing for the son she never had as blocks to further intimacy. Their relationship was always to be uneasily platonic, even after Sophie settled into the role of Gaudier's 'sister', a fiction in which many of their mutual friends still believed until well after his death. It is difficult to know at this distance whether Sophie's insistence was an exercise of choice or a necessity because of circumstance. Given her constant state of poor health, it seems she had genuine physical reasons for abstinence, although Gaudier's age and her learned reticence may have disinclined her to jeopardise a promising friendship.

10

Being Mrs Artist

For Ida, Paris had represented artistic and personal freedom. Her return to England forced her to face the question of her future and whether or not to ally herself, legally or otherwise, with the man she loved. Her cherished belief in the female artist's ability to maintain both marriage and career must have suffered a blow when, reconnecting with old friends she had left behind, she experienced second-hand the alarming way in which a husband could curtail a woman's aspirations.

Promising Slade artist Edna Waugh had fulfilled Tonks's fears and left the school six months before her term of study was up, in order to marry William Clarke Hall. Visiting her at Red Cottage in Thames Ditton, Ida found an alarming change in her friend, who now frequently spent her days alone, unable to continue with her work. In the days before their marriage, Willie had convinced an increasingly doubtful Edna that her status as a wife would not interfere with her career; indeed, he had often encouraged her work and accompanied the girls on their country rambles with sketchbooks. Upon their engagement, he had written, 'If you do me the great honour of marrying me you must have no trouble about domestic affairs at all. I want you to consider Art your profession and I will not have you hampered in any way by stupid household details. We must have a housekeeper to do all that sort of thing.'[1]

However, following the ceremony, Willie had become hostile to Edna's work and did not want to see it around the house; he asked her to remove the pictures she had hung and was angered by the 'rubbish' of her pens and paints lying about. Instead, he wanted her to focus on running the household and forget 'the part of (her) that was so inspired' in favour of the 'small tyrannies of everyday life'.[2] Frequently alone while her husband was working in London, Edna was isolated and unhappy, her days occasionally brightened by visits from her old Slade friends, timed to coincide with Clarke Hall's absence. For Ida, who had witnessed their early courtship and Edna's considerable talent, this must have provided shocking confirmation of how masculine adherence to convention could stifle female creativity and raised questions about men's trustworthiness. In comparison with Edna, Ida may have felt fortunate to be wooed by a fellow artist, himself sympathetic to the plight of female aspiration; he had encouraged his sister Gwen's work and modelled for Edna at Red Cottage. Surely the wife of Augustus John would not suffer in the way Edna was?

John's career had been advancing swiftly while Ida was in Paris, moving from end of year Slade prizes to acceptance by the New English Art Club. He had moved through a string of studios, initially shared with Evans and McEvoy and travelled about the country painting commissioned portraits, promoted by influential patrons including William Rothenstein and John Singer Sergeant, culminating in a one-man show at Fothergill's Carfax Gallery in St James's, which secured his reputation – and made him a more attractive proposition as a son-in-law. Conversely, his private behaviour had become more scandalous as he had thrown himself into new friendships, having been introduced by Charles Conder to the Café Royal. That summer, had accompanied the artist William Rothenstein and his family on a painting trip to the Normandy coast. Increasingly, his drinking and associated exploits became more outrageous, ending his evenings in police chases or dancing on church roofs,[3] news which inevitably found its way back to the Nettleship parents.

Nor did Augustus' feelings for Ida preclude romantic escapades; in fact, one liaison threatened to jeopardise the hope of any relationship entirely, when he attempted to elope with the parlour maid of Mrs Everett's new boarding house in Swanage, a Viennese girl named either Maria Katerina, or Anna Carolina, who 'escaped' from John after the landlady 'enlightened' her as to his character. That August, John returned to Paris, where he failed to keep an engagement with William Orpen because he was occupied with another 'lady'. He spent most of his remaining visit in the company of the dying Oscar Wilde and 'whoring' with Charles Conder in nightclubs until dawn. When he returned to London, he took up with a Miss Simpson, who dismissed him as too poor, chose a bank clerk instead and invited John to the wedding. His contact with Ida during this period was erratic, although mutual commitment to art maintained their connection: she was still a powerful muse for him, considering the portrait he painted of her clothed in scarlet. She proved willing to step in and model for his studio partner William Orpen's Hamlet, after Gwen John broke her nose. Back in France again with the Rothensteins, John's 'satyr-like' womanising became worse, making him almost unrecognisable to the old friends who witnessed his behaviour on this holiday. Also present, Michel Salaman was shocked to see him grow 'almost delirious' about women, one evening his 'temperature ... shot up to 104' and he complained of psychosomatic illnesses.[4] His disturbed, fretful behaviour reached a peak that summer and was beginning to deeply trouble him; he craved the stability he saw in the Rothenstein's successful marriage and his thoughts again turned to Ida.

Back in England, in autumn 1900, Ida and John resumed the more personal aspect of their friendship, despite her awareness of his recent behaviour, because 'although she had few illusions over the sort of life he had been leading, she still loved him' and Orpen was able to report that the union was 'complete'.[5] However, the Nettleships' resistance was still as strong, as was Ida's determination not to submit to an immoral arrangement, seeing a legal union as the only outlet for her to express her sexuality. Forced directly to choose between the wishes of her family and her desire to be with Augustus, Ida's final decision was a difficult, unhappy one, although she must have known she could rely on the depth of her parents' love; she was not to be rejected as Fernande was. Her rebellion was forgivable, as her choice to wed without their consent was a reinforcement of the strict personal morality of her parents' teaching. Around this time, John wrote a callous limerick:

There was a young woman named Ida
Who had a porcelain heart inside her

But she met a young card
Who hugged her so hard
He smashed up her crockery. Poor Ida ![6]

In the late autumn of 1900, John agreed to the only option Ida would allow him; that of a respectable marriage, although it would have to be a civil ceremony. Ida was deeply in love but had also remained constant to her principles for four years through his varying degrees of bad behaviour. John had strayed before at points when the relationship reached a stalemate, so this was the time for him to accede. Believing John's personality and success would win round her parents or, if not, a wedding certificate would give them no choice but to accept him, she consented to an elopement. On a misty Saturday morning in January 1901, 'which lent an air of mystery unexpectedly romantic,' they met outside St Pancras registry office, where Gwen John, Ambrose McEvoy and Ben Evans 'aided and abetted' Ida in becoming Mrs Augustus John.

Following their furtive ceremony, Ida and Augustus returned to Wigmore Street to present their wedding as a fait accompli to the less than impressed Nettleships. Neither Ada nor John was pleased to learn of their daughter's marriage and Ida must have felt their disappointment as she faced the difficult task of explaining her behaviour. It was a social and religious, as well as personal, betrayal. By eloping, she had rejected the grand-scale wedding with its rituals, family roles and public announcements in favour of a more intimate, private Slade-based affair, from which even her sisters had been excluded. It must have been a difficult few hours. By the evening however, the Nettleship parents agreed to attend a party held by the Rothensteins in the new couple's honour, although this too must have been fraught with emotion despite the riotous games of charades. In celebrating with an impromptu party rather than the traditional family reception, Ida and Augustus were reinforcing their choice of individual need over social convention. The early twentieth-century experimental freedom in personal relationships, marked by this elevation of individual happiness, was to characterise the marriage and claim its casualties.

The remaining hours of that day typified the roles each was to take in the coming years: Augustus disappeared, ostensibly to take a bath, reappearing that evening in outlandish checks and earrings, while the 'exquisitely virginal' Ida was informed about the secrets of womanhood by Alice Rothenstein and an employee of her mother's, rather than by Ada herself. Anticipating John's famous and insatiable sexuality, she confessed to fears about the approaching wedding night but had at least been able to plan the awakening of her sexuality by a man she loved, unlike Fernande.

The new couple honeymooned in Swanage, where they stayed at Mrs Everitt's guest house, the 'Pevril Tower'. Set on Dorset's Jurassic coast, on the eastern tip of the Isle of Purbeck, Swanage was a popular late Victorian holiday destination. The nearby Studland Bay was a favourite location of sisters Virginia Woolf and Vanessa Bell, along with their Bloomsbury friends. Swanage was noted for its clean air and fine weather, although Ida and Augustus can hardly have experienced much sunshine at that time of year.

On their return, John took a cheap flat comprising three rooms and a studio in Fitzroy Street, soon to become the centre of Walter Sickert's Francophile avant-gardism. In 1901, though, artists took studios there chiefly for the low rents. The poor conditions were rather a come-down for Ida after Wigmore Street and probably contributed to her immediate outbreak of measles. Her sisters, parents and even family servants were concerned by the conditions they found the newly-weds in; the cook was in tears at the state of the place. Perhaps fearing that she would catch 'a more contagious disease',[7] Ida returned home to be nursed by her mother in comfort. Her rapid return may have signalled some degree of regret or instinct to escape her new life and return to the security of her girlhood. Perhaps Ida had begun to get some inkling of the gulf her marriage had created between the two halves of her life. However, financial necessity was soon to take her further away from the safety and security of her family home and the lost innocence it represented.

Around the time of the marriage, John heard that his application for a British Institute Scholarship had been turned down. Instead, another offer presented itself. Through the influence of friends, he had been proposed for an art professorship at Liverpool University. It was too good an opportunity to refuse, especially for one so young, with the regular income plus an anticipated stream of commissions.

The transition to a new city beyond the reach of family and friends would have been more difficult for Ida than John, who had already severed his Welsh ties. Ida must have suspected it would put their love and commitment to the test but for the sake of that love, she was prepared to leave her former life behind and boarded the train from Euston at the beginning of March 1901.

John's first impressions of Liverpool were favourable. The architecture, docks and influx of immigrants excited him and he spent his first days exploring the Chinese quarter. In the eighteen months they spent there, he was to make influential new friends and develop life-long interests. For Ida, the time was to be less happy, associated with her descent into domestic drudgery and increasing loneliness in her marriage. Possibly she accompanied John on some of his rambles to explore their new home, or else stayed behind to help create the domestic environment that was to become her sphere. Initially they lodged at 9, St James' Street, where Augustus found it impossible to work, before moving to a large boarding house that combined numbers 10 and 12 Falkner Street, in Liverpool's Georgian quarter. Now a cobbled road of four storeyed brown-brick terraces, the two houses retain their wide, solid front doors, each topped with a semi-circular stained-glass window, their sash windows, stone steps and iron railings. The census of that year lists Augustus and Ida as residents along with twenty-three others, in a 'private hotel' run by a German widow named Rebecca Rodiek. Other boarders included an optician, a solicitor, a retired pawnbroker, a dressmaker, a physician and a German pastor. Augustus was listed as an artist who was working 'at home' on that day.[8]

The shared facilities at Falkner Street made it a difficult workplace and in April the newly-weds found rooms at 4, St James' Road, owned by John Macdonald Mackay, a professor who held the Rathbone Chair of History, a 'leading spirit' of the University. Augustus set to work on a three-quarter length view of their landlord, later exhibited by the New English Art Club where it won a gold medal. The University's art department proved less impressive, being little more than a collection of sheds, although Augustus threw himself headlong into his work there, seeming to Ida to be always busy. She found the new social regime taxing and she would have rather spent her time engaged in the pursuits of art than socialising with members of the university, and with much of her remaining time taken up by modelling for Augustus. She had managed to continue a little painting of her own since the move, using an old man who lectured on Dante as a model, but found the increasing intrusions difficult. As a new university couple, preceded by John's reputation, they were the cause of local curiosity and prompted visits from well-meaning academic families. The social dinners they attended usually proved a success and Ida made friends among the other university wives, but the visitors came to discuss art with John, while she worried about the room being untidy. She was marginalised as an artist and some were surprised to find their new colleague's wife able to converse with them on an equal footing. She 'dreaded' return visits and would 'rather hide', even contemplating escaping to London for a visit without her husband.[9]

Overcoming Ida's initial shyness, the Johns' most significant friendship was with John Sampson, the university librarian. He was 'big and monumental, clad generally in a velvet jacket, with a strangely gentle voice and insight into character of friend and foe.'[10] Sampson's interest in language and folklore influenced Augustus hugely, leading him to introduce the artist to the gypsies and tinkers of North Wales and discuss his work on a Romani dictionary, which would be published in 1926. Sampson's work stirred in John a passion that was to profoundly influence the course of his life and Ida became friends with his wife, Margaret. They stayed with the Sampsons in Liverpool's Chatham Street, with Ida writing to inform her mother they were 'delightful people'. The feeling was reciprocated, as their host was fascinated by Augustus' talent and charisma, writing that he had 'certainly been favoured by the Gods. Strong, handsome, a genius, beloved by many men and women, with a calling which is also his chief pleasure and allows him the most entire freedom, successful beyond his dreams or means and assured of immortality as long as art lasts.' Ida and Margaret were often thrown together while their husbands were exploring the gypsy camp, Cabbage Hall, on waste ground outside the city. John was drawn in by their exotic names, their speech and customs.[11] Here, he found a more authentic and less self-styled form of bohemianism, of a nomadic people who rejected the material trappings of an artistic existence that had been made fashionable by Mugler and Du Maurier as a shabby-genteel style choice.

Ida also developed a close friendship with Mary 'The Rani' Dowdall, née Borthwick, the beautiful and charismatic wife of the future Lord Mayor of Liverpool, Harold Chaloner Dowdall. Mary and Ida were both twenty-four in 1901 and she provided the new wife with a much-needed confidante. Augustus painted her husband, Harold, in his mayoral robes in 1909. Mary cut a flamboyant figure in a short striped skirt, kerchief over her head, bare legs and sandals, and Augustus found her 'the most engaging person in Liverpool'.[12] Once, the two families scandalised the city by riding down the aptly named Bold Street 'at the fashionable hour' in a caravan, with Mary 'seated stockingless – a first class event in those days – on the steps and behind her the Sampson and John families, with Dowdall, a rising young barrister ... and John riding on nags behind'.[13]

In late spring, Ida fell pregnant. Confirmed in the early summer, this news must have delighted her, as she had been writing to friends about her desire to start a family. However, her months of pregnancy did not run as smoothly as she might have hoped. Alarmed by a doctor's warning of possible complications, her predictable reaction was to flee south; first to her parents, who feared that Augustus would not look after their daughter and then to stay with Edwin and Winifred John in Tenby. Augustus joined her there in the summer, before they left for New Quay in Cardiganshire, where they planned to spend a month resting and painting. In reality however, this turned into John bathing and painting local girls in a disused schoolroom, while Ida sat at home making baby clothes. Judging the danger to have passed, they returned to Liverpool in late September and moved in briefly with the Sampsons, as the stairs at the Mackay's proved too much for Ida with her increasing girth. She wrote to her mother of growing very large and that her general health was good. Two weeks later, following a pay rise from the university, they moved to the more pleasant, middle-class Canning Street near to where John had found a suitable studio. Also in the Georgian quarter, it comprised a terrace of four storey red-brick townhouses, with porticos, steps and iron railings, giving way to a larger, more angular cream-fronted terrace, and a number of considerably larger houses, with a central entrance balanced by windows on both sides. During their residence, the city ran a competition for architects to design the cathedral that would shortly be built on St James' mound at the end of Canning Street. The Johns had moved away by the time work began on Giles Gilbert Scott's design.

Augustus' attitude to Ida's pregnancy fluctuated. Never one to appreciate restrictions, even those of his own making, her absence in the early summer had renewed his taste for freedom. For a short while, he had again tasted the life of a single man, taking himself off on jaunts; one of which ended up abroad. In early autumn, he settled down again and became intensely curious about the baby and tender towards his wife, but events in October brought about another change. In a bizarre parallel with his youthful head injuries at Tenby, another accident dramatically altered John's behaviour. While painting in his studio, he fell from a ladder, breaking his nose and putting a little finger out of joint. Again, his accident made him something of a celebrity, which he exploited by parading his bandages in front of anxious students, a 'sartorial accomplishment'.[14] More worryingly for Ida, he grew impatient with her pregnancy, seeing it as a personal restriction. The imminent baby prevented him visiting London and increasing work commitments made him distant and irritable.

As a young expectant wife affiliated to the university, Ida received a steady stream of well-wishers bringing gifts. Augustus resented the gossipy female atmosphere and spent more time away from home. In her loneliness, the approaching event sparked nightmares in Ida, of strange, savage looking babies 'most astonishing to us' and tiny children lapping milk from saucers, leading her to muse to her father about whether the baby will be a 'lunatic, having such a mother'.[15] Llewelyn de Wet Ravachol John (later called David Anthony) arrived promptly on 6 January 1902 and, for a few weeks, both Ida and Augustus were caught up in the excitement of parenthood. He was probably born at home, as was usually the custom, with the assistance of a midwife or doctor. The capable Ada Nettleship came to stay, bringing a nurse to allow Ida the relief of two weeks' bed rest, followed by Augustus' younger sister,

Winifred John. Ida's initial instincts were maternal and loving, if full of disbelief at the new life she had created. She described the time as 'lovely', writing letters full of details and praising her son's 'wonderful mixture of Nettleship-John'.[16]

After Ada's departure, another move to the less salubrious Chatham Street followed and the baby's constant crying affected both parents deeply. Ida wrote honestly about her despair to Alice Rothenstein, who had also recently given birth: 'Ours howls ... I have done all I can for him ... I suppose the poor soul is simply unhappy.' Their new rooms were not clean and Ida seemed to spend all her time in housework; a new puppy adding to their 'difficulties' and made life 'perplexing'.[17] The noise drove John away, leaving her increasingly alone with a baby she was now unable to bond with, marvelling at the maternal feeling she witnessed in others; 'I do not think we feel about our babe like you do about yours,' 'I love only my husband and the children as being a curious ... part of that love.' Even her letter writing was curtailed as 'there are so many things to do.'[18] There was no question of Ida doing any painting.

Only a year since their marriage, Ida's vision of two self-supporting artists working side by side had been derailed by reality. Her isolation from family and friends, coupled with John's frequent absences must have left her despairing and disillusioned. John's ability to separate the domestic and work spheres allowed him an escape that Ida could never realise; her living quarters were also her work space. There was to be no separate studio in which she could forget her commitments. From her own accounts, it sounds likely that she was suffering from post-natal depression, complicated by losing hold of her preferred self-definition as artist and model, rather than mother. Her children were the necessary 'curiosities' arising from their union, almost a price to pay for being John's wife. Social expectations of married women and the attentions of fellow university wives must have exacerbated her feelings of alienation, cast in a role to which she felt unsuited. The inexperienced Ida had had no way of anticipating the dramatic changes brought by a child and for her, the reality that motherhood was not initially instinctive or enjoyable, but proved very difficult. A visit from Gwen John provided welcome companionship and support, reminding Ida of what she was missing and prompting a visit to her sick father in April. Their isolation in Liverpool was proving too much; Ida from the support of family and John from artistic and amorous opportunities. After eighteen months away, they returned to London in July, to live at 18, Fitzroy Street. The house no longer stands but it was probably in the same style as the Georgian terrace that survives further down the street in the direction of Fitzroy Square.

Ida's awareness that she 'certainly was not made for a mother' highlighted other changes in her identity and relationships. Marriage and motherhood had transformed her from the mysterious muse into a predictable, solid, domestic figure. Her previous role as John's mistress was incompatible with that of his wife. The over-protected, dreamy girlhood, wrapped in poetry, art and romantic friendships had failed to prepare her for the realities of life. In her naivety she had pictured a future that had little to do with the real nature of financial struggle, domestic drudgery and the extent of her husband's excesses. It was one thing to be the object of John's attentions and know him for a 'rogue' and quite another to be his neglected wife, faced with all his failings. Additionally, Ida was about to lose the second most significant figure of her life. On the last day of August 1902, John Nettleship died at the age of sixty-one.

Six months after bearing David, Ida was pregnant again and her life became increasingly entrenched in the domestic routine and severed from her husband's. While he was busy cultivating his role as King of the Bohemians at the Café Royal, Ida was washing, sewing and baby-minding, beginning her day at 5.30am. The home environment itself, in which painting now seemed impossible, became her canvas. She tried to make a pleasant home in Fitzroy Street, importing old pieces of furniture once belonging to the Nettleships, papering the walls white and hanging up baskets of roses; but still John stayed away. Ida tried to comfort herself with her maternal duties, excusing her husband on the grounds that he was an artist, a viewpoint which returned her to the traditional female role and completely overlooked her own talent and ambitions. She prioritised Augustus as a 'spirit of the highest order' who needed his freedom' even if the cost was her own.[19] The proximity of her mother, sisters and ex-Slade friends was certainly an improvement on her Liverpool isolation but the discrepancy between Ida's girlhood dreams and the lonely future of maternal drudgery spread out before her made this a difficult time.

On occasion John still used his wife as a model, producing the beautiful, earthy 'Merikli' portrait, voted picture of the year by the New English Art Club. Romany for 'jewel', which may refer to her jewellery or herself, Ida symbolises fertility, holding a basket of fruit and flowers, yet this image is associated firmly with the past through its obvious debt to the old masters. The fixed pose and dark colouring create a traditional and artificial effect as opposed to the radiating light of from a 1903 portrait John painted of the beautiful Estella Cerutti, who lived below them in Fitzroy Street. Estella or 'Esther,' after whom John wished to name their child, was too frequently present in their lives for comfort during the autumn of 1902 and following spring. Her name was never to be used though, as Ida's second child proved to be a boy, Caspar. The 'nice fat slug' arrived on 22 March 1903 and doubled her commitments. 'As with one I was tied,' she realised, 'so with two I shall be bound and can have no pretences of being a mere woman without a family.'[20]

Domestic pressure was becoming intolerable. Work was impossible. As Ida wrote to Mary Dowdall, 'there is nothing else to do now that painting is not practicable' and 'I have a great deal of sewing to finish and when that is done, a great deal of washing to do.' She was forced to dismiss Caspar's nurse because it was too expensive to keep her and felt herself returning to an 'original state of serfdom' in which she was constantly tending to the needs of her children for around fourteen hours a day, getting only an average of three hours' sleep at night.[21] John avoided his growing family by visiting Wales, then Liverpool and Ida sent the children to her father-in-law at Tenby, finding things 'most delightful without them'. Apart, the cracks in their relationship deepened and, after experiencing jealousy over his intimacy with Esther, Ida may have been painfully aware that John was falling in love again, this time with the woman he was soon referring to as his 'spouse'. Their early closeness was almost completely eroded by the time Dorothy McNeill entered their lives, altering their marriage forever.

11

Love and Poverty

Poverty and ill-health made happiness elusive for Sophie Brzeska and Henri Gaudier. Soon after their meeting in Paris, Sophie's poor diet and miserable lodgings led to the recurrence of her previous health problems. Her doctor urged her to spend some time at a coastal resort in order to rest and recover, or else she would suffer more serious consequences. In July 1910, she headed south to the Atlantic coast and the fashionable town of Royan, known for its sea bathing. Situated between La Rochelle and Bordeaux, Royan sits on the mouth of the Gironde Estuary, surrounded by sandy beaches. Once a convalescence centre for Napoleon's armies, it had become the most luxurious resort on the coast in the last decade of the nineteenth century, rivalling Deauville and even Biarritz for a while. Sophie headed initially for the new suburb of Pontillac where villas had been laid out to the north-west; but finding this area too expensive, she took simpler lodgings in the main town. Here, she spent a few relaxing months, writing to Henri, still in Paris, sea-bathing and walking among the pines and dunes.

That autumn, Gaudier succumbed to anaemia, undoubtedly exacerbated by the same unhealthy conditions of dirty rented rooms and poor nutrition, and received similar advice from his doctor. Through the past months of separation, he had written regularly to Sophie of nose bleeds, asking to join her. Afraid of getting too close, she sent him a few francs and urged him to look after himself, but while working he barely managed to eat, even when Sophie was there to watch him, surviving on coffee, neglectful of his own health. Visiting the expensive Royan was not possible for Henri and, because of Sophie's fears of 'being let down again', she suggested he visit his parents, to be nursed in St Jean de Braye. He urged her to join him, refusing to take no for an answer. Thus two maternal figures were on hand to comfort Henri in the countryside; his horrified mother welcomed him home to St Jean-de-Braye 'ashamed' and scarcely knowing 'whether to laugh or cry' at his emaciated appearance, while from Royan, Sophie gave notice to her landlady and hurried north to nurse a 'gravely ill son'.[1]

Her reception from the Gaudier family was less than warm. Meeting her at the station around midnight, Henri and his father conducted her to a hotel; Sophie only met Madame Gaudier once but an immediate and possibly predictable antipathy sprang up between them. Not that far apart in age, they were close rivals for the figure of mature female authority to balance Henri's naïve masculinity: both wanted to be the only mother to the sickly young man. They bestialised each other: Marie saw Sophie as a 'lard' or pig; Sophie described Marie as dressed in a bat-like cap. Henri had to listen to his mother's crude suggestions and criticism of his new friend which, by association, he felt as criticism of his own judgement. In *Matka* she described Marie as 'very coarse' and similar to her own mother in despising and mocking her son's distress.[2] A letter Henri wrote to Sophie relates how his father explained the situation, in 'a nice little speech about what women think about themselves' and identified the 'source of the evil' as 'feminine jealousy'.[3]

Sophie had forebodings about staying so close to the Gaudier family. A 'cabin' was rented by Henri on her behalf in Combleux, a tiny pretty village two kilometres to the south-east of St Jean de Braye, stretching over two arms of the Loire. Henri walked the distance every day to see her, arriving early, while she was lying down to rest. Sophie tried to discourage him from visiting so often, in order not to displease his mother who was now accusing her of debauching her son and making him ill. She also hoped to buy herself a little time to write. H. S. Ede's account of their time at Combleux provides a chaste picture: Henri was allowed to kiss her tenderly but never 'as a lover'.[4] In *Matka* she explained she had ruled out any passionate amorous kisses but could not deny him the 'little caresses he seemed to need.'[5] Due to their difference in age, the thought of a physical liaison with him still felt inappropriate to her, which makes the subsequent scandal even more ironic.

One afternoon, the local police arrived at the house in Combleux. Sophie's landlord knocked on the door to warn them while the pair were resting after dinner: Sophie's act of reclining on her bed to aid digestion was an unfortunate detail that appeared to corroborate local rumours of immoral conduct. An anonymous letter had been sent informing the police that a stream of men was constantly visiting Sophie at home, threatening the respectability of the village. Indignant and angry, Sophie and Henri denied the accusations and explained their position, in which local people supported them, agreeing that Gaudier was her only visitor. A number of written statements were taken, from Sophie, Henri and other villagers, accusing a local well-known poison pen-writer of sending the letter. Sophie's innocence was formally established but her efforts to secure a conviction against her persecutor, a local man named Coutau, were dismissed by the Deputy Prosecutor.

The frustration and indignation they experienced during this episode so unsettled Henri and Sophie that they decided to leave France. Gaudier wrote bitterly to Uhlemayer of a 'lovely country' full of 'utterly degraded' people, 'malicious, treacherous ... miserly ... grasping', who had mixed him up in an 'abominable business'. He saw the French as 'rotten to the core' and the country in an 'advanced state of decadence'. He was about to leave it 'to the Furies' and head 'quickly to the frontier'. An additional reason for flight was the imminent commencement of the military service Henri was determined to avoid. The notorious French 'Biribi', the harsh punishment in Algeria for army shirkers disgusted him and persuaded him to leave the country in order to avoid 'years of slavery'.[6] His memories of England suggested the pair would be happier in London.

The incident had profoundly shaken Sophie and broken her health again. No matter how Henri reassured her, their twenty-year age gap always weighed heavily on her mind. She insisted they return separately to Paris, mindful of Henri's legal status as a minor and fearing public misunderstanding and censure. Sophie temporarily took up her old rooms in the Rue Cujas again and for two months they survived on her 'slim' and rapidly depleting savings; after their recent stay, Henri did not wish to ask his parents for money. That December, Gaudier went on ahead to London to find work. In early January 1911, Sophie Brzeska followed across the Channel and became, in the eyes of English society, Gaudier's sister. For the first time, they took rooms together in a furnished lodgings house on Edith Road in Hammersmith. A road of unbroken grey-brown brick terraces, it was a more respectable, pleasant environment, with some pretentions to gentility suggested in the wide bay windows and large porticos. Yet the new arrivals did not feel welcome.

After two months, Henri was still trying to find work, 'in spite of all (their) approaches' and the advice of new friends. Sophie felt, whether correctly or not, that they were unwelcome because of their nationalities. The 'English brutes ... the odious English,' she wrote, 'kept everything for their own race exclusively' and swore at Henri because 'his shoes were not polished or quickly dispatched him as a foreigner' in favour of 'their species of dirty Englishmen.'[7] Experience had taught Sophie the harsh lessons of poverty, coupled with consistent rejection on the grounds of her background and gender, but work really was difficult to come by. Statistics for unemployment through the previous decade indicate that the usual rate of 3-4 per cent had suddenly doubled in 1908 and 1909, and was still high at 4.7 per cent in 1910.[8] The 1901 census had recorded 1,596,160 men who were not employed and not retired or living on private means; by 1911 that had risen to 1,710,678. As to Sophie's comments about the English, a race she felt 'stinks out the whole world', it is sadly plausible that she and Henri met with hostility in the capital city of the British Empire. That year, the First Universal Races Congress met at London University with a view to greater understanding and co-operation but the reality of xenophobia on the streets and in the job market must have been a daily occurrence. Increasingly desperate, Henri sketched locals in a pub for a penny a time and Sophie was driven to begging, with a rag 'baby' wrapped up in her arms. It earned her sixpence.

Eventually, Henri found a position as a clerk and translator at Wulfsberg and Company, a Norwegian timber merchants in St Mary Axe, for a salary of six pounds a month. All his painting was relegated to evenings and weekends. Coupled with the recent pressure, this created a sort of desperate hysteria in him. He could not sleep, raged and argued with Sophie, threatening to kill himself and running out into the road. Violent, emotional quarrels and the need to restrain each other's suicidal excesses drained their energy. Henri was also frustrated by the lack of physical contact in their relationship, although they were now living together, but Sophie still felt this was impossible. Instead, she encouraged him to visit prostitutes 'to relieve his feelings' and 'strengthen his nervous system', although she regretted the loss of five shillings each time he went. Sophie recognised they might be better apart – 'it was not surprising that we poisoned each other's life' – so when she was offered a temporary position as an au pair in a school in Felixstowe, in exchange for board and lodgings, she accepted. It is likely to have been Neuheim, a school run since 1899 by a Mrs C. J. Jutson, situated on the corner of Queen's Road and Orwell Road. The red-brick building has corner turrets and an elaborate ironwork porch extending into a first floor balcony and, although now divided into several flats, extends back a fair way, with a second entrance along Orwell Road. It was listed in Whitaker's Almanack for 1907 as a school for 'the daughters of gentlemen' and, again in 1914 as a 'high class home school for girls' paying particular attention to 'character, culture and health'. The census of 1911 lists Elizabeth Jutson, a widow of fifty-seven, as the head of a private girls' school, along with her mother Elizabeth Scammell and an elderly boarder. On the night of April 2, when the census was conducted, though, the school was quiet. Easter fell on April 16, so perhaps the holidays had already begun as there was only a cook and a parlour maid, a Dutch teacher of languages by the name of Anna Ohmstede and two resident pupils, one of whom was Jutson's own niece.[10]

Felixstowe, on the southern tip of Suffolk, was quiet and had many of the features of the healthy coastal resorts Sophie liked. Situated on the estuary between Suffolk and Essex, it was popular for seaside holidays and catered for its visitors with imposing hotels, landscaped spa gardens, a long iron pier and bandstand. Contemporary postcards depict Edwardians on the pebbly beach among rows of bathing huts, promenading along the Cliff Gardens, watching steamboats dock, or taking tea in the Spa Pavilion. Children sailed model yachts on a large pond and took rides in goat carts. Yet Sophie's experiences in Felixstowe were not all positive ones. Besides her unhappiness at being parted from Henri, it is possible to reconstruct a little of her difficulties from his letters. He wrote to her as 'Mamusin Dearest,' 'Matka,' 'Zosienka darling' 'Beloved' or 'Adorable Maman' and signed himself 'your own Pik' or Pickaninny.[11](sic)

On April 22, Henri wrote that he had been feeling miserable but had slept well and had a quiet time. He related how he had seen Michelangelo casts at the museum, told her gossipy stories and updated her about his drawing. His subsequent letters touched on the weather, the birds singing, art, literature, learning Polish, his diet, his exploration of the countryside and how pleased he was to receive her letters. 'We shall be happier soon,' he assured her, 'so have courage ... Let's keep our spirits up with the big sun as our guide.' He also urged her to 'consider her Pik as part of herself' so she would not talk as if he were two different people, 'a fellow who had a woman for his kitchen and for his bed' and 'implored' her 'on both knees' as 'the only creature who loves me, for the good of us both, to promise to think of yourself as part of your Pik, Otherwise ... he will go to the dogs through depression and disgust.'[12]

Sophie's health was still fragile; she was 'tormented by illness every month' and in April 'had to stay in bed three days this week' but gradually she recovered with regular sea bathing and bracing walks. Her teaching job was a struggle and the school did not feed her much. In response to her letters, Gaudier refers to the 'idiots' she worked for, 'those swine who upset you' and the capriciousness of pupils who can 'laugh and make pretty faces' but cannot disguise their 'filthiness ... vileness ... stupidity ... malice'. Even though Sophie apparently loathed 'brats' and teaching, necessity made her look for a permanent position for the coming winter.[13]

Between lessons, Sophie was writing a novel she called *Trilogy*. She was to work on this for many years, dividing it into three sections: the first, entitled *Outcast*, recounted her early life, the second, *Hysterical Woman*, described her travels abroad and, finally, *Matka*, which covered her relationship with Henri.

He responded that 'you write what you know about, what you have lived,' adding that she 'cannot choose' but write about her suffering as it 'burns' within her. Sophie may have been concerned about the obvious personal connections it raised, as Gaudier wrote suggesting she altered the setting to Greece, as the fundamental tragedy remained timelessly the same. He was keen to see the novel was 'well written' and woven with 'many sensations' uniting imagination and observation: to facilitate it, he was prepared to sacrifice 'art, study and everything'. Encouraging her through a bout of self-doubt, he likened Sophie's magnum opus to Harriet Beecher Stowe's creation of *Uncle Tom's Cabin*, when she was 'a little bit of a woman somewhat more than forty, about as thin and dry as a pinch of snuff, never very much to look at in my best days and looking like a used-up article now,'[14] remarking that Sophie was just the right age and appearance.

Henri was living in Kensington, then part of the borough of Fulham, where he is listed in the 1911 census. He was boarding with the German Heitzmann family, an elderly couple whose children had been born in England, and were all resident at 4, Applegarth Road, West Kensington. Described as 'single' and a 'sculptor' he somehow entered the records as being a Dutchman, although it is not clear whether he intended to deliberately mislead or if this was an assumption on the part of the census collectors. The street leads across to a Haarlem Road, offering a prompt if Henri had been trying to conceal his French roots, perhaps out of fear that official documentation may have led to him being recalled home for national service. A typical London terrace, number four stands next to the end house, up wide steps, with four storeys including a basement. It is a ten-minute walk from Hammersmith tube station, making it just a five-minute journey westbound to Richmond, where Henri loved to explore the park.

A visit from Henri was proposed for the end of term, when they could walk by the sea and bathe in the 'swift' waves. He wrote giving details of his proposed arrival on Thursday 22 June, benefiting from an extra day off following the coronation of Edward VII, returning to London the following Sunday. However, at the last minute these plans changed; either he was put off by the distance or Sophie feared further scandal. After rejecting the noisy, busy Southend as an alternative location, Sophie travelled to the quiet yachting town of Burnham-on-Crouch and took cheap lodgings with two 'old maids' who appropriated her food supplies. Henri joined her the following morning and they spent four days bathing and running in the fields, avoiding the muddy ditches. He had taken care of himself in her absence and was feeling much stronger. During this holiday, the nature of his affection became clear, altering the dynamic of their relationship. Sophie had somewhat naively maintained the pretence of her maternal relationship to Henri but, in Burnham, his 'passionate' embraces shocked her as a 'dangerous game'. He admitted having sexual desire from their first meeting but feared a confession might send her away. Sophie was unable to respond. She was flattered but feared being unable to satisfy him 'in our situation', with 'our illness'.[15]

With her Felixstowe commitments at an end, Sophie planned to remain in Burnham until the end of August and seek another teaching post. Gaudier worked hard to try to dissuade her and on his return to London, found cheap, unfurnished lodgings for them both and persuaded her to join him by weaving tenuous connections with ancient Greece: a fig tree by the door, a statue in the garden. However, their 'hoped-for Paradise was a regular hell'. Henri's letter failed to mention the large, noisy garage next door, or the lack of gas, the fact that the rooms were damp and smelled, and the smoking lamps.[16] Sophie was unhappy with the squalor of their ill-equipped rooms and the necessity of housework. Given their precarious states of health, she felt unable to compromise on food expenses. After sleeping on deckchairs and dealing with an infestation of bugs, they moved again at the end of September to Paulton's Square in Chelsea. After this, they began a nomadic, unsettling existence, moving every three or four months, arguing and struggling against poverty and illness. Sophie cooked a large meal of meat, potatoes and herring every Monday, which they ate cold for the rest of the week, augmented with bread and milk.[17]

*

Poverty also dictated the conditions Fernande found herself living in with Picasso. Although the young Spanish artist's reputation was spreading, he was to remain in Montmartre until 1910, when recognition and financial success allowed him to move into better accommodation in the Boulevard de Clichy. The Bateau-Lavoir studio they shared contained a mattress supported on four legs, a little iron stove covered in rust and an earthenware bowl, with a scrap of towel and stub of soap. The dirty studio with the rotting floor and sparse furniture was no worse than the rooms of other artists she had recently lived in, although Picasso had added an extra surprise by decorating an alcove or 'votive chapel' in her honour, containing objects belonging to her – sketches, flowers and a packing case draped with cloth to make an 'altar' set with lighted candles. It was a flattering discovery. Fernande was touched and amused by his mysticism and 'mocking self-irony' but not blinded to the dilapidated state of the rest of the studio. Picasso had practically no furniture but, instead, a huge assortment of objects: buckets, easels, paint tubes and pans overflowing with dirty water, all animated by the 'wild colour and confusion' of large canvases.[18] A rusty frying pan served as a chamber pot. No curtains hung at the windows. On cold days they would remain in bed as they could not afford to buy coal and tradesmen demanding payment received no reply to their knocking. When silence no longer worked, Fernande would call out that she was naked and unable to come to the door; good relations with creditors were maintained with a flash of her beautiful smile. Inside, the pair were poor but happy. Picasso worked mainly at night while Fernande lay on the divan, drinking coffee, smoking Turkish cigarettes and reading novels. Never one to enjoy housework, she was delighted by Picasso's insistence on taking over the cooking and shopping himself, although his unwillingness to let her leave the house sprang more from a 'morbid jealousy' and lack of trust. He kept her almost in harem-style, depriving her of shoes so she could not go out, sketching and worshipping her as she lounged about, exclusively his.

Picasso's early fears of Fernande's faithlessness may have paralleled his own recent behaviour. It suited him to keep her at home whilst he maintained his connections, or finished, with other women. During the early part of that year, he had still been involved with his previous muse, the slender, ethereal Madeleine, who had aborted his child in 1904. Other lovers included the beautiful Germaine, over whom his friend Casagemas had committed suicide; Alice, the future wife of Andre Derain; a teenaged flower girl named Linda and Margot, stepdaughter of Frédé at the Lapin Agile. He was also aware of her many liaisons with the artists of Montmartre, including those like Debienne and Sunyer still under their very roof. They did not remain in total isolation though. Friends were regularly invited, including the Canals, Paco Durrio, the young Spanish sculptor Manolo, the witty Max Jacob, poet Andre Salmon and art critic Guillaume Apollinaire, who lent Fernande books. Since Pablo's arrival in Paris, the 'band à Picasso' had been gathering in his studio or in local bars, especially the colourful Lapin Agile, the Closerie de Lilas and at the home of the American collectors Gertrude and Leo Stein. Riotous evenings were spent in talk and drink and the spare mattress on the floor was often occupied. Surviving on fifty francs a month, they ate out at local restaurants on credit, cooked meals for friends and visited the circus Medrano. As the winter progressed, keeping warm proved more difficult and tea left in cups overnight froze. However, Fernande was still able to write 'I'm happy in spite of this. We're not miserable; we love each other.'[19] When Picasso sold a drawing, often of her, there was money to afford food and wine to celebrate.

Fernande appears in Gertrude Stein's fictionalised account of the life of her lover, *The Autobiography of Alice B Toklas*, published in 1933. She describes Fernande upon their first meeting as 'a tall, beautiful woman with a wonderful big hat and a very evidently new dress'. She and Picasso were late for their visit, which upset Picasso, who was 'never late', but it was due to Fernande having ordered a new dress that they did not arrive on time. Fernande became 'calm and placid' after she had been paid a number of compliments. Stein also identified Fernande in a portrait by Picasso, by a 'characteristic gesture, one ringed forefinger straight in the air' and remarked how she had the 'Napoleonic forefinger', as long or longer than her middle finger, and when she was animated, 'which … was not very often as Fernande was indolent,' she always put it straight up in the air.[20] She spoke 'very elegant French' with some 'lapses into Montmartois' and, due to her education to be a schoolteacher, Stein wrote, 'her voice was lovely and she was very, very beautiful with a marvellous complexion.' She was, Stein continued, 'a big woman but not too big … and she had the small round arms that give the characteristic beauty to all French women.'[21] Her favourite topics were hats and perfumes; knowing how much she loved fashion, Gertrude once gave her a Chinese gown from San Francisco. When Stein posed for her portrait in Picasso's studio in 1906, Fernande read aloud from La Fontaine's stories to help amuse her.

Fernande too was still painting. She had recently discovered an 'eye for colour' and, in later life, would describe herself as being 'gifted'. Living with Picasso she would have welcomed his guidance and frequently sought his advice, except he refused to oblige, only telling her to enjoy herself. In the 1960s, John Richardson was shown a folio of her work, Fauvist in style, primitive and mask-like with echoes of the style of her friends Kees Van Dongen and Marie Laurencin, which led him to suggest that Fernande's artistic credentials should be taken 'more seriously'.[22] Her portraits and still-lifes certainly have a vitality about them and she undeniably had a sense of colour and composition. Taken to galleries by Charles Petot as a child, she had been particularly attracted by the Impressionists, whose work she described as a revelation. She adored Manet and Cezanne and felt drawn to the Primitives, although her uncle had always rushed through that section in favour of more classical, Academy-approved artists. However, she would never warm towards the angles and planes of cubism, understanding their importance but preferring the colours and fluidity of the Fauves.

Yet in spite of her abilities, Fernande was not dedicated to art. She lacked the vision and determination to succeed in the face of pervasive national mistrust of the female artist. She felt crippled by 'a tendency in France ... to regard women as incapable of serious thought' and therefore serious painting. Picasso's attitude that women 'should not trespass on men's preserves' deeply affected Fernande to the extent that she only felt able to join in when the great artists became playful or childlike, when she was not seen as a serious competitor. However, Picasso kept many of her drawings, admitting later that they were 'very beautiful' and that she was 'very gifted, but she didn't possess that sacred fire of work. Her work resembled Marie Laurencin's a little, but Fernande had a more vigorous line, less pretty-pretty.'[23]

As Germaine Greer has explored in *The Obstacle Race*,[24] many women were enabled to paint through their close relationships with practising male artists. Ida's parents had supported her ambitions and education but she soon found that motherhood and life with Augustus left her little time to put them into practice. Sophie was fortunate in finding a young man who valued her literary efforts although her poverty curtailed her time and ability to work. Picasso did not extend the benevolent hand that could have encouraged and enabled Fernande to explore or realise her potential.

There were female artists within Fernande's social circle. The contemporary successes of Montmartre artists Marie Laurencin and Suzanne Valadon were partly due to the force of personality, circumstances and the compliance of men in their lives. Fernande later claimed, with some justification, that Laurencin's success had been dependent on the support of her influential lover, the poet Guillaume Apollinaire, and described how the Steins bought one of her first works 'for fun'. Marie had also been mocked as a lone female during her studies at the Académie Humbert although she had persisted and tempered Picasso's more masculine, harsh cubism with feminine curves and softer lines. In 1908, Marie painted 'Group of Artists' which included herself and Apollinare, Picasso in profile with one, large, ringed eye and Fernande, her features elongated, her eyes sloping. Marie would also draw a sly-looking Fernande wearing the gold hooped earrings Pablo bought her, with a wide, dark querulous mouth, a work she labelled as 'Madame Pickaçoh'.

Fernande was also aware of Suzanne Valadon's paintings hanging on the walls of the Lapin Agile, as well as her walks around the Butte of Montmartre, which often concluded in the discovery of her drunken son Maurice Utrillo, and her home in the Impasse Guelma, near the Place de Pigalle. The older woman's magnetic personal charm and strength of character were exceptional, enabling her to impress her early mentors without relinquishing her independence. But these were exceptions. Fernande's own dedication to art, like the promise she had shown in her school work, did not seem strong enough to survive social disapproval or overcome personal discouragement. She never pushed to exhibit her art or to take part in the male-dominated arena that made the names of her friends.

Picasso's band of friends continued to meet regularly at the Lapin Agile, or Lapin À Gill, so named after a previous tenant, although it was now owned by singer Aristide Bruant, the subject of posters by Toulouse-Lautrec. A cabaret bar on the Rue de Saules decorated with Eastern and European statues and dominated by a huge crucifix, it had a reputation for rowdiness and violence. The owner's son was shot and killed by the till one night, razor blades were often produced instead of payment and even Picasso was known to fire a pistol to disperse idle chatter. There was a comic side to the Lapin Agile too. The most famous incident involved the owner's donkey, Aliboron, Lolo or 'Boronali', that was encouraged to produce the modern works of art that impressed the 1910 Salon des Indépendants by means of a carrot and paintbrush tied to his tail. This irreverent poke at the vagaries of artistic acceptance was to find echoes in the work of Picasso and his friends. On a visit to the Bateau-Lavoir, Lolo would eat some Spanish silk scarves Fernande had used to brighten the studio. Riotous nights and opium-smoking provided a release from the claustrophobia of the studio. Derain, Matisse, Jacob, Apollinaire, Marie Laurencin and Modigliani were among the Lapin Agile regulars. Here also, Picasso's close artistic friendships with Georges Braques and Juan Gris developed, leading him in a new direction, away from the acrobats and harlequins of 1905-6 into something altogether more angular and revolutionary.

Life with Picasso was not easy. His jealousy intensified over time and caused arguments. Fernande was still not allowed out alone; even when they visited the Lapin Agile, he accused her of flirtatious behaviour, despite having another girl sitting on his knee; on another occasion she went out to hear news about an attack upon the Lapin Agile, whereupon Picasso followed her, slapped her and pushed her roughly home. Once she was locked in the studio when a fire broke out below, although on that occasion the danger passed her by; a little later, she recorded that she had not been out for a week. Undoubtedly Fernande stirred Picasso's jealousy with her threats to return to modelling, especially when the Bateau-Lavoir was full of her admirers and past lovers. In spring 1906, their situation began to change as Picasso's work attracted wealthy patrons and their finances improved significantly.

Picasso had initially been reluctant to show his work in public; dealers had to come to him. On their first visit to his studio, Gertrude and Leo Stein had been sufficiently impressed to part with the unheard of sum of eight hundred francs – this was topped by dealer Ambroise Vollard's offer of two thousand. The unexpected windfall brought a welcome touch of luxury and paid for a holiday to Barcelona and Gosol, to satisfy Picasso's Spanish yearnings. Fernande spent three happy months with Picasso in Spain. Initially, travelling made her nervous; it was the first time she had left France and the longest journey she'd ever made; at one stage she begged to return to Paris but the next morning's sun renewed her courage. In 'cheerful, lively and colourful' Barcelona, Fernande visited Picasso's family and friends as his fiancée, finding him transformed into a more cheerful, calmer person by his native country. After several weeks they headed for Gosol, a remote and beautiful little village in the Pyrenees, a dozen stone houses set around a square. The journey by mule was uncomfortable but they received a warm welcome at a clean, rustic inn, where traditional customs were preserved.

Both Picasso and Fernande were in their element; he painted all day, listening to the old men's stories whilst she walked, posed and read; often they joined excursions into the mountains and ate huge meals with the local families. Fernande only objected to the discrepancy she saw in status between the genders; women never ate with men, standing in a corner with left-overs and too ashamed to eat in public, which she found 'offensive and intolerable', insisting that their hostess join them. Apart from that, she loved the simplicity of their life there, with the pure mountain air and everything gleaming in the sunlight against a soft, pure blue sky; she loved walking in espadrilles, with the wild roses brushing her legs and lizards racing past. She believed they had found 'true happiness' there, but in mid-August 1906, the idyll was broken by an outbreak of typhoid. Fernande discovered the extent to which Picasso feared illness when he insisted upon their departure, at five in the morning, across the mountains on mules.

Back in Paris, they found the studio overrun with mice which had eaten an umbrella. (Perhaps surprising then, that Picasso contributed so little to surrealism.) Their bed was infested with bugs. Life only settled down again after the burning of sulphur in an attempt to fumigate the place, allowing Picasso to resume work. Soon after their return they heard of the death of Paul Cézanne. It is difficult to overestimate the importance of his reduction of form into the cylinder, sphere and cone, in terms of the development of modern art. Picasso was to acknowledge him as his 'one and only master', developing Cezanne's tenets to an extent that permanently redefined the visual and plastic arts.

After Cezanne's death in October, a huge retrospective exhibition was organised, with 56 pictures hung at the Salon d'Automne, which was attended by Picasso, Matisse, Braque and Apollinaire. Perhaps of them all, it had the greatest significance for Georges Braque who, in the summer of 1907, made his own visit to L'Estaque, where he simplified and restricted his palette to create sculptural scenes, which were exhibited in the Salon des Indépendants of that year. Braque and Picasso had met in the spring and were soon working so closely together on their 'little cubes' of landscapes that their work was often indistinguishable. Soon Fernande was to witness the completion of possibly the most important painting of the twentieth century, although she was not to understand it.

Guillaume Apollinaire was one of the first to see the completed angular, tribal figures of the 'Demoiselles d'Avignon'. The simultaneously voluptuous and terrifying women with their African mask-style faces rendered the normally verbose poet speechless, whilst Braque told Picasso 'it's as if you are making us eat rope and drink turpentine'. Violent reactions to avant-garde developments were de rigueur among newspaper critics and the general public, but the Demoiselles received censure and misunderstanding all the more harsh for having come from the artist's friends: Matisse thought it was a hoax satirising his own work and commented to Leo Stein that Picasso would be made to pay for it. Stein himself laughed at it as a deliberately humorous attempt to paint in the fourth dimension, then was horrified. His sister Gertrude never mentioned it. Art dealer Vollard refused to buy any more works. Critic Felix Fénéon told the artist to stick to caricature and Fauvist Andre Derain said that 'one day we shall find Pablo has hanged himself beside his great canvas.' Fernande was silent. These reactions and Picasso's disappointment guaranteed the picture a limited exposure; first shown in 1916, then purchased in 1923 by patron and designer Jacques Doucet, it was acquired by a New York Gallery and finally bought in 1937 by the New York Museum of Modern Art. Now it is considered critical to the development of modern art but in 1907, Fernande can hardly be blamed for failing to realise its importance. In her 1933 memoirs, she confessed to being unable to explain or admire cubism but that habit and success 'encourage indulgence' for work that once met with vilification.[25]

At this point in time, Fernande's story ties up unexpectedly with that of Ida, but only through their men. One day, a mutual friend brought 'a rather silent young man to meet Augustus John at his studio. The visitor pronounced his name, 'Picasso,' with some hesitation, as it was 'beginning to be mentioned as belonging to a new Spanish painter of mark'. After examining John's work, he invited him to visit his studio, which must have been at the Bateau-Lavoir, where John was struck by Picasso's 'unusual gifts' and, in particular, a 'large canvas (of) a group of figures which reminded one a little of the strange monoliths of Easter Island.' This must have been the Demoiselles, as John cited the Musée Ethnographique as his inspiration and described how it may 'at first sight disturb or even horrify, but which, on analysis, reveal elements derived from remote antiquity or the art-forms of primitive people.' During the course of their conversation, Picasso explained that he was 'seeking freedom'. John's comment on his 'ceaseless industry' and talent, is that during his youth, Picasso was 'preoccupied by the macabre' but he had now learned 'in his maturity, to wink the other eye'.[26] Picasso and Augustus John met in front of that transforming masterpiece, but no mention is made of Ida and Fernande. It seems a significant metaphor, in terms of their marginalised biography, that they were elsewhere, whereabouts unknown.

12

Ménage à Trois

The pressure on Ida, which had seemed intolerable following the birth of her second child, was set to worsen early in 1903. Never one to conceal his amorous adventures from his friends or wife, John had plans for a new liaison which would involve his new lover in their lives to an unprecedented degree. As with Ida, he chose a beautiful but essentially malleable woman, capable of great depths of emotion and endurance, willing to make sacrifices in order to promote his freedom. Initially it seemed unclear whether this new woman would return his affection but the eventual longevity of their relationship allowed her reputation as John's model and partner to far outstrip biographical memoirs of his wife. More significant perhaps, was the solidarity and support that she was to offer Ida, when John would appear to fail them both.

Dorelia (Dorothy) McNeill was almost five years younger than Ida, having been born in December 1881. She was raised in a quiet, middle-class family in Camberwell and juggled her work as a secretary by day with evening classes at Westminster Art School, where she met Gwen John in 1903. Her 'sphinx-like' presence and dark good looks attracted John at once, who saw her beauty as a perfect ingredient in his evolving gypsy aesthetic. Even before she became the icon for his new lifestyle, she dressed 'artistically' in long skirted dresses, with her hair drawn back into a bun and believed herself destined for the 'world of art'. It is unclear exactly when they met but contact was certainly established when mutual friends invited Dorelia to a party attended by Gwen John, to whom she confessed having been 'riveted' by a sighting of Augustus at an exhibition of Spanish paintings. Perhaps she then introduced the pair, but soon brother and sister were both fascinated by the young woman.

Ida had known about Augustus' roving eye long before their marriage and although he had openly indulged in flirtations and affairs with models, most had quickly burned themselves out and no serious rival to Ida had previously emerged. Now, honest to a fault, John confessed his infatuation to his wife and arranged a meeting between the two women. Hard as this must have been, Ida was favourably impressed by Dorelia and immediately realised that this threat to her marriage was serious. She still loved Augustus but the two children left her exhausted and she was side-lined artistically as Dorelia became John's new principal model. Ida saw the young woman usurp her cherished position as John's muse and was enlisted to help dress her up in colourful petticoats and ribbons or 'ransack' local shops in search of further adornments. Witnessing the development of her husband's fixation with a younger, beautiful woman, only two-and-a-half years after their marriage, proved painful. Such was Ida's dependence on her fading role as John's muse that later she would believe it preferable to lose a child rather than the ability to sit for him.

There is little doubt that Ida suffered intensely during this period; not only was her jealousy roused over the new relationship but after giving birth twice in as many years, she could not help feeling less attractive and useful. Her innocent dream of a union of artistic freedom, where she painted and acted as John's muse, was exposed as hopelessly idealistic. Now she found herself humiliated and restricted by the bonds that her husband appeared to disregard; by the summer of 1903 he was writing to Dorelia as his 'sweet girl-wife'.[1] Counselling herself to remain stoical and unwilling to let jealousy distance her from John further, Ida saw her pain as the direct result of sexual inequality – 'men must play and women must weep' – rather than blaming her husband for his behaviour or calling for a redefinition of their relationship. However unconventional their sexual openness, Ida was still shackled to the Victorian imprimatur by enduring and accepting his choices.

Ida had few people in whom she could confide. Having defied her family in order to marry John, she was reluctant to admit the deep sense of failure she now felt so soon afterwards. Her husband's behaviour was so flagrant, though, that it was impossible to maintain secrecy in the face of spreading rumours. Feeling her situation to be in painful contrast with the domestic happiness of Alice Rothenstein, Ida found her friend's questions and judgements difficult to bear. The older couple's more traditional marital arrangements represented the social ideal she had rejected in favour of a life that now began to incite their disapproval. Again, Ida wavered between the desire to remain truthful and the conflicting urge to avoid censure for the 'secret agreement' suggested by Dorelia's presence at the dinner table. As with their clandestine wedding, Ida had to compromise her ideals in order to retain her husband's affection. Other friends voiced their disapproval, with their former teacher Henry Tonks describing it as a 'sad state of matrimony', forcing Ida to admit that 'the communicable part of my life is very narrow' and 'as to the other', she must remain silent or lose friends. To Alice, she explained 'we are not a conventional family ... my only happiness is for him (Augustus) to be happy and complete ... far from diminishing our love it appears to augment it.' To herself, Ida admitted 'the mistake I made is considering Gus as a man instead of an artist-creature ... he's a poet and he knows no more about actual life than a poet does.'

For the time being, the only answer was flight. For a month that summer, Ida escaped to Tenby with the children and returned to find the prospect of approaching respite, as Gwen and Dorelia had begun to plan a European excursion. The details of their ambitious desire to walk to Rome engaged Ida less than the opportunity to have some time with Augustus to repair their relationship. However, by the end of the year, after the travellers had left, Ida was forced to recognise that rather than driving a wedge between them, Dorelia's presence might actually be keeping the marriage from fragmenting completely.

In November 1903, Augustus, Ida and their two young boys moved to Elm House, in Matching Green, Essex. Between Harlow and Chelmsford, just off the modern M11, the tiny village has changed little after a century, set around a triangular green surrounded by fields. Standing next to what is now the Chequers Inn, its orchards, trees and stables delighted Ida, although she found the house itself ugly. Built from warm yellow brick, the house was originally a symmetrical rectangle, with a window either side the front door, extended on its left hand wing to include a garage and room above. It has a white gable and lintel above the door, its windows and porch gently curved and what is a small driveway today sets it back a couple of metres from the road, which immediately gives onto the green. Surrounded by pigs, dogs, cats, geese and horses and canaries, enjoying the views and the birdsong, Ida settled happily into country life with Maggie, their cook from Fitzroy Street and Lucy, a local girl of fourteen who gave occasional help. With this support, Ida was able to enjoy a little more space, finding her new pursuits of cooking and gardening more creative and fulfilling than child rearing. As well as employing the dressmaking skills learned from her mother, she made puddings and pastry and polished furniture. The 'bald' little house became increasingly hospitable with shelves of books, papered white and hung with paintings. Soon after Christmas, she was pregnant again with her third child and was hoping for a daughter.

While Ida was establishing their new home, Augustus was dividing his time between Elm House and Fitzroy Street. In conjunction with old Slade friends Gwen Salmond, William Orpen and John Knewstub, he opened the Chelsea Art School in Flood Street, retaining the old flat as his own office and studios. Following Slade lines and employing ex-pupils as teachers, the sexes were strictly segregated and clarity of line was emphasised. In a revealing scene reminiscent of Tonks, John reduced one female student to tears by suggesting some of the ladies might be better engaged in domestic work such as childcare. For all his supposed 'enlightened' or 'bohemian' thinking, his belief in traditional gender roles remained unshaken. A decade after his own art school education, with a wife and family ensconced in the country and a mistress abroad, he was not inclined to make a stand for female emancipation.

John did not relish his time in the country. He was listless and edgy, staying in bed, going for long walks or withdrawing by drawing or reading. A deep depression settled on him which permeated their country life, leaving Ida in despair. His regular letters to Dorelia in Paris pleading for her return received little encouragement. Partly through her pragmatic generosity and partly frustration, Ida suggested he spent a week in Paris that May, combining a visit to the other woman with the opening of an exhibition of Post-Impressionist Primitives. Seizing the opportunity of an emotional reunion, John hurried to France, only to find that behind Dorelia's short replies to his letters lay a worrying development. A young Belgian farmer named Leonard had attracted her attention and, soon after John's arrival, the pair disappeared together to Bruges. In danger of losing his latest muse, he confided again in the pregnant Ida back in Essex, conscious that her happiness depended upon his. After all his sexual betrayals, or perhaps because of them, Ida listened as her husband explained his fears; the lack of secrecy allowed a greater degree of intimacy than might have otherwise remained. If she was losing one role as his muse, she could at least hold on to that of confidante. Through that summer a barrage of letters crossed the channel as Dorelia attempted to cling to the freedom the Johns wanted her to relinquish. Convinced that Augustus and therefore she, could not be happy unless Dorelia returned and resumed her own lost role of muse, Ida herself wrote to Paris. Dorelia was to live with them at Elm House and provide the anchor around which their marriage would hold fast.

It was an unconventional move for 1904. Those in the know – Augustus, Ida, Dorelia and Gwen – described it in terms of beauty, possession and nobility. Gwen wrote that it 'took her breath away' when Ida promised to 'haunt' Dorelia until her return and desired her presence [?] 'passionately' for the sake of their 'worldly welfare'. Without Dorelia at her side in the country, Ida feared she may lose John completely. She felt she had made the mistake of considering him as a man rather than an 'artist-creature' subject to different rules.[2] That summer, she had planned to visit Gwen in Paris, perhaps to relive happier days spent in the Rue Froidevaux but was forced to abandon the plan when one of her boys became ill and her pregnancy rapidly advanced. Instead, Gwen came to Essex for a few days that September, concerned by the desperation and exhaustion in Ida's letters. Emotionally drained and carrying an unusually large child, Ida was close to breaking point. She wrote to Mary Dowdall that she was 'hungry and thirsty, but for ethics and life and rainbows and colours butterflies and shimmering seas

Above: A bohemian dinner party from 1887, featured in *Harpers and Queen* magazine. Towards the end of the nineteenth century, the image of the impoverished bohemian, sacrificing all for art, living in poverty, had taken hold of the imagination and become a fashion. (LoC)

Right: James Whistler's less glamorous image of bohemian life. The reality of bohemian living was often far removed from that depicted in magazines and fiction of the era. Poor nutrition and frequent ill-health could lead to premature death, as in the case of Henri Murger, the original creator of the bohemian ideal in Paris, who died penniless at the age of thirty-eight. (LoC)

Sophie Brzeska, 1872–1925. Original artwork by Geoff Licence.

Krakow, where Sophie's father, Mieczyslaw Brzeski lived as a young man and later practised law, and where she would go as a young woman to escape the family home. To the right is the Jagielle statue, symbol of Poland's greatest royal dynasty. (LoC)

Immigrants from Eastern Europe at Ellis Island in around 1910, awaiting the boat to take them to Manhattan. The scene would not have changed in the few years since Sophie sailed to New York and was processed in the same way. (LoC)

The impressive Sainte Geneviève Library, Paris, an engraving from 1859. In 1910, Sophie returned to Paris, where she attended lectures at the Sorbonne and spent her evenings reading in the library. There, she met Henri Gaudier, and persuaded him to show her his sketch book. (LoC).

Left: The rosarium at Baden bei Wien. Sophie travelled to the spa town of Baden, just south of Vienna, in order to recover her health. Renowned for its fresh mountain air, the town offered a range of diversions for the visitor, including the rosarium, which had been opened in 1820 as an 'English garden' and included a swimming pool and skating rink. (Lucy Green-Watt)

Below: The East Cliff, Felixstowe, on the Suffolk coast. In April 1911, Sophie took a position as a teacher at 'Neuheim', a school for girls, situated near to the seafront. Picturesque as the location was, she was unhappy there and only remained until the summer term. (LoC)

098. - FELIXSTOWE, EAST CLIFF.

Katherine Mansfield, the New Zealand short story writer in whom Sophie hoped to find a friend. Unfortunately, Katherine did not warm to her, finding her intensity and confidences stifling. (New Zealand Archives)

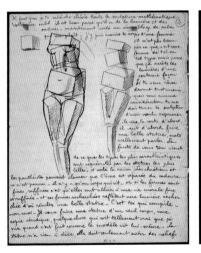

Above left: Letter from Henri to Sophie, dated June 1911, featuring the sketch of a female figure broken into cubist blocks. (Reproduced by kind permission of the Albert Sloman Library, University of Essex)

Above right: Letter from Henri to Sophie in 1912, with a sketch by Henri alluding to their lack of sexual contact and her encouragement of him to resort to prostitutes. (Reproduced by kind permission of the Albert Sloman Library, University of Essex)

Above left: 45 Paultons Square, which Sophie found too noisy a location to remain in for long. (Courtesy Google Earth)

Above right: Sketch of a woman, probably Sophie, by Henri. (Reproduced by kind permission of the Albert Sloman Library, University of Essex)

Sophie's poetry notes. (Reproduced by kind permission of the Albert Sloman Library, University of Essex)

Taking ammunition up to the front at Neuville St Vaast for the Canadian Field Artillery. Henri Gaudier was killed in the battle to capture the town on 5 June 1915, long before this picture was taken. (Archives of the National Library of Canada)

Ida Nettleship, 1877–1907. Original artwork by Geoff Licence.

Above: 58 Wigmore Street, home of the Nettleship family, where Ada ran her costume making business and John painted. (Courtesy Google Earth)

Left: The actress Dame Ellen Terry, with whom Ada Nettleship worked to create costumes for the stage, including her famous dress as Lady Macbeth. Ada also made items for Ellen's personal wardrobe, and was remembered in her autobiography. (LoC)

Female students at the Académie Julian, Paris, c. 1885. This was the first choice of Ida but she couldn't afford the fees and enrolled instead at Colarossi's. Clive Holland observed that 'a year or two at Julian's, the Beaux-Arts or Colarossi's is worth a cycle of South Kensington with its "correctness"'. (LoC)

Henry Tonks sketched by John Singer Sargent in August 1918. A surgeon, Tonks became a war artist, recording battle sites and the reconstructed faces of the wounded before returning to become Slade Professor of Fine Art in 1918. Ida worked hard to please him. (Courtesy Fitzwilliam Museum, Cambridge University)

The Slade School of Art, at which Ida enrolled in 1892, and where she would meet her future husband, Augustus John. (Courtesy O. Usher)

Paris, 1900. When Ida arrived in Paris in 1898, with her Slade friends Gwen John and Gwen Salmond, it marked an exciting new chapter in her life, seeking artistic inspiration and a freer, bohemian life. (LoC).

Elm House, Matching Green, Essex. Ida moved here in November 1903 with Augustus and their children, but she was isolated and unhappy, then felt obliged to invite Dorelia to join them. They left in the autumn of 1905. (Courtesy Paul Fairbrass)

Augustus John, 1878–1961. Increasingly, Ida realised that although she loved him, she was 'better alone'. (LoC)

Fernande Olivier, 1881–1966. Original artwork by Geoff Licence.

The Bois de Boulogne c. 1900, the most famous park in Paris, where Fernande agreed to go with Paul Percheron. It had a reputation for lovers' trysts. (LoC)

Le Chalet des Isles, the restaurant on the island within the Bois de Boulogne where Paul Percheron took Fernande, and where she stayed too late to return home. (Courtesy Roger W.)

The town hall, or mairie, in arrondissement 14, Paris, where Fernande and Paul Percheron were married on 8 August, 1899. (Courtesy F. Challiss)

A window dedicated to the Bateau Lavoir, the artists' colony in Montmartre, where Fernande lived with Laurent Debienne before moving into Picasso's studio in 1905. This isn't actually the entrance to the colony but a building adjacent to the 'cité d'artistes'. (Courtesy David McSpadden under Creative Commons)

Above: The Lapin Agile, the cabaret bar in the Rue des Saules, frequented by Picasso, Fernande and their friends, where Fernande would later earn money by reciting poetry. Here photographed in 1905, Raoul Dufy, Adrien Barrière (who would become famous for his Pathé film posters) and other artists listen to guitarist Frédé Dad. (Courtesy Montmartre Museum)

Above left: The Moulin Rouge, photographed around 1900. Situated on the Boulevard de Clichy, this was one of Montmartre's most famous nightspots, frequently depicted by Henri Toulouse-Lautrec. Picasso painted it first in 1901. (LoC)

The village of Horta, Spain, where Picasso and Fernande spent the summer of 1906 and Picasso produced a range of important works in the transition to Cubism. (Courtesy Tijs B.)

11 Boulevard de Clichy, where Picasso and Fernande moved in 1909. (Courtesy Google Earth)

Gertrude Stein, photographed in her house in the Rue Fleurus, under the portrait Picasso painted of her in 1906. (LoC)

A group of the Futurist artists who came to Paris in 1912. Left to right, Russolo, Carrà, Marinetti, Boccioni and Severini. Fernande met them at L'Hermitage, the venue opposite her flat in the Boulevard de Clichy, and began an affair with Ubaldo Oppi. (LoC)

Above left: Fashion designer Paul Poiret admired Fernande's artwork while she was still living with Picasso, and gave her a job in 1912, when she was in financial need. (LoC)

Above right: Denise Poiret, Paul's wife, wearing the fashions of 1912, when Fernande was employed as a manager in the shop of the Atelier Martine. Fernande had always had a passion for clothes and perfume but, for reasons unknown, she did not work there long. (LoC) and human intercourse'. Instead she was 'alone and alone and alone', her 'usual happiness is unhappiness ... how pleasant it seems it would be to die.'[3]

A full-length portrait made of her by Augustus as this time shows quite a different figure from the alluring 'Merikli' of Fitzroy Street days. The two works may stand as emotional representations for how his vision of his wife had changed. 'Ida Pregnant' is a sketchy, almost coarse work, in earthy tones. The dominant brown palette creates a muddy feel and, in places, Ida's fluid gown and dark hair blend with the abstract surround from which she appears to have sprung. Half turning away from the viewer, she rests one hand on her stomach in a gesture that could be pride, protection or reproach. Equally, the enigmatic smile spread across her thickened features may be accompanied by a slight lowering of the brows and is difficult to read. Ironically, given her pregnancy, the figure appears almost childlike in stance and expression. The painstaking detail of the sultry 'Merikli' is lacking; the 1902 hands, so clearly delineated with their wedding ring and gentle grip on a flower stem, have been reduced to smudges barely visible beyond her cuff. Fabric folds are no longer sharp and the contrasting colours of Ida's 1902 black eyes and red lips have been replaced by paler orange-browns. In two years, Ida has faded on canvas. The work seems hurried, as if John's attention is not fully engaged; was the portrait his attempt to appease Ida and compensate her for the arrival of Dorelia? If so, Ida must have felt the difference given the intense and sultry portraits he was producing of 'Ardor', her rival.

Dorelia NcNeill moved into Elm House in August. The Johns' cook was disgusted by the new arrangement and left but Ida remained confident that, in spite of the criticisms of friends and society, the ménage à trois would be a success and empower her as its driving force. She wrote to Alice Rothenstein describing Dorelia as 'augmenting' rather than 'diminishing' her happiness and that the 'beautiful' arrangement could be appreciated by the 'large minded', although to her aunt she confessed the difficulties and the days when she had to 'fight to keep where I am (like the) saints and martyrs ... suffering everything for their idea of truth.'[4] She was determined not to apportion blame and to maintain the image of a forward-thinking, enlightened life style, which her friends were too traditional and conservative to understand. In truth though, Ida was sinking into a deep depression and frequently experiencing emotions of desperation and frustration. She longed for stimulation and company but still awaiting her child's birth, John and Dorelia would leave her in Essex while they pursued the artistic society she greatly missed.

After Robin's birth on 23 October 1904, Ida undertook a short visit to London on her own, but became strangely 'hysterical' as she drifted listlessly and avoided friends.[5] Returning home, she found John had painted her out of a double portrait featuring her and Dorelia, a symbolic gesture she refused to overlook. She felt isolated and rejected, considered suicide and took pain killers for a number of minor physical ailments that sound like the symptoms of exhaustion. For a while, death seemed to offer the peace she craved but she resisted the laudanum bottle. Unsettled by terrible arguments, all three were unhappy. The house Ida had worked hard to make a comfortable domestic retreat was turning into a prison; Dorelia and John both made regular threats to leave and her new role as mediator gave Ida additional status in the trio. No matter how hard she tried, though, her natural feelings of jealousy and neglect could not be so easily disregarded. Writing to Dorelia that 'nature was the enemy to our scheme,' [6] Ida was about to discover that nature had bound them even more closely together just at the point the ménage seemed about to disintegrate. At the end of 1904 or early in 1905, Dorelia confirmed the pregnancy she had been concealing from Ida.

The new year was to mark an unexpected shift in the power of the John triangle. Just as Ida believed the situation could not worsen, she found the solidarity and support she had craved in the most unlikely place as a familiar pattern began to emerge. As the months progressed, Augustus found the pregnant Dorelia less appealing; his physical relationship with Ida was reignited and in February, she conceived her fourth child. Predictably, he left the two pregnant women alone together more often, sharing the maternal bond and preparing for the new arrivals. However, Ida was entertaining her mother alone at Elm House in the late spring when a telegram announced the birth of Pyramus. Dorelia had accompanied Augustus on one of his gipsy jaunts, but was apart from him and given birth in a remote caravan on Dartmoor. Ida responded at once, travelling overnight by train and arriving before Augustus, whose concern to spare her feelings manifested itself as disinterestedness towards the new baby. Between painting and loafing, he redoubled his attentions to his wife and the irony was not lost on her: 'He is (or acts) in love with *me* for a change.' In favour at last, she realised that in the triangle, one woman's happiness would always come at a painful cost to the other. For practically the first time, Ida's usual spirited defence of her husband slipped and the 'artistic creature' became a 'horrid beast'.[7] The bohemian vision had soured.

Ida's painful situation regarding her own creativity finds some echoes in the relationship of two of her contemporaries, writer Ford Madox Ford and artist Stella Bowen, who lived together and had a daughter. Stella:

> My painting has been hopelessly interfered with by the whole shape of my life, for I was learning the technique of quite a different role: that of consort to another and more gifted artist, so that although Ford was always urging me to paint, I simply had not got any creative vitality to spare after I had played my part towards him and Julie.[8] [If Stella had painted] I should not have been available to nurse him through the strain of his daily work ... to stand between him and circumstances. Pursuing an art is not just the matter of finding the time, it is a matter of having a free spirit to bring it on ... there was no room for me to nurse an independent ego ... A man writer or painter always managed to get some woman to look after him and make his life easy and since female devotion, in England anyhow, is a glut on the market, this is not difficult.[9]

It seemed that in the cases of domestic experiment, the advantages, the freedom and, therefore, the artistic success, were unevenly shared. While men might escape the routine of childrearing and throw themselves into their work, this was only possible, for John and Ford, because there were dependable women in their lives who created an environment, a stability, on which they might lean.

In the summer of 1905, the Johns remained for a while on Dartmoor. Ida loved the outdoor life, with the children running wild and the beautiful countryside. They washed in the nearby stream, cooked over open fires and gathered at dusk before retreating into a gypsy-style tent built by Augustus. The exhilarating new freedom Ida felt, coupled with her increasing solidarity with Dorelia, made her determined to seize back control of her life and loosen the marital bonds that weighed her down. She rejected the role of wife to Augustus, which she considered a 'mockery' and cast herself as his mistress, experimenting with different identities, calling herself Anne or Susan. Determined to shrug off the weight of imposed dishonesty and reject any social censure, she confided the true state of her marriage to her mother. Predictably, the response was disapproving but Ada was disappointed more with her daughter for having countenanced such behaviour and having brought the taint of scandal upon her unmarried sisters. Letters from Ursula and Ethel Nettleship provoked Ida to a defence of her misunderstood 'beautiful' life but their dramatic avowals to forego marriage after her example deeply shocked her.[10] She wrote to Augustus explaining that she wished to live apart from him, as the daily struggle with their incompatibility was too much of a strain. When the lease on Elm House came up for renewal that autumn, it was the seven-months pregnant Ida who travelled and made the necessary arrangements for their move; in September, she, Dorelia, the children and dog crossed the channel and headed for Paris.

*

For Sophie and Henri, their escape from Paris to England brought new friendships and influential connections. Determined to settle in London, they began to seek out the like-minded friends they had been unable to find elsewhere. An article by ex-colonial Haldane Macfall in January edition of *The English Review* interested Henri to the extent that he wrote to the author, who in turn invited him to attend one of his Wednesday evening 'at homes'. The initial meeting went well and he soon returned with Sophie, who was keen to meet fellow writers, yet anxious about her reception. Over the coming months, they met more of Macfall's circle, including designer

Claude Lovat Fraser, ex-army Major Smythies and writer Enid Bagnold, who described the tense energy of Gaudier's presence. Her account gives some idea of his prickly intensity and pugilistic nature: he 'shot' into the group 'like a mechanical wasp ... all stings and ceaseless quiet noise,' the 'wheels' inside his head 'never at peace'. From his lips poured 'invention, criticism, intolerance, jibes, enthusiasm.' Talking to him was like 'stepping on a thorn'. He 'burnt his black eyes' into his friends and 'jabbed and wounded' them when they replied. On a station platform, as Gaudier poured out to them 'his future and his past and his passion', she and others tried to back away from him out of the wind, to which he reacted by throwing his arms round them so they should not move and distract him. Bagnold presents an intense, passionate youth whose hunger for ideas and sense of purpose and disadvantage could easily offend the sensibilities of the more reserved.[11]

Bagnold found Sophie a difficult dinner companion – 'treacherous, suspicious, easily affronted, violently hurt' – and constantly 'pestering' Gaudier with imagined slights she perceived in people's behaviour. Sophie was not slow to notice Bagnold's dislike or communicate it loudly to Henri within earshot: 'That Bagnold despises us ... Did you notice?' Another friend, Dolly Tylden, recorded that Sophie 'looked at least twenty-five years older than (Henri)' and that Sophie was 'obviously an "exaltee" and she talked of philosophy and poetry in the grand manner, but without being in the least ridiculous.'[12] They must have been prickly and uncomfortable guests; Sophie's insecurities led to jealous responses and she would frequently create 'scenes' before and during social occasions although Henri could more than equal her propensity to take offence. Many potential friendships were spoiled by their rash intolerance, for which Sophie was entirely blamed after Henri's death. When Enid Bagnold visited them in their new apartment to model for a bust, Sophie was ill, lying down in the next room, perhaps in a deliberate attempt to avoid company. Bagnold described the 'little bare room at the top of a house' in winter, where she posed while Henri suffered a nose bleed and watched dogs fighting in the street outside with dark, fascinated eyes, wrapped in bloody bandages.[13] Later, Enid recalled the scene differently, making herself the sufferer of the bleed, but the bohemian image remains, of art created out of stark poverty tinged with violence.

A more significant friend emerged for Gaudier during 1912, whose connections would lead him into contact with some of the leading artists and poets of the day. Jacob Epstein was an American who had moved to England in 1902 and was currently sculpting a tomb for Oscar Wilde in his Cheyne Walk studio. With its distinctive winged figure, it would be erected in the Père Lachaise Cemetery in Paris the following July. Epstein saw Henri as 'a picturesque, slight figure with lively eyes and a slight beard', warming to him at once.[14] He gave an account of Henri in his autobiography as wishing 'to be always in the vanguard of the moment' with 'any amount of talent and great energy' but also captured his confrontational nature, the heart of his bohemian difference, in that he loved to shock people, declaring that he was homosexual 'expecting us to be horrified' and he often had a black eye from 'fights with Cockneys'. Epstein's response to Sophie was similar to that of many of their friends of the time. Writing in retrospect, he saw her 'outbursts of frenzied jealousy and hatred of anyone who approached Gaudier' as a sign of mental instability. Epstein dined with the pair in their flat, observing that Sophie sat and talked whilst Henri cooked a stew. 'We got on very well,' he wrote about that meeting with her, 'although Sophie had it always in the back of her mind that I was standing in Henri's light.'[15] By 1912, with the various difficulties and trials she had been through, the cruelties, criticisms and desertion by friends, lovers and family, coupled with her ill-health and depression, Sophie had become 'difficult'. Emotionally volatile and defensive, she elicited strong reactions among Henri's friends, often creating social situations that they both found awkward. She both longed to connect with like-minded friends and rejected them, imprisoned within her own cage of opposition.

Paulton Square was a pretty and salubrious part of Chelsea, with neat Georgian terraces facing each other across narrow gardens. Sophie and Henri moved into part of number 45. It is a five-storey house, including cellar and attics with the front door situated on the right, across a path of black and white tiles. The first floor has long sash windows with iron balconies and on the top floor a little round window set between the standard two differentiated the house from its neighbours. It is today a pleasant, leafy, well-to-do neighbourhood but it proved to be far too noisy for Sophie. Perhaps the fact that their front door was immediately opposite the entrance place to the square's gardens was the problem. The next few months of their lives are poorly documented, as they struggled with loneliness and poverty, while Gaudier drew small, satirical posters and made sketches of Sophie, none of which appealed to potential new employers.[16]

In February 1912, Henri and Sophie relocated half a mile west to the narrow Redburn Street, which appeared quiet, and where the flat roof of their property could be used as a sort of open air studio in good weather. Here, at number 15, they were just a short stroll from the Chelsea Physic Garden, Cheyne Walk and the Albert Bridge Road. On the day of their move, they attended a play with the Hares, friends of Macfall, which led to a commission for Gaudier and an invitation to their home. The process of sculpting this Madonna soon filled the new rooms with intolerable noise and dirt for Sophie; Gaudier was ashamed about having plunged her into 'such a damned mess' and children also living in the house proved noisy enough to drive a 'lunatic's asylum sane'. The 'beastly' children with 'monkey's faces and 'frog's eyes ... never close their mouths for a minute,' making 'savage yells ... wild shoutings and inhuman hollerings.'[17] For Sophie, other people's noise was to be a life-long intolerance; after her experiences of teaching, children were the worst. More commissions for Gaudier, including busts of Macfall and Major Smythies, created even more mess in their tiny living quarters, although this was compensated for by the money they eventually brought in. By the summer of 1912, Sophie was finding the degradations of poverty damaging to her health. It was fortunate, then, that a new friendship began around this time, briefly renewing her hope for sympathetic human contact.

Katherine Mansfield and John Middleton Murry had plans brewing and debts mounting. She was a short story writer of twenty-four, originally from New Zealand, who had lived a bohemian life of heterosexual and same-sex love affairs, followed by recuperation in European spa towns, a miscarriage and a fleeting marriage to an older man, whom she left just hours after the ceremony. Now she was determined to write and displaying the beginnings of what would become considerable talent. She had met Murry the previous year, who had confounded expectations of a glittering career when he dropped out of Oxford and headed instead to Paris. As editor of the avant garde magazine *Rhythm*, he had rejected Katherine's first contribution, only to be impressed by a second, darker story which he went on to publish. By 1912, they were living together in London but were on the verge of bankruptcy, trying to resurrect the doomed magazine as *The Blue Review*. Mansfield had recently published her first collection of short stories, *In a German Pension*, and was a regular contributor to A. R. Orage's influential *New Age*. She was petite, neat and strong-willed, dressing in simple dark clothing, bobbing her hair, projecting an elusive, almost oriental façade in the formal passport photographs of the decade.

Gaudier met the pair first. He sang with Katherine and began work on a sculpted head of Murry, discussing art enthusiastically and imagining a life where they lived on a Pacific Island.[18] To him, Murry had the 'refined features and ... magnificent head of a Greek God, an Apollo or Mars', while Katherine 'was not at all silly or vindictive' and found English women 'heartrendingly conventional'. Henri was 'enchanted' and told Sophie he had 'never met anyone so charming or so sympathetic'.[19] It was awkward then, that when the two women met, Sophie thought she had found a kindred spirit, to whom she could unburden her troubles, while Katherine found her 'Dostoyevskian' character too intense and neurotic, fearing she would be 'strangled by her tentacles'[20] and shuddering at her heart-felt confessions about the past.[21]

On paper the two women had much in common despite a disparity in ages. Like Sophie, New Zealand writer Katherine Mansfield travelled independently before settling in London; she was sharp, intelligent and a devoted, talented writer but her constant poor health affected her badly, necessitating moves to healthier dwellings. Like Sophie, she was insecure in her own skin, constantly challenging and experimenting with her identity and adapting the truth to suit her purposes. Both women refused to conform to social conventions that might have brought them an easier life; unconventional personal relationships and the centrality of their writing brought financial hardship and public disapproval. Katherine and Murry were both in their early twenties, making them closer in age to Gaudier by a decade, which was a difference Sophie was to come to feel. Increasingly, invitations were sent to Gaudier alone, excluding Sophie, who responded by sending a telegram to withdraw an offer of tea she had made to Katherine.

In the summer of 1912, though, Sophie was still hopeful about the friendship. When Katherine and Murry left London for a cottage outside Chichester, promising to invite their friends as soon as it was ready, Sophie was keen to escape London and accept their hospitality. That September, Sophie sent Henri into the countryside to investigate, hoping that she might soon follow. However, as he approached the house, Gaudier overheard the pair inside talking about him and Sophie. When Murry suggested it was time to invite them, Katherine replied, 'Oh no, I don't want to see her here, she's too violent, I won't have her.' When Murry tried to persuade her that this wasn't the case and he could see no reason not to invite Sophie, Katherine added 'I don't like her and I don't want to see her, she'll make me ill again.'[22] Henri was furious and stormed away without declaring his presence. Back in London he wrote an aggrieved letter to Murry describing Katherine as 'wicked' and 'fiendish',[23] requesting the return of three books Sophie had lent them, including the 1905 *Bubu de Montparnasse*.[24] The following summer he burst into the offices of *Rhythm* magazine, attacked Murry and demanded payment for some sketches which, according to Murry, had never been agreed. By mid-1913, the friendship was effectively over.

While Gaudier sketched and sculpted, Sophie was still writing. She sent a specimen of her work to the wife of the art critic Thomas Leman Hare, Clemence E. A. Pascal, born in Haiti, whom he had married in 1887. Clemence was three or four years older than Sophie but, instead of offering her advice about her work, Mrs Hare suggested that she should take a large house and open it up to a few paying guests, so as to live more comfortably. Sophie took this as a 'direct reflection on the quality of her work' and was 'bitterly hurt'. (Which does not seem to be unreasonable – no one told the George Eliot she would be better off as a landlady; perhaps they would have, if introduced to Miss Evans.) As H. S. Ede explains, Sophie was convinced that she was 'a great writer' and spent all her energy 'trying to crystallize her ideas' but was able to achieve nothing because of her surroundings and lack of food. Haldane Macfall encouraged her as best he could but, other than Henri, she was not 'fortunate enough to meet anyone ... who would encourage her in her work' and, as Ede adds, 'her insistent nature drove people away from her.'[25] However, the Hares were swifter to encourage Henri, buying several works including a 'Woman and Child', for which they paid three pounds. Gaudier was indignant on Sophie's behalf, believing her as good a writer as he was an artist, but also emphasising her centrality to his output, as 'without my Mamus I should have had nothing to show anyone, for as soon as I have done anything it disgusts me and if you had not saved all my works, I should have destroyed them all.'[26] Sophie frequently posed for Henri, during which she sang old songs from Russia and Poland and they were 'both for the moment in a frenzy of delight, and forgot that any cloud had ever dimmed the edge of their horizon.' Sophie was usually exhausted afterwards, but the portrait turned out to be 'a miracle'.[27]

That summer, a letter Henri wrote to his German mentor, Dr Uhlemayr, helps clarify his feelings about Sophie. He feared that Uhlemayr had been offended to learn of their friendship, thinking 'Gaudier ran away from his parents to have fun with an ordinary woman and it is not very honourable' so he was 'not worth the trouble to write to'.[28] He reassured his friend that there was more to his relationship with Sophie and explained her character and abilities as he saw them:

Zofia Brzeska is more than my friend – this is certain – without her financial and moral help in Paris, I would have been dead long ago and her help is even more valuable as Brzeska herself was also poor and ill. For two years now we have lived together, we pooled our efforts and together keep up the struggle against life. For eight months now our finances have improved by sheer energy ... She is writing much better now that when I first met her, we are certainly very happy but our happiness is peculiar, not sentimental, we do not spare ourselves and work incessantly. Nature has created man and woman in order to complete themselves and know how to fight better ... Brzeska is 40 years old, I am 20, therefore each one of us is 30 ... I can only congratulate myself to have met Z. Brzeska and to have decided immediately to join my fate to hers. She is very energetic, serious, and as a writer she possesses amazing power and technique; she is very experienced, understanding good and true feelings, but very particular about cleanliness; she can feel a deadly hatred to anyone who offends her. She does not represent 'Eternal Femininity' but a new feminine type, made of steel, strong as a man, having the same temperament and each forgiving the others' faults to love one another gradually more, with a love built on friendship, giving sexual passion second importance.[29]

In October 1912, Sophie set off alone for the countryside, to recover her nerves amid peace and quiet. In his last letter to Murry, Henri commented that she was 'in a most lovely Worcestershire cottage, on a hill, where she works' and was free. From there, she moved first to an old house in Frolesworth, Leicestershire, where she lodged with a Mrs Newett and then on to the village of Dodford, in Worcestershire, by the end of the month, where she was at Ambrosia Cottage with a Mrs Hollyoak. On Friday 11 October, Henri wrote to Sophie from Redburn Street. He was receiving a summons from France to take up his military service, which preyed on his mind, but he was working well, producing a composition for Thomas 'Tomsy' Hare. The touching bucolic image he had woven for Murry was far from the realities of Ambrosia Cottage. Sophie had clearly written to him already, as he commiserated with her that everything was so dirty in her boarding house, and that her luggage appeared to have been lost on the train. He suggested she might prefer to go to Belgium, to visit the Ardennes, which was like the Black Forest. 'I wish,' he wrote, 'that I was ten years older in order to be richer and that my Sik had a lovely country house of her own.'[30] Two days later, after he had heard from her again, he wrote that she seemed 'to have got into a beastly hole', listing the reasons, which included 'the old woman with cancer, the workhouse, the Vicar', a woman named Niemczura, 'bad food and a rotten bed'. By October 16, he was urging her to return after a month in the country, instead of her planned three. He couldn't live without her and missed her so much that he cried at night in his sleep, waking with a wet pillow and swollen eyes. This elicited a cross response from Sophie, in which she accused him of being conceited and changeable, which made him 'very unhappy'.[31] His response was to explain the frustration of his situation, followed by criticisms of her character:

You don't, I think, realise that I have to be in a filthy office all day long, and that every minute I am devoured by the most torturing desire to be cutting stone, painting walls and casting statues? You always seem to forget this, and that isn't at all nice of you … You have ruined the best part of your life because of this pride which you place above the work which you could and should accomplish.[32]

He also responded to her accusation that her work meant nothing to him:

You insist that I am not sufficiently interested in your work, that I don't ask you questions, that I haven't read anything of yours since people here said it wasn't worth anything. That is a hideous lie … during the two years that we have been together your work has only been in a state of preparation and but for slight alterations, is always practically the same … Since I know the story from A to Z, what is the use of asking you questions about it? I have … read all the little notes you put in the margin and that is more than you can say for yourself about my drawings, which you never dream of looking at.[33]

In 1912, however, Gaudier had designed a cover for a family history that Sophie was writing. Featuring two hostile looking figures, a man and woman of elderly years, it was titled '*Histericzki od Zofii Breskiej*' (A History of Sophie Brzeska) with the subtitle '*Polska KZiazka we Warszawie*', which roughly translates as a Polish book set in Warsaw. This is an interesting detail, which may suggest Sophie was tracing her roots back to older family members who originated from Warsaw, although her life was spent closer to Krakow, or it may have been an assumption by Gaudier, or a deliberate artistic choice to gain Sophie some distance from surviving family members whom she disliked.

By early November, their grievances had been put to one side. Henri wrote that 'not only are we of different sexes, but also of different nationalities.' Nor were they of 'the same age, nor have we had the same experience, nor do our talents follow the same course.' But in spite of this, he continued, what remained was their love for each other. 'So let's finish all these harangues,' he pleaded, 'and we will always love each other, just we two, because this is the only happiness on which we can count.'[34] Soon afterwards, on the second weekend in November, Henri went to visit her in Worcestershire. She had found 'nice rooms at a farm house', where they talked late into the night, enjoyed a long country walk and, in the garden, they found some old jars and a fifteenth-century Christ which they tried to purchase. 'Dear, you are in such a charming place ... all the lovely country, not grand, but very intimate, very human, and rather Celtic, with a gaiety of its own,' he wrote. Sophie had also spent thirty shillings on four Indian curtains to hang in their London home.[35]

Henri was back in London for the opening of the Futurist Exhibition at the Sackville Gallery, which was causing some ripples of hostility in artistic circles. On 20 November, he attended a supper party hosted by Wyndham Lewis in his flat at Greek Street, after which the group of friends went to the Doré Gallery and heckled the leading Italian artist, Filippo Marinetti. As Lewis recalled, 'Gaudier went into action at once. He was very good at the parlez-vous ... sniping him without intermission, standing up in his place in the audience all the while ... the Italian intruder was rousted.'[36] This was quite a different Henri from the one who returned to Worcestershire to visit Sophie that Christmas. It rained the whole time and both of them were ill. After four days spent largely in silence, he urged her to come back to London. Early in January, he found a new studio, 'a marvellous place', Studio 5 454a Fulham Road, where he felt 'lifted from Hell into Heaven'.[37] In addition, Sophie was worried to read in his letters that he had made friends with a number of young women, whom she feared would steal him away from her. She packed her bags and returned to London in February 1913.

13

Madame Picasso

Soon after the return to Paris from Gosol, Picasso and Fernande settled into a new domestic intimacy. A drawing he made of her in the autumn of 1906 shows her bent over her sewing, plying her needle as he sketched, others showed her partially dressed or draped in scarves or her favourite mantillas. Her cooking was improving as she grew more adept at economising and she was pleased to find her meals appreciated by visiting friends. They bought another dog, Frika, to replace Fernande's fox terrier that had died, a great shaggy creature who makes an appearance in studio photographs of this period, and a cat to get rid of the mice. Resting after dinner one evening, Fernande was overcome by happiness: it did not matter that 'day-to-day life (was) difficult' or that they lacked 'furniture or comfort': Picasso's bare studio contained all she needed: 'Where would I be better off than at his side?'[1] The grinding poverty, the bedbugs and their lack of space could not detract from the depth of her love for Picasso, an emotion she had not previously experienced. If it hadn't been located amongst the privation of the Bateau-Lavoir, Fernande's bohemianism might have approximated to an imitation of bourgeois domesticity. But there was one missing ingredient that would make the picture complete.

After Fernande had suffered her miscarriage in 1899, she suspected she was no longer able to bear a child. By spring 1907, after eight years of being sexually active, with a number of partners, she had not conceived again. Pictures of Fernande that year show her posing with Dolly, the young daughter of their neighbours Kees and Augusta 'Guus' Van Dongen. The two are in close physical proximity but there remains an awkward formality and distance between them. In one, Fernande is looking away down the street with one hand extended out to the dog, which has become the point of their shared focus: an indoor shot shows her holding Dolly stiffly, while the girl's face is a picture of distress. The photographs portray Fernande in an ambiguous maternal light but this did not prevent her from wanting a child. Another photograph dating from their later visit to Horta de Ebro shows Fernande holding the hand of one of the village children, a small girl in white. It may be significant that the desire for motherhood is absent from Fernande's diary, as she approached her twenty-sixth birthday and faced the reality of childlessness.

On 9 April, 1907, Fernande and Picasso visited a Montmartre orphanage run by the Sisters of Mercy in the Rue Caulaincourt. It was Fernande's idea; her desire for a child may have been an attempt to bind her closer to Picasso, whose artistic focus had shifted from her in recent months. Instead of being his inspiration, appearing in most of his work as she had in 1905-6, she was now being replaced by angular, unrecognisable female forms, derived from the African masks and statues he had seen at the Ethnographic Museum. It may have been that she wanted a child as the final element to complete their world. Pablo accompanied Fernande to the orphanage reluctantly, wary of the way that a child would disrupt his work. He waited while she chose Raymonde, the playful, intelligent and beautiful daughter of a prostitute, one of the many born in such conditions in that district and left to the Montmartre nuns. The girl may have been as old as thirteen, although Guillaume Apollinaire described her as being younger and other sources suggest she was around nine years old.[2] She had already been adopted and rejected once by a journalist with unrealistic aspirations of making her a musical talent.

At first, Raymonde was welcomed in the Bateau-Lavoir, given presents and fussed over by the couple and their friends. Fernande enjoyed the role of mother, dressing her up and brushing her hair as she would a doll, reminiscent of her aunt Alice Petot's treatment of herself. They 'played' together, trying on clothes while Picasso made sketches to amuse her; she met Fernande's friends Gertrude and Leo Stein and the poet Andre Salmon, who later romanticised her in verse as 'Léontine'. Salmon brought her sweets and the poet Max Jacob arrived with the gift of a doll. But the whole episode was 'play,' a game for Fernande, an experiment in parenthood that did not last long. This doesn't mean that she didn't take it seriously, or truly desire a child, but more that she underestimated the reality of the situation, of bringing a third presence into their small room, which would change the dynamic of their union. Perhaps her maternal instincts were insufficiently strong or she found that the poverty and intensity of studio living did not lend themselves to child rearing. It is possible that, like Ida, she was unprepared for the life-changing experience of parenthood. Picasso's biographer John Richardson[3] has suggested Fernande was made uneasy by certain inappropriate drawings made by Picasso of a precociously nude Raymonde. His previous sylph-like images of girls pre-dating their relationship may have incited Fernande's jealousy or her protective instincts towards the girl. It is impossible now to know her motives but, unlike the unhappy Ida, Fernande took the opportunity to relinquish her maternal role when it did not suit her. That July, she attempted to return Raymonde to the orphanage, which refused to take her back. In the end, Raymonde was adopted by a concierge near the Sacré-Coeur but appears to have remained in touch with Fernande, sending her a postcard in 1919.

The episode opened cracks in Fernande and Picasso's relationship. Writing to Gertrude Stein, she explained how that summer had been especially hard 'from a physical and psychological point of view'.[4] If the adoption had been Fernande's attempt to repair developing fissures in her relationship with Picasso, it only served to create further distance between them. At the end of August they agreed to part and Fernande soon moved out of the Bateau-Lavoir, going a three-minute walk away to the small 2 Impasse Girardon, which was hidden away beside 5, Rue Girardon. Apparently Picasso had 'had enough' and was not 'cut out for this sort of life'; he always found Fernande beautiful but was irritated by her habits and their proximity in the studio made the relationship very intense.

Fernande clearly believed their separation to be permanent at the time, although it turned out to be short-lived. Downhearted at the break-up, she described herself to Gertrude Stein as 'truly devastated' and felt her future looked hopeless. She was hurt by the 'light' way Picasso had taken the separation, seeming dismissive of the time they had lived together and placed herself above reproach for never having 'restricted his life or interfered with his work'. In an attempt to move on, she threw herself into the decoration of her new home, hunting for bargains and enjoying the sunshine that flooded it. She also returned to her own painting, part-Fauve in a similar style to works by Marie Laurencin, winning 'outrageously high' praise from Gertrude.[5] As a child, she had been drawn by the primitive art in the Parisian galleries and now her old friends Dufy and Friesz, were working in the new sauvage-naïf style. The Fauve's controversial exhibition at the 1905 Salon d'Automne had seized the interest of most of Montmartre's young artists and produced their own imitators. Yet Fernande lacked the commitment, courage or enthusiasm to attempt to equal their efforts. She identified a lack of confidence underpinning her failure to create, wishing that she had received even a minimal amount of encouragement to continue. She may have suffered from the limitations of the identity she had assumed so far, as the artists' model, muse and lover; the transition to creator may have been too difficult, too alien for her, in an environment where female painters like Impressionist Berthe Morisot and post-Impressionists Suzanne Valadon and Marie Laurencin were still very much in the minority. Enlightened and bohemian as Montmartre was, it still had a clear gender imbalance: with a few notable exceptions, women were friends and mistresses, partners in crime at the Lapin Agile, dancers at the Moulin Rouge or prostitutes in the many brothels around the Butte, catering to the needs of the men who made art.

Gertrude Stein was to prove a friend to Fernande during this difficult time and Fernande would come to consider the mannish poet from Pittsburgh as something of a mentor. She wrote to Gertrude that August, telling her that summer had proved 'particularly hard' for her 'both from a physical and psychological point of view' and that she was bored and depressed. During this period, she signed her letters as Fernande Belvalet and Belvallé, as if toying with the notion of returning to her former identity. Gertrude describes how she tried to help Fernande in *The Autobiography of Alice B Toklas*. Picasso suggested that she and Alice might take French lessons from Fernande, to help her out financially, 'because she and Pablo have decided to separate forever' and' she wants to install herself in a room by herself.' They went to visit her in a little house, down a little street, where they asked for 'Mademoiselle Belle-vallée' and were sent 'into a little corridor'. Fernande received them in a 'moderate-sized room in which was a very large bed and a piano and a tea table.' Also present as guests, funnily enough, were two of Picasso's former loves, Alice Princet (later Derain) and Germaine Pichot. As Gertrude related, the conversation around the tea table 'was not lively, nobody had anything to say.' Fernande complained about her charwoman's dusting and the annoyance of arranging to buy a piano and bed in instalments, before becoming angry 'like a lioness defending her cubs' that Picasso had refused to give her the comic supplements of the newspaper.[6]

Living alone was financially difficult for Fernande. Had she wished to purchase art materials, it would have become even more tight. A sum of money Picasso had given her in August began to run out and she was driven to pawning a favourite pair of gold earrings he had given her as a present. In preparing for her new-found independence, she also looked backwards. She wrote to her Aunt, Alice Petot, and was sad to learn of her Uncle Charles' death two years previously. Alice suggested a meeting but Fernande was reluctant and probably did not accept that offer, once reunited with Picasso. She did, however, partly take up the career her aunt had once destined her for, offering French lessons to Gertrude Stein's American friend Alice B Toklas at fifty cents a time. The helpful Gertrude proved instrumental in her reconciliation with Picasso by inviting them both to her home in the Rue de Fleurus for dinner. Fernande moved back into the Bateau-Lavoir at the start of December 1907.

A change had taken place in Picasso's direction during Fernande's absence. Now he was working increasingly closely with Georges Braques, developing a post-Cezanne, pre-Cubist style. Braque had moved to Montmartre in 1902 and established himself by adopting the uniform and behaviour of an avant-garde artist; blue overalls, canary coloured shoes and one of a hundred identical hats he had literally purchased for a song. He was known for his dancing, his strength and build as a boxer and for singing aloud from the tops of omnibuses, accompanying himself on the accordion. Like Fernande, Braque had been attracted to the vigour of the Fauvist style, which he called 'physical painting' and, following trips to

Normandy, Antwerp and L'Estaques, worked their influence into his landscapes. Like Picasso though, he had also been deeply moved by the 1907 Cezanne retrospective exhibition and returned to the dead artist's home in L'Estaques with Friesz, to 'translate emotion into art', developing a darker palette of muted greens and browns quite distinct from bright, pure Fauvist colours. In attempting to model the countryside in a three-dimensional way with colour, he was reinterpreting Cezanne's 'passage' technique of running planes together; key steps which moved Braque into the angular landscapes of proto-Cubism. Now he brought these techniques into the Bateau-Lavoir studio and worked closely with Picasso.

Picasso's style had been rapidly evolving since settling in Paris. A comparison of the blue self-portrait influenced by Van Gogh he completed in 1901 and the Demoiselles of 1907 underlines his speedy progression as well as drawing attention to the rapid assimilation of new influences. The paintings and drawings he had completed in Gosol had already made use of Cezanne's landscapes and nude bathers; Picasso united these monolithic figures and blocks of colour with his own interpretation of the exotic. Just before Fernande had left in August, he had seen African tribal masks at the Musée de l'Homme which he began to merge with, and then replace, the faces of his subjects. The angularity of his new works outstripped even Braque's expectations and tolerance.

Intense discussions took place in the studio. Braque had 'abandoned' his previous friends Friesz and Dufy as reactionary and imitative but was still to be wholly convinced by Picasso's new direction. Quietly witnessing these debates, Fernande once summarised Picasso's argument as being put with 'great reasonableness and clarity' and was not surprised when Braque was won over. Picasso could be very persuasive. Even if his artistic choices were baffling, she recognised and respected his desire to create a 'new kind of art' and saw him as an innovator, although she could not help but comment that he could have 'enjoyed great success as a traditional artist'.[7] Biographers and friends of Picasso have been critical of Fernande's 'bourgeois values' but, without the benefit of hindsight, her concern over his future and potential earnings must be seen in the context of their relationship as man and woman, rather than overshadowed by her lover's immense reputation.

Leisure hours were spent together too; Fernande, Picasso and their friends continued to visit their favourite haunts of the Circus Medrano and local cafés and bars. Through her friendship with Guillaume Apollinaire, Fernande was thrown together more often with Marie Laurencin and featured as a coquettish beauty in a couple of her large group portraits of the time. Her own sketch of Marie shows a witch-like face set under a mass of curly hair, not too dissimilar from the slanting eyes and mask-style features of Picasso's work. This may be more due to the initial dislike Fernande took to Marie; in many ways they were opposites; she found the other woman affected, irritating and unnecessarily self-advertising. Marie was also the dedicated artist that Fernande was not encouraged to be. Interestingly, among their circle, Fernande was known by her Christian name, denoting her intimate role, while Marie was always referred to by her surname, placing her on an artistic level with men. Her works hung regularly in the Salons and later, unjustifiably, in Cubist exhibitions, due to the encouragement and nepotism of her lover Guillaume Apollinaire. His support of Marie must have underlined the lack of encouragement Fernande received from Picasso, whose attitude was that 'women, if not inferior, should not trespass on men's preserves'. Guillaume also lent Fernande books from his 'excellent' library, which contained 'works by almost all the important authors from the eighteenth century to the present day'.[8] There was an uncomfortable moment when they were visited by fashion designer Paul Poiret, who was then at the start of a career that would see his contributions to couture likened to Picasso's contribution to art. He elaborately praised a small gouache of Fernande, believing it to be a work by Pablo, only for the artist to confess it was a self-portrait painted by his mistress. But the enthusiastic and innovative Poiret took to Fernande and would assist her later in life.

In April 1908, Picasso was visited in his studio by Inez Haynes Irwin, an American author whose description gives an impression of the man and the world he and Fernande inhabited at the time:

Picasso turns out to be a darling: young, olive, with bright, frank eyes, each with a devil in it, straight black hair, an overcoat and a blue sweater ... the filthiest studio I have ever seen; a mass of bottles, rags, sketches, huge unfinished paintings, easels covered with paint, canvases turned to the wall, stove with a pile of ashes in front of it, paint brushes and bowls of water on the floor, one vast melee of dirt, disorder and disorganisation. [9]

Picasso had a consummate and exclusive focus on his own vision. Through the spring of 1908 he worked on post-Demoiselle figures in 'Three Women' and 'The Offering,' pushing his angular female forms further into the early deconstructive stages of cubism. Sometimes the only way Fernande could detach him from his work was to coax him out to dine in Vernin's, a local restaurant which gave them credit, then walk to the top of the butte of Montmartre, before the Sacre-Coeur and observe Paris stretched out before them, sleeping, when he seemed 'less anxious, less ferociously silent … more cheerful … more interested in things around us'.[10] When they did not venture out, evenings were spent in the studio with friends, drinking cold lemon tea and smoking opium. Fernande describes the mood of those occasions, when the effects of the drug tinged their vision with 'special beauty and nobility' and nights slipped 'away in a warm, close intimacy'.[11]

In June 1908, the peaceful mood was shattered when Picasso discovered the body of the German painter Karl-Heinz Wiegels, whom he had taken under his wing and moved into the Bateau-Lavoir two years earlier. Before hanging himself, the opium-addicted artist had experienced hallucinations and made suicidal threats. The shock was still severe enough for Picasso and Fernande to permanently give up smoking opium. For a long time afterwards, Wiegels' studio was a place of 'terror' for them and reopened old wounds for Picasso over the death of his Spanish friend Casagemas six years earlier. As the summer days grew hotter, he entered a nervous depression and felt unable to be alone. At the recommendation of his doctor, they left Paris for a remote village named La Rue-des-Bois, in the forest of Halatte in Picardy, on the River Oise. Sixty kilometres out of Paris, they rented a little outbuilding on a farm, with no facilities, so they felt as if they were practically camping. There were only ten houses in the hamlet but they bought eggs, milk and vegetables from the farm, spending no more than three francs a day. They enjoyed the beauty of the forest and the visits of friends but Picasso was 'quite out of place', finding the environment too damp and monotonous and smelling of mushrooms. However, he still managed to complete a dozen paintings, a brief 'green period' that reflected their surroundings. In contrast, Fernande would have happily remained, looking to rent a large, neglected property with lots of land, but Picasso announced that he finally felt free 'of the obsession that had been torturing him' and 'wasn't prepared to settle down in this remote corner' which was too far from Paris.[12] So, in the autumn of 1908, they returned to the Bateau-Lavoir.

That year, Picasso and Fernande met the self-taught painter Henri Rousseau, 'a poor, charming man of unimaginable candour and naivety ... an artist with a unique gift, a kind of genius'.[13] At his studio in the Rue Vercingétorix, they met the young artist Robert Delaunay, later founder of Orphic Cubism, which used abstract geometric designs and bright colours, along with the German art dealer Wilhelm Uhde and his talented wife Sonia, who would soon divorce him to marry Delaunay. At the end of 1908, Picasso hosted a banquet in the Bateau-Lavoir in Rousseau's honour, decorating his studio in greenery and constructing a throne from a crate, set against a backdrop of paper lanterns and flags. A long board was set up for a table, with chairs, plates and cutlery borrowed from a nearby restaurant. The guests arrived, but the food from a Montmartre caterer did not materialise until midday the next day. Picasso and Fernande had to send out for sandwiches and cakes from the patisserie. The evening, which had been intended as semi-serious ended in hilarity, with drunkenness, jokes, song and melted candles dripping down upon the guest of honour, and Fernande became very cross with Marie Laurencin who sat on a plate of cakes. Rousseau took it all in good faith and was touched by the gesture. He died less than two years later, in September 1910.

In May 1909 Picasso and Fernande returned to Barcelona. The artist's sister Lola was due to marry, even though Picasso was reluctant to attend the ceremony. They found the large family welcome overwhelming and Fernande in particular disliked the city and its heat. She had been suffering from a kidney complaint in Paris and now conditions conspired to bring about its return.

She began to haemorrhage. Advised by a doctor to remain in bed, she was stuck in the city, while Picasso had hoped to travel on to Horta de Ebra and escape his family, who were critical of his work and of Fernande. He became increasingly frustrated as the days passed until Fernande was finally well enough to embark on the journey on 5 or 6 June. Picasso had spent time as a teenager in Horta, which was the home of his friend Manuel Pallares and where he had taken important artistic steps, later claiming he had 'come of age' there. Now the Pallares family welcomed him back, but their deep conservatism meant they would not extend the same welcome to his lover. However, Fernande's charm captivated the local mayor, so they were not ostracised and spent their evenings playing cards with his daughter and had a local piano mended, hoping they could play it and dance, although most of the time Fernande was too ill and unhappy to do so. While Picasso was busy executing a number of Cezannesque views of the town, the pain in her kidneys intensified and she passed blood, leaving her cold, weak and exhausted, unable to do anything else except lie in bed, not even able to sew. Her condition made Picasso grumpy, as she confided to Gertrude Stein: 'Pablo is no help, he doesn't want to know anything. He's too self-centred to understand that it is I who now need him.' His neglect made her feel completely abandoned:

> It's largely he who reduced me to this state last winter. He has completely demoralised me; all this is nerves, I know, but I don't have any nerves left. I can't go on … If I'm sad he gets furious … it's far from certain but I may be pregnant … only eight days have gone past since my first inkling, but what will I do, pregnant and sick as I am? … Although I believe that he loves me, I feel so wretched, so lonely. Pablo would let me die without noticing my condition.[14]

As it transpired, Fernande was not pregnant but Picasso's neglect of her was something she would never forget. He no longer cherished her or cared for her comfort, as he had at the start of the relationship, when he laid gifts at her feet and constructed a shrine of sketches and objects relating to her. She appears in some of his works at Horta, including a *Head of Woman with Mountain,*

Fernande in a Mantilla and *Female Nude* but, symbolically, all traces of her voluptuous curves from former works have been replaced by fragmented planes and her features slip across hard lines as if her misery has been caught in paint. The distance between them in Horta was exaggerated by Picasso's intense, all-consuming passion for the new method he was exploring. As would be the case with his life-long artistic development, a new style required fresh inspiration and Fernande's influence belonged to the flourish that had led him out of the rose period. She was a muse of the past: now he was looking in a different direction.

In the autumn of 1909, Picasso decided to leave the Bateau-Lavoir and move to an apartment on the Boulevard de Clichy, near the Place Pigalle. In an attempt to placate Fernande[15] the lease was taken out in her name, indicating that Picasso was still committed to their relationship. The art critic Maurice Raynal considered that they must have 'hit the jackpot'[16] when he helped them to move:

What a change! It was Picasso's first 'middle-class' home in Paris. A large, airy studio in the north, an apartment that was sunny at noon, looking out onto the trees of Avenue Frochot. The building belonged to a minister ... and he lived in it too. Apart from the canvases, we did not have much to transport. The few shabby furnishings barely filled the servants' quarters.[17]

This was more than just a physical relocation, it represented a shift up the social scale, the attainment of respectability, the entry into a more bourgeois world. The broken floorboards, flat bedframe and dripping tap of the Montmartre slum were to be replaced by a heavy copper bed, an inlaid cabinet, couch and piano, mahogany furniture, a maid in a white apron and a view over the leafy square outside. In a chapter entitled 'Picasso Becomes Respectable' Fernande describes how nothing in his new studio could be touched, how the maid got used to his character, but that he was 'less happy here than he'd been before.' The new apartment represented middle-class security, a compact that was equivalent to the marriage she could not have with Pablo, even though she was regularly signing herself as 'Fernande Picasso'. Immediately after they had moved in, Picasso invited all his friends and patrons to the flat in order to purchase work he had produced in Horta. Gertrude Stein and the dealer Ambrose Vollard made considerable purchases, and Pablo put aside this money for Fernande to have an operation to cure the kidney pain she had suffered that summer. She underwent the procedure in January 1910.

Yet the physical structure of the new apartment, with its increased middle-class privacy, continued the new element that had been introduced at Horta. Picasso decorated it with the primitive masks and statues that were his new inspiration, hung with beads and jewels, almost shrine-like – as he had once honoured Fernande. Picasso would shut himself away in his studio from two in the afternoon until dusk and Fernande was not permitted to enter. This established a new demarcation between art and life, which relegated Fernande from the role of muse to mistress only. His art was no longer integrated in her life as it had been at the Bateau-Lavoir, where she had slept or read as he drew, or while she cooked surrounded by the instruments of his trade. Now, art was happening elsewhere, behind a closed door, leaving her bored and excluded. As Picasso threw himself more fully into the development of cubism, so his relationship with her began to evanesce, at least for him. Gertrude Stein noticed that things were changing. She wrote that now Fernande had an apartment and a maid 'who served up souffles ... she should have been happier than ever before, but she was not.'[18] In the eyes of the American, the problem lay with Picasso's dislike of the social conventions that Fernande increasingly favoured, like going out or hosting an 'at home', which they did for a brief spell on Sundays, although this soon petered out. Fernande, puzzled by his distance and silence, would ask whether he was bored or ill, to which he would look at her in astonishment and reply that he was thinking about his work.[19] A picture of them at the dinner table, taken in 1910, shows Fernande leaning across to put her arms around Pablo's neck and press her cheek against his with a wide smile, but there was an increasing gulf between them.

14

New Loves, New Homes

In September 1905, Ida arranged a sale of her furniture and set out for Paris with Augustus, Dorelia and the four children. Formerly the scene of her youthful adventures as a young bohemian hoping to become a great artist, she was returning as a disillusioned wife and mother, with a sense that her unconventional marital arrangement had not brought them happiness. Seven years since that first wide-eyed arrival, she was hoping to recapture a little of that Parisian magic and regain the identity that had become subsidiary to John's.

As their first base, Ida took two rooms at the Hôtel St Pierre, situated at 4 Rue de l'Ecole-de-Médecine, in the Latin Quarter. It was a ten-minute walk away from the Bibliothèque St Genevieve, where Sophie would meet Henri and an hour's trek across the river to the Rue Ravignan, where Fernande had just moved in with Picasso. Incredibly, the hotel still exists, offering fifty rooms, with the gold initials HSP monogrammed on its tall windows, the curving staircase and tiny, art nouveau cage lift. Ida wrote to her mother to reassure her that the food was good and the 'very kind' hotel staff were treating them well.[1] Ida forbade Augustus from visiting the Louvre until he had found somewhere for them to live and, although he could not avoid buying himself a 'brown plush hat with a feather', he managed to find 63, Rue Monsieur-le-Prince, near the Luxembourg Gardens. They had moved in by mid-October, with a maid called Clara and another old servant, meaning Ida and Dorelia were free to explore and 'saunter' around the city. Tall and narrow, with its front door opening directly onto the street, the house was in a busy, bustling location. Ida was excited to have Paris on her doorstep. At first, the city worked its magic.

Heavily pregnant, Ida spent her days reading, drawing, making clothes and listening to music. She was in good spirits, able to state that 'life is pleasant and exciting,' after the quiet and seclusion of Matching Green. Ida cut her hair short but it curled under to her disgust, so she did not look very 'new womanish'. When the artist William Rothenstein visited he found them in a long room with bare boards, a large bed in an alcove and a table where the children had lessons. The boys were being very boisterous and Rothenstein considered that they were living in terrible poverty, in comparison with his own spacious residence in Church Row, Hampstead. Of more concern, though, was his observation that when Augustus appeared, the young 'acrobats' were clearly afraid of him. 'He is very impatient with his children,' he wrote, although by way of compensation, 'anyone may be considered richly endowed who has such a mother as Ida.' The new addition to the family arrived that November, when Ida gave birth to 'Susannah,' who turned out to be another 'beastly boy ... a difficult child' who snored loudly. At first the baby was called 'Quart Pot,' before becoming Jim, and finally, Edwin, a 'long, thin cross creature (who) howled independently in toothless rage'.[2] They took it in turns to take the children out and, as Ida commented, Dorelia was the only one who never lost her temper.

By January 1906, three months of sustained noise finally proved too much for their neighbours, who complained to their landlord. Recognising it was time to move on, they feared they wouldn't find anywhere as good but, after a little while of searching for a 'small house' in the area, they looked at the ground floor flat of 77 Rue Dareau, conveniently near the place where John had already rented a studio for the spring. There were three living rooms and a garden, kitchen and scullery, still near enough to the Luxembourg Gardens, and no objection to the children. The only concern was whether their presence would prove too disruptive to Augustus's work, but he urged them to take it. As the apartment wouldn't be ready until April, Ida accepted an offer to accompany her mother and sister Ursula on a trip to Menton in the south of France. Early in March, she left Edwin with his nurse and set off with the three older boys.

Menton, on the French Riviera, between Monaco and the Italian border, had become a very popular destination for English and Russian tourists at the end of the nineteenth century. It was particularly favoured by sufferers of tuberculosis, after the 1861 publication of Dr James Bennett's *Winter and Spring on the Shores of the Mediterranean*, and Sophie Brzeska's one-time friend Katherine Mansfield would stay there in 1920, seeking relief from the illness that would kill her in 1923. Since being widowed, Ada had been moved along the road to the Tudorbethan Norfolk Mansions, a flat at 28, Wigmore Street, where she lived with Ethel and Ursula above shops on the ground floor. Ada's visit to Menton had been planned for health reasons, but whatever she was suffering from was not critical, as she was to survive another twenty-five years. Their hotel was full of genteel British women and their daughters, but the magnificent scenery made up for the company in Ida's eyes, with sunlight and flowers, olive groves and snow-topped mountains. Yet Ida could not relax. All the time she was worried, and jealous, about what was going on in Paris, with Augustus, Wyndham Lewis and Dorelia still there. 'I am biting my nails with rage and jealousy and impotence,' she confessed, 'because if I were there it would spoil the fun.'[3] She returned to Paris to take up residence in the Rue Dareau early in April 1906.

That summer, Augustus carried them all off to the remote village of St Honorine-sur-Mer in Normandy, situated between Cherbourg and Caen. A tiny, rural and inaccessible place with a population of around 400, he had chosen it in particular because of the presence of a band of gypsies, and the fact that there were 'wonderful sea-women who collect shellfish ... tall and quite prehistoric.' Postcards of the time show children in summer whites on a small shingle beach, with cliffs rising behind or climbing on the seaweed-covered rocks, and depict the road that entered the village, lined by walls on both sides, with tree branches spilling over. There was an old church and a small square in the centre of the village, with a shop or two. Travelling by cart or steam tram, they arrived at the home of a Madame Beck: Augustus, Ida, the pregnant Dorelia, Clara, the older lady Félice and five children. Ida wrote to Mary Dowdall that 'the kids ought to enjoy it'[4] and they soon took on an unkempt, unconventional appearance, with loose smocks and long hair, spending their days sliding down the cliffs, picking blackberries and collecting seaweed in which to bathe the baby. 'It is very relaxing,' Ida admitted but, apart from the children, they all felt 'awful'. Amid the holiday, Dorelia gave birth to her second son, whom she named Romilly.

Augustus' friend, the writer Wyndham Lewis, arrived at St Honorine-sur-Mer and stayed for five weeks. Ida enjoyed his company, saying she loved him like a brother. He let off cheap fireworks and made them all laugh. Gwen John also stayed with them for five days, from where she sent her lover Auguste Rodin three letters a day. Yet Augustus was moping around the place, miserable, making little effort to enjoy himself. In fact, he had had another motive for bringing them all that way into the middle of nowhere, no matter how beautiful it was. He had found a new mistress, Alice Schepeler, whom he hoped to install on the island of Jersey, just a few miles away by boat. However, Alice had refused to comply and John was in a bad temper as a result. He announced to Ida and Dorelia that it was impossible for him to paint without Alice and that they must accept her into their ménage.

This proved to be the final straw for Ida. She confided her dilemma to Mary Dowdall: 'I can't leave him and take his money, and I can't keep the kids on what I have, and if I left the kids I should not find peace.' She had no choice but to stay out of financial necessity; 'I am bound hand and foot ... how will it all end? By death or escape?'[5] By the time they returned to Paris, Ida was pregnant again with her fifth child.

*

In 1913, a third person threatened to upset the balance in Sophie and Henri's relationship, though not to the extent that Dorelia was involved with Ida and Augustus. Nina Hamnett was a colourful figure in a visual and metaphorical sense. She was close to Gaudier in age, having been born in 1890, in Tenby, the Welsh coastal town where Augustus John had grown up. She was studying at the London School of Art and, as a disciple of the most famous recent alumnus, would follow Augustus down the street. At this time, Slade students would stand 'in silent homage' when he entered the Café Royal 'like a pirate king getting onto his quarterdeck'.[6] Another individual who typified the notion of bohemian living through her travel, friendships, affairs and the pursuit of art, Nina provides a link between all three women we are following. As well as being Henri's friend and an admirer of John, she was a resident of Montparnasse in the years that Picasso and Fernande were living in the Boulevard de Clichy, and once visited their favourite haunt, the Lapin Agile; in later years, she would spend an evening drinking champagne with Picasso and the writer Jean Cocteau in the Rue Boissy d'Anglais.

Nina had seen some sketches Henri made for Murry's *Rhythm* magazine that 'interested (her) very much'.[7] When Henri exhibited the statue of a wrestler and four others with the Allied Artists Association in the Royal Albert Hall, he and Sophie observed a young woman looking intently at his work and christened her 'la fillette'. In her autobiography, *Laughing Torso*, Nina described a 'young man, looking like a foreigner with a little beard', whom she was too shy to tell how much she admired his work. However, when she went upstairs, she was delighted to find him 'standing in front of my pictures'.[8] Later, a mutual friend introduced them in a bookshop and she posed for him in his studio:

> I went one day to his studio in the Fulham Road and took off all of my clothes. I turned round slowly and he did drawings of me. When he had finished he said 'now it is your turn to work.' He took off all his clothes, took a large piece of marble and made me draw, and I had to. I did three drawings and he said 'now we will have some tea.'[9]

On another occasion, they went foraging in some Putney stonemasons' yards, returning at night so that Henri could take a piece of marble that was within reach of the railings. It was small enough that he could fit it in his pocket and he used it to sculpt a torso of Nina. During 1913, Henri and Nina spent every Sunday together, roasting chestnuts on the stove in his studio while he drew her, eating dinner and walking in the park.

Sophie was aware of the growing friendship. Henri and Nina's closeness, their shared passion for art and their age parity made it difficult for Sophie to bear, fearing that Henri may decide he preferred the younger woman and leave her. When Henri praised 'my Nina', she replied with the question 'perhaps she wants to seduce you?' In reply, Henri snapped 'well, why not? I intend to make love with her. You're useless, you make me wait too long.' Sophie said she would give him her blessing if that was what he wanted and Gaudier, only half-joking, cruelly suggested that she might hide behind a screen and watch if it did not make her too jealous. Sophie said she could 'ask for nothing more' and that it would 'amuse' her. She had told Henri 'a hundred times that since I can't give you what you want I am not so selfish as to try and stop you finding it elsewhere.'[10] The exchange raised the uncomfortable but constant sexual tension underlying their relationship. As previously posited, Sophie's reluctance to sleep with Henri may have resulted from a number of concerns, including the age difference, embarrassment about disclosing the true nature of their relationship, health concerns and fears of pregnancy. It has been suggested that Sophie suffered from some sort of sexually transmitted disease, although this had been ruled out by the doctor she saw in Paris in 1910; there may have been another infection or condition that made her self-conscious about her body, such as the genetic trimethylaminuria, the bacterial infection gardnerella or a simple case of recurring thrush or cystitis, which may have led to discomfort or odour. Additionally, the extent of her sexual experience is uncertain. Her accounts of her young Polish lover only hint at a possible consummation and she appears to have given Mr 'M' in Baden satisfaction in a way that did not include penetration. It is not impossible that she remained a virgin all her life. Although a deeply emotional woman, with passionate moods, it does not follow that she experienced a particularly high libido. The other alternative is that she did desire heterosexual or lesbian sex but suppressed this and, to follow the Freudian line, this suppression manifested itself increasingly in hysterical behaviour and contributed to her later instability. But these are all theories: Sophie maintained that she could not sleep with Henri, and did not leave a full explanation as to why.

The first meeting between Sophie and Nina was difficult. Henri brought Nina home one evening, unexpectedly, when Sophie was recovering from the flu, sitting facing the wall so as not to see the squalor in the room.[11] Sophie reacted defensively to her rival by deciding in her diary that Nina was 'ungainly' and 'common-looking', asking whether this was 'the young girl who is supposed to be so brilliant and perfect in every way.' However, she invited Nina for lunch the following Sunday, when she was keen to observe that her hair was unwashed, her nails dirty and her blouse torn. The return visit they made to Nina was just as awkward, with Sophie accusing Nina of copying Henri's style of drawing and a misunderstanding over whether they had been invited to eat or not. Sophie later regretted confiding in Nina, considering her to be typically reserved and superficial as she experienced with many of the English, and still believing her to be concealing her true motives for her friendship with Henri. Like many of their London friends, Nina found Sophie hard to like, believing Henri's story at first that they were brother and sister. She was intimidated by her intensity and her need to find sympathetic listeners, pouring out her heart with an emotional honesty that many, like Katherine Mansfield and Enid Bagnold, had found difficult to bear. To Nina, Sophie was 'terrifying and Polish', adding that 'at that time young men had the idea that Polish women were the only women in the world. They certainly had brains, but also temperaments and many complexes.'[12]

On one occasion, when Nina had sold some of Henri's sketches, he told her, 'Don't tell my sister you sold six, say it was only five and we will go to the "Swiss" in Soho and have some drinks.' Another time, Nina dined with them both in their rooms in Putney, during which Henri and Sophie had an argument and threw food at each other, after which Sophie said, 'You bore me, take Nina away and give her something to drink.' When they did, drinking beer at the Swiss, Gaudier confessed, 'She is not my sister, she is my mistress.'[13] Although this not entirely accurate news shocked Nina and made her sob, she recognised that Sophie was not jealous of their closeness, but actually encouraged it. Sophie also urged Henri to visit prostitutes at this time, and may have believed that he was sleeping with Nina, although Nina's otherwise explicit memoirs offers no evidence that they were. Early in 1914, Nina left England for Montparnasse, but she would return to play a significant role in Sophie's later life.

Also present at the Allied Artists' exhibition of 1913 was the American poet Ezra Pound. Then in his late twenties, Pound had been in London for five years and was the author of *Ripostes*, a collection of his first Imagist poems. Pound described Henri as 'a well-made young wolf or some soft-moving bright-eyed wild thing' who darted before them as they admired his sculpture, a 'figure with bunchy muscles done in clay painted green.' When he heard the poet attempting to pronounce his name, as he had hyphenated his surname with Sophie's, Henri explained that it was 'Jaersh-ka' and then 'he disappeared like a Greek God in a vision.'[14] Pound invited Henri to dinner, but he did not appear and, according to Sophie, she had 'prevailed with him to intend to come, but that there was a row at the last moment and that by the time he had got himself ready it was too late.' Pound also relates how Henri made 'parodies' of himself and Sophie in wax, 'which parodies she either threw at him or at the stove.'[15] That year, Pound commissioned Gaudier to sculpt his head, in a work that became the Hieratic Head of Ezra Pound, a phallic marble monolith, which Pound had asked him to make 'virile'. Henri appears in two photographs of himself at work during this period, one of him carving the head and a second where he stands behind the completed 'Bird Swallowing Fish' of 1914 displayed on a plinth; he looks proudly on in a tie, with wild hair.

In the same year as the Allied Artists' exhibition, Nina Hamnett introduced Henri to Roger Fry, who ran the Omega Workshops in Fitzroy Square. Fry's reputation preceded him, whose second Post-Impressionist exhibition of 1912 and writing Henri had admired. It was essentially a concern of the Bloomsbury Group, the literary and artistic circle centred around Fry, Vanessa Bell, the sister of Virginia Woolf, Vanessa's husband, the art critic Clive Bell and the artist Duncan Grant, but its intention was to draw in a new generation of young artists and provide them with an income to work under a collective name, such as the Wiener Werkstatte in Vienna in 1903 and Paul Poiret's 1911 Ecole and Atelier Martine, where Fernande Olivier would later work. The Omega artists gathered to design and execute functional and decorative items for the home, reflecting a new simplicity in modern living. Henri produced some designs for trays, including one that reflected his current sculpture, 'the Wrestler', ornaments, boxes and a bird bath that stood in Fry's own garden. In November, Henri took up the lease of a studio under a railway arch in Putney, which was cold but very spacious. There, inspired by Pound's poetry, he worked on a new carving, 'Redstone Dancer', which Fry included at the Grafton Group's exhibition at the Alpine Gallery in January 1914. Sometimes he worked so intensely that he slept in a deckchair in the studio rather than walk home to Sophie in Fulham. His new direction in art alienated Sophie too. When she was confused by the geometric yet erotically charged 'Redstone Dancer,' he told her 'if you can't understand it, I can't explain it to you. I just feel it and there's an end of it.'[16] It was a blow to Sophie that Nina could share Henri's artistic vision, from which she was sometimes excluded.

Early in 1914, though, a new artistic group emerged in direct conflict with the Omega workshops, dividing Henri's loyalties. His fellow artist Wyndham Lewis, the friend of Augustus and Ida John, had a dramatic disagreement with Fry over the ownership of a prestigious commission, so departed Fitzroy Street in order to establish the Rebel Art Centre in Great Ormond Street, and the Vorticist movement. The new spokesman of the Rebel Art centre was the critic and poet T. E. Hulme, with whom Lewis was working on a new manifesto, later launched as *Blast: Review of the Great English Vortex*. The first edition was planned for June, with contributions by Lewis, Pound, Epstein and others, including reproductions of drawings and sculptures by Gaudier, as well as something between an essay and a manifesto, entitled 'Vortex.'

While Henri was racing along in this tide of avant-garde art, Sophie's concerns were more domestic. Just as Fernande had been marginalised by Picasso's shift from softer, rounder representations of the female form to more shattered planes, and the energy and isolation this required, Sophie was excluded from the race towards modernism of Henri's new friends in the first part of 1914. That summer proved to be very hot, and their rooms in Fulham studio were infested with bugs, so Sophie headed to Littlehampton and lodged with a Spanish woman, whom she greatly liked. It had been a popular nineteenth-century holiday destination, with a pleasure pier and walks through the West Sussex countryside. By the time of

Sophie's stay, the resident population of just over 6,000 benefited from a railway connection and a cross-channel ferry to Honfleur.

Money continued to be a problem for both Sophie and Henri. He wrote to ask her to send him something: 'For the last four days my cat and I have lived on milk and eggs given me on credit.'[17] Sophie spent her time by the seaside thinking of different ways to solve it and returned to London with a plan. In Littlehampton, she befriended a French teacher named Mademoiselle Borne, whose sister was coming to England and Sophie intended to rent a larger house and take in the two women as lodgers. The house was found, equipped and prepared. The two girls arrived and settled in, but then, after only a week, war was declared.[18]

*

War of another kind was brewing between Fernande and Picasso in 1910. Itching to return to his Spanish roots for inspiration, Pablo arranged for them to spend the summer in Cadaqués, on the coast north-east of Barcelona. Clustered around a tiny beach, with white-washed houses and sloping roofs, it is a picturesque little town on the modern Costa Brava but, arriving after a long train journey, Fernande found it small and disappointing. Nor did she like the house in the bay that Picasso rented, considering it too expensive at a hundred francs a month for such a tiny, sparse place. 'There is nothing but the sea,' she wrote to Gertrude, 'some wretched little mountains, houses that look as if made from cardboard, local people without any character ... the only beaches are small and cramped, nothing to eat except fish ... fruit hard to find and mediocre and life almost as expensive as Paris.'[19] There was little for her to do but gossip with the other women while he devoted full days to work or went out on the fishing boats. She did not appear in Picasso's work that summer nor does it seem she had the impetus to draw or paint herself. As Picasso's biographer John Richardson comments, 'intellectual isolation was a major operational hazard of cubism.'[20] It was to prove fatal for his relations with Fernande too.

The fragmentation of Fernande's relationship with Pablo was marked by their choice not to spend the summer of 1911 together. He went south to Céret while she hoped to visit Holland with the van Dongen family. The plan did not work out and, from early July until the first half of August, she remained in Paris alone. But Picasso wrote to Fernande on 8 August 1911, saying that he loved her, asking her to join him, and to come soon. She took the train from Paris and appeared in Céret on 15 August. A week later, news reached them about the biggest art crime of the century: the Mona Lisa had been stolen from the Louvre. Early in the morning of 21 August, a young Italian by the name of Vincenzo Peruggia had slipped in through the workers' door at the back of the museum, wrapped the painting in a smock and hurried out with it. The situation was made more complicated by the role played by Apollinaire's secretary, a desperate man by the name of Géry Pieret, who had been asking for work and had also been taking advantage of the lax security at the Louvre. He had stolen several Iberian carved stone heads, which he had installed in Apollinaire's apartment. Two of them had been given to Picasso. Fearing that he might be implicated, Picasso packed up at Céret and hurried back to Paris. Apollinaire met them at the station on 3 or 4 September. Fernande described them as a 'pair of contrite children, terrified and thinking of fleeing abroad.' They planned to put the heads in a suitcase and throw them in the Seine but, after walking the streets with them all night, Picasso could not bring himself to do so. The following morning, Apollinaire handed over the statues to the *Paris-Journal*, under a promise of secrecy. The promise was not kept. Apollinaire's name was passed to the police and both he and Picasso were arrested. Early in the morning of 8 September they arrived and Fernande had to help him dress, as he was trembling so much. Eventually, Picasso was released without charge but Fernande said he never forgave her for having seen him 'reduced to panic, his pride in shreds'.[21] It left him deeply shaken, desperate to escape from the public eye into some sort of respectable, irreproachable life. The Mona Lisa was returned to the Louvre in 1913.

'L'affaire des statuettes', as it came to be called, coincided with the arrival of a new artistic wave in France. The reputation of the Italian Futurists, led by Filippo Marinetti, with their emphasis on machine and movement, on technology, the urban, the man-made and on violence, had already reached Paris. Their work used a technique called divisionism, breaking planes into stripes and dots, in a way that fuelled their interest in Picasso's developing cubist methods. When Marinetti and his friends arrived in Paris in October 1911 on a visit in advance of their exhibition scheduled for the following February, they were keen to meet Picasso. They visited L'Ermitage, the bar opposite the apartment on the Boulevard de Clichy, where Fernande met them. Feeling excluded from Picasso's work, and hurt by his long silences, she particularly enjoyed the attention of one of the Italian painters, a handsome twenty-two-year old called Ubaldo Oppi. Born in Bologna, he had studied in Vienna in 1907-9 under Gustav Klimt, then returned to Italy to do a year of military service before arriving in Paris. His work belonged to a *novocento Italiano* movement, a neo-quattrocentro realist style, and his 'Figure in Red' with its distinctive hair and slanting eyes is clearly Fernande. Severini describes their meeting: 'La belle Fernande, who was always very flirtatious, went on the attack, partly as a joke, partly to practise her powers on a boy from the provinces.' Oppi 'couldn't resist at all' and they 'embarked on a passionate affair'.[22] Another version of the story is told by Jean-Paul Crespelle, author of *Picasso and his Women*, which has Fernande seducing Oppi in an attempt to make Picasso jealous and win him back from another woman who had caught his eye.

Fernande made a mistake in choosing a confidante as a go-between for herself and Oppi. She turned to a new female friend she had met recently, who is described by Gertrude Stein in *The Autobiography of Alice B Toklas*:

> Fernande had at this time a new friend of whom she often spoke to me. This was Eve who was living with Marcoussis. And one evening all four of the came to the Rue des Fleurus; Pablo, Fernande, Marcoussis and Eve ... I could perfectly understand Fernande's liking for Eve ... [her] great heroine was Evelyn Thaw, small and negative. Here was a little French Evelyn Thaw, small and perfect.[23]

One night at the Cirque Médrano, Eve and Marcoussis entered into conversation with Apollinaire and Picasso's fellow Cubist, George Braques, who introduced the young sculptor to Picasso.

A friendship developed between the two women and Fernande enlisted Eva's help to carry notes between her and Oppi. This element of subterfuge was to set the tone for their connection. Just as Fernande had changed her name from the original Amelie Lang, so Eve, or Eva Gouel, as she came to be known, had been christened Marcelle Humbert. She had been born in 1885, making her four years younger than Fernande, twenty-six to her thirty when they met. She was the mistress of sculptor Louis Marcoussis, a Pole whose story united elements of Sophie's and Ida's world, having attended the Krakow School of Fine Art before moving to Paris in 1903 and studying at the Académie Julien. The attraction between her and Picasso was established on the evening they were all invited to Gertrude's.

Soon afterwards, Picasso took a studio in the Rue Ravignan, close to the old one he had recently left. This served to distance him from Fernande in the Boulevard Clichy and was a place to meet Eva. When Gertrude and Alice visited in the spring of 1912, they noticed he had incorporated the motif of 'Ma Jolie' into his latest work, and Gertrude remarked that it did not refer to Fernande.[24] The very friend Fernande had trusted to facilitate her affair was having one of her own with Picasso.

On 18 May, Picasso told Fernande he had discovered that she was sleeping with Oppi and was leaving her. Two versions of the story survive: either that Eva simply passed one of Fernande's notes to Pablo or else Fernande had discarded one, which he subsequently found. Either way, her secret was out. Picasso was resolute that the relationship was over; he later admitted that he had grown tired of Fernande and that this event provided him with the excuse he needed to be rid of her. His dealer, Kahnweiler, would sublet their Boulevard de Clichy apartment, as it was in her name, but she had little choice except to leave. She went to Oppi's studio. Picasso wrote to Braque: 'Fernande ditched me for a Futurist ... What am I going to do with the dog?'[25] Picasso and Eva left Paris for Céret and, realising that she had lost him, Fernande pursued them there with the Pichots, angry with her friend and hoping to win Picasso back. There were unhappy scenes, but the relationship was over. Picasso and Eva moved on to Avignon and Fernande was left to return to Paris.

The Montmartre grapevine quickly spread the gossip. Picasso wrote to Braque in June: 'I'm really annoyed by all this because I don't want my love for Marcelle [Eva] to be hurt in any way by any trouble they (the press) could make for me.'[26] Matisse wrote to Gertrude's brother, Michael Stein:

> It seems that F had been going with the Futurist for some time, and a note she gave her woman friend, who is always with her to deliver to the Futurist, the friend gave it to P because she wanted P herself. So P confronted F and they split. P ... cleared all his things out of Ravignan, discharged the maid, locked up the other place and decamped to Céret with the friend, where he is still working. The Futurist has no cash so F poses ... and says she is going on the stage and is living with the Pichots.[27]

Penniless and uncertain of her position, Fernande had little choice but to recognise that after seven years, her relationship with Picasso was finally at an end.

15

Mortality

On 3 August 1914, Germany declared war upon France. The following evening, Britain declared war on Germany. The situation for Sophie and Henri, as foreigners in England, was a complex one. As a young, fit Frenchman, it would be expected that Gaudier would fight, although at least he would have been on the side of the Allies. Henri had refused to do his military service so was considered absent without leave but almost at once he decided to go and join his regiment and 'defend his county from the barbarian hordes'. Just five years after staying with the Uhlemayr family in Nuremburg, he performed a complete volte-face and fully embraced the stereotype of rushing off to kill some 'filthy Boche'.[1] Sophie was in a more difficult position; as an eastern European immigrant, she was technically Polish, but her birthplace and culture had been under the crushing German control that reactionary groups had fought against. This was typified by the life of Franz Thomas von Brzeski, a possible relative who sat in the Prussian House of Representatives in Berlin, where he was one of fifteen members representing the Poland Party, arguing for equal rights for the Polish language and Polish-based education in the post Franco-Prussian empire. However, to the English public, the finer points of this struggle were nothing in comparison with Sophie's strange foreign accent and customs. She was also dependent upon Gaudier, with few other friends of her own, and did not relish the idea of being abandoned in England.

At first Sophie could not accept Henri's intention to fight, as she had known his pacifist principles before the war, but she soon saw his intentions were serious and 'took fright'.[2] Writing in *Matka*, Sophie realised 'it was only then that I knew and felt how very dear he was to me.' She 'repented of having so often been hard on him' but dared not 'hold him back'. In spite of his recent involvement with the Omega workshops and the Vorticists, Sophie believed that Henri was 'disgusted with England' and wanted to return to France, 'the only country of Art and above all sculpture' but her 'prophetic' dreams kept haunting her. Both had previously dreamed of Henri being killed in war, with Henri even imagining suffering a head wound. Sophie's superstitious nature was particularly troubled that war had been announced at the time of a full moon. Nothing could change Henri's mind though. He simply said, 'One has to die some time, if it is in bed or in the war, what does it matter?'[3] Before he left England, Henri signed a deed of gift, dated 5 August 1914, leaving everything he possessed to Sophie. Written on a small piece of green paper, with his signature over the one penny stamp, it was to prove an invaluable document for Sophie in the coming years.

Days after Henri's departure, Sophie went walking in Richmond Park thinking of him, only for him to appear, like a ghost. He told her: 'When I arrived in France I was told that I was a deserter and that I should get twelve years' imprisonment. They didn't want my kind at the Front. So they whisked me off to a prison and told me that I should be shot by the sentry outside if I attempted to escape.' However, escape is exactly what he had done, using his sculpting chisels to work loose the bar across the window. Then he ran for hours across country until he reached Calais and caught the night boat.[4]

Henri was critical of Sophie during this period of return. He criticised her clothes, her shoes, her appearance, but still tried to encourage her to become his lover, which she resisted. Ill and tired, she offered him her 'intellectual and spiritual love', nothing more.[5] He went off to his studio and she stayed in the house.

Early in September he came to say goodbye. He had obtained a better passport and was heading for the front. Sophie thought he was trying to trick his way into her room so she refused to open the door. After half an hour he went away but she called him back from the window. Their last two days were spent together. Friends tried to dissuade him from going but he replied that 'I'm going, I absolutely must, there's no more to be said about it, and nothing else to do.'[6] Jacob Epstein provides a description of Henri's departure, having been one of the friends who gathered at Charing Cross station as he boarded the train. 'The turmoil was terrible. Troops were departing and Sophie was in a state of hysterics and collapse ... Gaudier himself, pale and shaken by Sophie's loud sobs, said goodbye to us.'[7]

Left behind in England, Sophie was powerless to do anything but sit and await news from Henri. His letters to her were either lost or destroyed in subsequent years as none of them appear to have survived, although she did paraphrase some of them in her writing. It is fortunate, therefore, that Henri's correspondence with his parents, art collector Edward Marsh, Ezra Pound and others help build a picture of Gaudier's experiences in France, and indicate the sort of information Sophie was receiving. By 1 October Henri had been at the front for two weeks and seen 'both latent and active fighting'. He took part in a night attack against the Prussians, creeping in the darkness through woods and fields, shooting for around a quarter of an hour against an enemy who was only a dozen yards away. Only five of the men survived out of twelve.[8] On 4 October, his 23rd birthday, he informed his parents that he was resting with his battalion in a little fortress where they slept in the cellars. 'Life is very monotonous and animal, one hasn't the energy nor the desire to think and one is too disturbed to concentrate anyhow.'[9] A week later, he was a foot deep in mud not far from the German frontier, waiting for the order to advance, hoping to bring back some Cezannes and Rousseaux.[10] In mid- November Henri told his father cryptically that he was in front of the 'town sacred to the Kings' and that the Cathedral burned before his eyes. This meant Reims, where the French Kings were traditionally crowned in the Cathedral of Notre-Dame, an oblique reference in case the letter was intercepted. The Cathedral had been opened as a hospital on the outbreak of war and was shelled by the Germans that autumn. The north tower caught fire and the lead on the roof melted, dramatically pouring through the gargoyles and destroying the bishop's palace. On 8 November, Henri was sent on a mission to repair wire in no-man's land. When the Germans fired on him, the 'entanglement' of barbed wire and debris above collapsed and trapped him, but he escaped by cutting his way out with a knife and crawled back to safety. He sustained two wounds, one tear on the right leg made by wire and a bullet to the right heel, describing this experience to Pound as 'the greatest fun this night of all my life'.[1] If he told Sophie about this incident, it must have added hugely to her anxiety.

Sophie referred to one letter, in which Henri described to her 'a dreadful place in the close neighbourhood of a cemetery, where everything looked dreary and disheartening. There were poor fellows under a constant murderous fire, scarcely having any food and already for seven days without any relief at all.' He told her he was 'exhausted with fatigue and hunger, enervated through the continual rain of shells and bullets from the enemy's trenches, distant only a few yards.' On other occasions, he wrote to her as if 'ready for the last stand', filling her with dread, but then a letter would arrive in which he assured her 'of his invulnerability and faith of coming out safe and sound from the struggle', so that she began to 'take assurance in our good star'.[12] Sometimes two weeks would pass without a letter and she supposed he was lost. There was little sympathy for her among their friends, which made her bitter. 'When I went among the so-called artists and spoke with feeling, with passion about war or life, they looked at me with condescension, if did not treat me as a fool.'[13]

A week before Christmas Henri wrote to Pound that 'no one foresaw the awful ground we had to defend. We must keep two bridges and, naturally as usual, "until death". We cannot come back to villages to sleep and we have to dig holes in the ground which we fill with straw and build a roof over, but the soil is so nasty that we find water at two feet six inches depth.' In the New Year, Sophie recorded that he was made a corporal and then a sergeant, but conditions did not improve. In March he told Pound 'it is again bloody damp ... and I indulged in the luxury of mud baths, very good for rheumatism, arthritis, lumbago and other evils ... I have experienced all sorts of weather in these hellish places so that I can stand a night under a heavy rain without sneezing the next day and sleep beautifully a whole day on hard frozen ground without any ill result to the abdominalia'. Then came the prophetic comment 'It's so calm today ... but I have some presentiment it is the great calm preceding violent storms.'[14]

Sophie longed to leave England, hating being left there alone among the unsympathetic English. 'I was prepared to go if possible anywhere, to the end of the world, if it were even to the south or north pole.' Her brief moments of cheerfulness were only 'artificial nonchalance, trying to keep from despair' as her thoughts turned again to suicide. Once more, Sophie found herself in a position of poverty, illness and desperation, as she had in Poland, Paris and New York, feeling that she had been betrayed by a place and its people, and that her only options were death or flight. Unable to gain a passport and leave, she remained alive in spite of her wishes, and found work teaching in a girls' school in the country. As she had found in Felixstowe, the food and noise proved intolerable to her so she handed in her notice after a few months. Instead, she found a 'small attic in the neighbourhood for very little money' and six days a week she gave French lessons to the children of a Lady G, five miles from her lodgings.[15] She had to leave at eight in the morning to walk two hours through the mud of the country lanes but Lady G was kind to her and she earned six shillings a week. This arrangement was exhausting though and Sophie returned to London in the early summer of 1915. Later, Sophie described the nine months from his departure in her diary:

You left for the war, tearing my heart in pieces. The country air, where I had gone, calmed my nerves, your letters from the front reassured, the sun filled me with confidence. All through the winter you wrote me rather scrappy letters, mostly talking of your military exploits. We did not indulge much in affection, I, because I was thrown out by your conduct during much of the previous year.

I thought you did not really love me any more, a little yes and that truly from the depths of your heart, but my candour and the fear I had of realising an ugly truth held me a little on my guard. You did not write to me nearly as often as I wanted and all that gave me great cause for apprehensions more or less precise.[16]

After what Sophie perceived as a period of coldness, there came a change:

> Then, as the spring came, your love, sweet dear, renewed itself. You began by sending me letters more often and less cold. And my heart took fire and as the spring advanced was aroused more and more, to a loving and ardent sensibility; I had died so without friends, without lover. I wanted so much to see you again, to press you in my arms and fondle you on my breast, pent up with tenderness so long unspent.[17]

Henri wrote to her that he wanted to return and for them to be married. Her reaction does not survive, but she was angry and rejected him, writing in unhappy terms about how he had abandoned her. Almost at once she regretted posting it and quickly sent another, in which she accepted his proposal. In spite of everything, she would become his wife.

Between 9 May and 18 June, 1915, Henri's regiment was engaged in the Second Battle of Artois, as the French army sought to gain ground up to the infamous German-held Vimy Ridge. Henri saw action in the area between Vimy and Arras, near a place they christened the Labyrinth, a German area of tunnels and trenches to the south of Neuville St Vaast, with obstacles, dugouts and machine gun posts. The shelling was intense, with periods of shooting and hand-to-hand combat, resulting in 102,500 Entente casualties, of whom 35,000 died, according to French sources. In the first days of June, Henri described the scene to Pound, after having endured ten days of shelling:

> We shall be going to rest sometime soon, and then when we do come back it will be for an attack. It is a gruesome place all strewn with dead, and there's not a day without half a dozen fellows in the company crossing the Styx. We are betting on our mutual chances. Hope all this nasty nightmare will soon come to an end ... You asked me if I wanted some cash not long ago. No, not here but as you may imagine things are pretty hard and I should be thankful if you could send what remains to my sister.[18]

Henri died from a head wound at one o'clock in the afternoon, on 5 June 1915. He was twenty-three. The official account of his death stated that 'in a single attack by the first and seventh on the village of Neuville St Vaast, Houses D3 to D12 were captured, taking over also the left of the main street and the houses bordering on it. This result was achieved by 3.30pm on June 5th 1915. The ninety-five men killed in the action included the Sergeants Rocher, Buisou, Gaudier ...'[19] Twelve days later, the French succeeded in capturing the Labyrinth and the town, although the Germans were to hold Vimy Ridge until it was taken by the Canadians in April 1917. Henri Gaudier was buried in one of the 15,000 graves at the military cemetery of La Targette at Neuville St Vaast.

*

In September 1906, when Ida returned to Paris, her thoughts were becoming increasingly morbid. She believed that she had failed in her marriage to Augustus, and in her relationship with Dorelia, which was no longer as close as it had been. Her driving purpose just five years earlier had been to facilitate her husband's work, by inspiring him and creating an environment conducive to creativity. Creating their lifestyle was to have been her art. She had tolerated – and then even welcomed – Dorelia into their intimate life, at the cost of great personal pain and public censure, because she had believed it essential for his work. Now she seemed to do little but take it in turns with Dorelia to bear an endless stream of children while Augustus was chasing yet another woman. 'I believe my raison d'être has ended,' she wrote mournfully to Mary Dowdell, 'I am no more the inspired one.' She felt herself growing resentful, stubborn with a 'wooden' head 'slowly being petrified'. Her spirit was gone. 'My lady, my light and help, has gone, not tragically, just in the order of things and now I am not sure if I am making an entrance into the world or an exit from it.' Ida seems to have been in a state of numbness, of depression, asking Mary, 'Are you in a state where the future seems hopeless? ... There is always death, isn't there?'[20]

Augustus was depressed, and talked of living with Ida again, in either Paris or London and, although Ida realised that she would comply with his request if he wished it, 'as some men are helpless when left to themselves,' she felt she was 'freer alone'. She lived very thriftily all autumn and winter, saving money, regretting the fact that she was financially dependent upon him. 'It may be I should come back to London,' she told him. 'You must tell me, I will come, only we get on so much better apart.' She sensed that his request owed more to the fact that John lacked a home at that point, rather than a real desire to be with her, and she knew the children would bother him. She felt 'duties beating little hammers about me' and assumed that she would be back in London in six months. 'It chills my marrow to think of living back in England,' she wrote to Alice Rothenstein.[21] That October John returned to London and Dorelia soon followed him for a holiday. Ida was alone with the children, pregnant, and her maid Clara was also expecting a child, the father Augustus. Ida passed the time by reading Balzac and her sister Ethel came to stay. David and Caspar were sent to the Ecole Maternelle of the Communal School but they weren't happy in their first experience of organised schooling, so Ida took them out. She craved a time when the children were older, more independent, and she could have some time to herself. She felt a prisoner to their demands.

In November 1906, Ida sublet the Rue Dareau, remaining there herself while Dorelia and her two boys moved to 48 Rue de Chateau, with two good rooms, kitchen and alcove, 'a lovely disreputable looking building, very light and airy, the view is of a few lilac trees, some washing hanging up and a railway, very pleasant and to our taste.'[22] John returned to France in December, and Christmas was kept in the Rue Dareau, with him Ida, Dorelia, the children, Gwen and Wyndham Lewis. John hung up mistletoe in the middle of the room, they ate plum pudding, cakes and punch, exchanged gifts and watched the boys playing with their new train set.

Although Ida remained fond of him, Lewis took on a new, hostile approach to Ida, a callous and shallow response to her pregnancy which might reflect more on his own problems with women at the time; especially Ida Vendel, who would undergo an abortion the following summer, at his insistence. 'Mrs John has changed very much and is no longer pretty, and I no longer have any pity for her,' Lewis wrote, 'I don't see how John could do otherwise than perquisition (sic) another woman, but she seems changed, I don't like her a bit.'[23]

In February 1907, Ida was referring to her unborn child as Susannah, just as she had with Edwin. She longed for a girl but admitted that the baby was 'pushing about in a fearfully strong masculine way'. It was a large child and she was not looking forward to the birth, feeling sorry for the baby already: 'What right have we, knowing the difficulties of the way, to start any other along it?' Clara was also expecting to give birth around the same time as Ida, but she left the Rue Dareau, along with the older maid Félice, and Ida hired a nurse named Delphine to care for the children during her absence. Ida had decided to give birth in hospital for the first time, as 'it is much simpler and I don't pay anything ... I just go when it comes on without anything but what I'm wearing.' She was looking forward to the arrival of spring, confident that all would be better when the sun came out. On the last night of her freedom, she attended a music hall with the young painter Henry Lamb.[24]

When her labour pains began, Ida walked around the corner to the Hôpital de la Maternité, at 123 Boulevard de Port-Royal, where she gave birth to Henry on 9 March, 1907. He was named at her mother's request, as a tribute to her friendship with Henry Irving, whose theatrical costumes she had ceased making upon his death two years before. However, some complication arose after the birth. Ada visited, bringing dill water and magnesia, soap and building blocks at Ida's request, writing to Ethel and Ursula that Ida was to have a 'slight operation ... It is serious but not very dangerous. In 48 hours she will be quite out of danger.' At the time, the doctors believed that an abscess was causing Ida to experience a fever and pain, but in fact it was peritonitis, a bacterial infection of the tissue lining the inside of the abdomen, and puerperal fever. She was transferred to a Maison de Santé in the Boulevard Arago and one of the best surgeons in Paris carried out the operation on March 10. Afterwards, there was a brief improvement in her condition but then she relapsed and hovered on the verge of consciousness for four days. Ada bustled about, doing 'everything that is possible', even though Ida wanted 'all sorts of things that are not good for her.'[25]

Her sister Ethel arrived from England. She wrote that 'Ida is not really conscious but she talks in snatches, quite disconnected sentences. Mother just sits by her side and sometimes holds her hand, she has some violets on her bed.' Ethel took the children for a walk; it had been agreed that they would not see her, they wouldn't understand and she couldn't recognise them. On 13 March, she rallied and drank a toast to her husband, to love and life, with a glass of Vichy water. She was determined to leave the hospital and go home, where she would cure herself with 'a bottle of tonic water, Condy's and an enema.' ('Condy's crystals' was a popular disinfectant brand name for potassium permanganate.) She had to be persuaded that she was not in a fit state to go anywhere, and the deflation of this last effort of hers seemed to make her give up. That night there was a terrible storm. Augustus sat by her bedside while she was feverish, and stayed with her, even though the staff tried to eject him. He described how Ida made jokes and looked at the stars. As Ida's condition deteriorated, Ada recognised 'we are just waiting for the end.'[26] It came sooner rather than later. Ida died around half past three on the afternoon of 14 March, 1907. She was thirty years old.

On the same day as her death, Augustus wrote to John Sampson, 'Ida has gone to some land of miraculous caves where the air is pure and light enough for her to breathe in peace.'[27] Ada told Ursula, 'She left off suffering and smiled but she never knew she was going to die. I could not tell her just to distress her. The nurses folded her hands with a bunch of violets Gus had brought her and put a crucifix and candles by her side.' The following Saturday, Ida was cremated at the Père Lachaise Cemetery in Paris. Henry Lamb was one of the few present who saw her coffin consumed by flames, and her skeleton drawn out on a slab from the furnace. Lamb related how her bone structure was 'recognisably intact' until a single tap from the attendant's stick made it crumble to dust.[28]

Ida's newborn son, Henry John, would be raised by her mother Ada, while the other children lived with Augustus and Dorelia. The pair remained together until John's death in 1961, fifty-three years after Ida's.

16

Afterwards

Fernande's relationship with Ubaldo Oppi did not last long. Almost at once she regretted the loss of Picasso; Oppi had been a diversion, a way of feeling desired again, while Pablo retreated to his studio or sat in silence at dinner. She and Oppi were in financial difficulties from the start and she was appealing to Gertrude Stein for help by the Christmas of 1912. She also appealed to Guillaume Apollinaire, in the hope of getting work as a secretary, but with little success.

It was the fashion designer Paul Poiret, who had once mistaken Fernande's art for that of Picasso, who came to Fernande's rescue. Poiret had recently established a school and workshop for interior decoration and furnishings, which he named after his daughter, Martine. It was something of an experiment to discover raw talent, being run for young working-class girls who were encouraged to express themselves freely. They were sent out to sketch plants and animals in the local park and zoos and produced some colourful, primitive-style patterns, not completely uninspired by the work of Henri Rousseau, who had died a year or two before. It opened on 1 April 1911 and comprised the Atelier Martine, École Martine and La Maison Martine, at 107 Rue de Fauberg St-Honaire, with a shop used primarily as an outlet to sell his new perfume, 'Rosine', named after his other daughter. At first they made textiles and wallpapers, before expanding to include carpets, lighting, glassware, ceramics and domestic items. Matisse, Dufy and Van Dongen were also involved. With Fernande's interest in fashion, she would have been delighted when Poiret asked her to manage the shop in 1912. She would have been witnessing the new designs being created and modelled; the fashionable large, heavy kimono coat, harem pants and sultana skirt and pantaloon skirt that set the pre-war trend. In her memoirs, Fernande recalled Poiret's talent for throwing successful parties 'free and easy, gay and animated, in pleasant surroundings which he knew how to make intimate'. He deserved his later fame, she believed, 'for his audacity, his generosity and his genuine feeling for art. He saw things on a large, a grand scale.'[1]

Soon afterwards, Fernande was also earning money by reciting poetry at the Lapin Agile and it was probably there that she met her next lover, the journalist and poet Jean Pellerin. Born in 1885 at Pontcharra in south-eastern France, Pellerin was one of a group of young artists and writers patronising the bar along with Francis Carco, who had arrived in Paris in 1910 and acted as a ghost writer for the novelist Colette. In 1913, Carco began an affair with Katherine Mansfield, who had recently arrived in the city and was staying in the Rue de Tournon, near the Luxembourg Gardens, a twenty-minute walk from Ida's final home in the Rue Dareau. Fernande described Carco in *Picasso et ses Amis* as 'very young then, almost a boy, but he was knowing and had already considerable experience of life.' He was perpetually 'on the defensive and jeering, with a vicious observant eye'.[2] When he 'used to perch on a table' at the Lapin Agile and 'do his bawdy song act, our enjoyment knew no bounds.'[3] Together, Carco and Pellerin established a poetic movement characterised by its use of the fantastic, writing about domestic and familiar situations in loosely structured verse. Pellerin appears slightly sardonic in one surviving photograph of him, dressed in a spotted bow tie, with his dark hair brushed across his large forehead. His mouth is twisted in a half-smile and his eyes are both laughing and intense. He was keen to marry Fernande, perhaps unaware that her union with Percheron had never been dissolved.

Fernande was still in touch with many of her former friends from the Bateau-Lavoir, especially the Van Dongens, who had prospered and moved to the Rue Denfert-Rochereau. Shortly before the outbreak of war in 1914, she attended a 'grand dance' there, welcomed by an Arab servant into a house 'transformed by shimmering drapery' and 'brilliant colours' contrasted with dark corners where 'one seemed to make out human forms buried deep in piles of cushions.' She observed that during the course of the party, a spectator 'might have seen examples of every deviation from normal human behaviour'.[4] Fernande and Pellerin appear to have been together until the outbreak of war. He went off to fight, serving at Ypres, and the relationship was not revived. 'Little by little,' Fernande explains, 'the gang divided up and dispersed.' 'Finally, the war widened the split and it became a crack. Anguish brought them together for a time but the rapprochement was not to last. More money meant more freedom and their differences began to make themselves felt.'[5]

Fernande moved from one job to another, working as a vendeuse, a shop girl, for an antiques dealer before his shop shut down, reciting Baudelaire and Duvigny at cabarets, as a nanny, a cashier in a butcher's, taking walk-on roles on the stage and reading horoscopes.[6] She may have heard of the death of Eva Gouel from cancer in 1915, and that of Guillaume Apollinaire during the outbreak of Spanish influenza in the autumn of 1918; and Ubaldo Oppi died from tuberculosis in 1921. At some point before 1932, she learned that her husband, Paul Percheron had died 'crazy'.

During the war Fernande had begun a relationship with the film actor Roger Karl. Born in 1882, he had acted on stage with Sarah Bernhardt, painted, published a novel, and then made the transition to the screen in a career that would span five decades. It was news of Picasso's marriage to Olga Khokhlova that spurred Fernande to move into an apartment with Karl in the Rue de la Grande Chaumière in 1918, but their time together was not easy for Fernande, due to his drinking, extravagance and habit of chasing other women.[7]

In 1927, Fernande began writing a memoir of Picasso which was serialised in six episodes in *Le Soir* before Picasso's lawyers succeeded in having it stopped. However, the writer Paul Léautaud offered to publish extracts in the *Mercure de France* instead. Léautaud's interest in Fernande was more than professional. He invited her to his studio, observing that she was 'really very pretty' and wondering whether he might offer to pay her fifty francs a time to pose naked for him, just for his personal enjoyment. Three further extracts appeared in the *Mercure*.

In 1932, Fernande contacted Picasso for the first time since they had parted in 1912, upset by his attempts to prevent her publications from going ahead. Her letter is full of dark threats and superstitions, its tone bitter and foreboding as it played on Picasso's worst fears, sounding like the settling of a curse upon his life:

> Until now I have never wished you anything but happiness. Now, every day, I shall make a wish for you to be hurt in the things you love most, affection, money, your health. And you will be punished for your utter heartlessness. I know it. I have only ever wished to see three people unhappy or hurt because they did harm to me. My husband ... died crazy. An aunt who cast a shadow over my life saw her husband die tragically and Eva Markousis ... as you know, met a miserable end. I am in an impossible situation ... Now I would like you to know unhappiness. At the first moment it arrives you will think of me ... Now remember that you promised me several thousand francs the moment I put my affairs in order. You never gave them to me. Remember that unhappiness awaits you and I know there is a curse hanging over you.[8]

Picasso et ses Amis was published in 1933 in spite of Picasso's best efforts to suppress it, and Gertrude Stein's issue of her own similar memoirs, *The Autobiography of Alice B. Toklas*, which Fernande angrily felt had been inspired by her own. Gertrude had initially offered to help Fernande secure an American publisher, but had later withdrawn the offer and declined to write a preface.

In her memoir, Fernande reflected on the bohemian life Picasso had lived and the contrast with his present bourgeois lifestyle:

> Could anybody ever have imagined Picasso as the man of the world he is today when they met him on the Butte, in espadrilles and plumber's overalls, his hair blown by the wind or stuffed into an old cap? He used to wear trousers and a short jacket made of blue canvas ... and a red and white spotted shirt I shall never

forget, which he had paid less than two francs for at the Sunday market in the Square Saint-Pierre.

How does Picasso feel now about those days when nothing in the world would have induced him to wear a proper shirt, a stiff collar or a hat?[9]

In contrast with her former lover's success, Fernande's financial situation was not greatly alleviated by the publication of the book, so she continued to give French lessons.

In 1938, Fernande and Karl moved to Neuilly, a suburb to the west of Paris. After war broke out, they lived in fear, both vulnerable because of their Jewish roots[10] and the relationship disintegrated. They separated in 1943. Fernande continued to eke out a living as a teacher of drawing, French and elocution. In 1957, she wrote again to Picasso, asking for help and threatening to publish more memoirs. This time, he agreed to pay support to prevent their appearance until after both their deaths. He saw her for the last time on his television screen in 1959 but they were never reunited in person. Fernande Olivier died on 29 January 1966 aged eighty-five. She was buried in the cemetery at Cognac. The manuscript of her diary, and other writings, was found in a trunk in her flat by her godson, Gilbert Krill. In the introduction to her diary, she had included the following message for Picasso:

So I owe you more than life could ever have allowed me to hope for. The only thought that comforts me during my lonely nights when in my despair I accept that it was my own fault that I ruined my life, my only comfort is to remember you, and the remembrance of you finally brings me calm and peace and I fall asleep at dawn because I can forget my present life as I am cradled by the memory of you.[11]

*

Sophie learned of Henri's death when her landlady brought her a note from T.E. Hulme. It said simply 'Your brother was killed.' She was already in bed, unwell, and the news plunged her into despair. 'Oh! That brutal note' she recalled. 'Should I live an eternity, I will never forget the blow … I do not intend to describe my feelings but as long as I'll live that horrible sentence will ring in my ears and cut my brain.'[12]

Grieving for Henri, Sophie underwent a crisis of faith. 'To Him [God],' she complained, 'I entrusted the very dear life of my Love, He takes him away from me after ten months of continual trance … and I take myself into the darkness, without even the consolation of the hope of meeting the spirit of my wonderful friend there, so good, so noble, so profoundly loved.' She was also distressed that she had sent him an unkind letter, which had somehow 'poisoned' his last days and sent him to his death; even though she had followed it immediately by another, Henri had not received the second one and Sophie could not shake off the image of herself as his nemesis.

'Why if this God exists did he allow, let me write, send this letter? What God is he then? What is his power?' She was tormented that she had weakened him with her cruel letter, that she had somehow been his 'executioner' and could not stop thinking about 'the bullet that he received in his beautiful head.' Then 'my violent crisis of despair had passed … I had a sudden inspiration, willing me to write, to continue my work. Ideas, vague until now became precise … a work completely new in concept and technique presented itself to my mind urgently and with precision – I saw myself again at a crossroads … At times I was drawn towards the infinite, and longed for calm, at times the voice of my très Cher seemed to call to me to continue our work.'[13]

In this new mood of inspiration, Sophie's mind turned to his artistic legacy, and hers. She wrote feverishly, in a number of languages, in a journal she addressed to Henri and referred to as 'Our Work', later evolving into the longer title 'To Your Dearest Memory'. In it, she asked him if he had forgiven her for her stupidity and professed her desire to sacrifice herself, to do whatever would make him happy. Without a passport, she was 'a prisoner of war, of body, of spirit' and might 'go into fits of dementia and rage, tear out the fibres of my heart, shake my fists at the implacable powers and curse them to Hell.' On 3 August, she wrote how she experienced 'such terrible pain at the very idea of telling anyone' of her loss that she avoided everyone she knew, including a young couple who now lived in the house she and Henri had once shared, before whom she wept and begged to leave her alone.[14] Still hoping that there had been a mistake, that a rainbow was a sign that he would return, she reflected upon her character, describing herself as 'an eccentric flower of trouble, an orchid of suffering, a flower which poisons everything without she herself being able to die because she is everlasting.'[15] That September she recorded that 'the beginnings of madness have haunted me for some time ... with such definite precision as in these last days ... I felt swamped by the avalanche of my sorrow.'[16]

She turned to a famous author for help, perhaps inspired by the novels, biographies and historical dramas he had written, which made her feel that he might be sympathetic. Romain Rolland had received the Nobel Prize for Literature in the year of Henri's death, when he had also published a Pacifist Manifesto. Sophie hoped that he would 'take the trouble to decipher all my scribblings and make from them a small work of art.' In her eyes he was the best person to do so; the 'master of fathoming and going into depths and illustrating exceptionally powerful suffering.' She hoped he would print some of her poems, excluding the 'coarse' ones which Henri had not liked. She asked Rolland to show some of her Polish writings to 'some modern poets'. Yet perhaps she never sent it, as Gillian Raffles, the editor of *Matka* suggests. Sophie admitted 'I write (sic) to unknown French authors feeling sympathetic to their works – and I returned once again to my death.'[17] She appears to have been seeking more than literary recognition, someone to act as an editor of her work, to analyse, rearrange and select the best parts out of a random collection, indicating her belief in her own abilities. She was looking for a big name, a figure of the literary establishment, to 'discover' her as a new talent. By selecting the recipient of a Nobel Prize for Literature, she was surely overreaching herself. Perhaps this realisation prevented her from posting the letter. If she did send it, Rolland did not respond.

Sophie may not have sent her work to Rolland, but she definitely gave it to Stanislawa de Karlowska, a Polish artist descended from nobility, who was married to the Camden Town painter Robert Bevan. She later summoned Bevan to return her papers and apparently a revolver that was also in the packet, commenting,

'What a relief to have the instrument that gives peace and forgetfulness.' Around the same age as Sophie, Stanislawa also visited and wept with her over Henri's death. 'I was grateful to her, there are still good hearted people.'[18] But when her friend offered Sophie some money from the Polish refugee fund, Sophie reacted angrily and rejected it. Although her financial situation was dire, she was determined not to ask for or accept help, unless she was left with no other choice.

In London, Sophie received well-meaning visits from Ezra Pound, T.E. Hulme and an unnamed woman, 'Countess X', enquiring about Gaudier's work. Sometimes they offered her money, or sought to help her arrange Henri's legacy, but she frequently took offence at their suggestions or feared that they wished to claim aspects of Henri and his work. On one occasion, Ezra Pound made her an offer on behalf of a wealthy American collector, John Quinn, who was interested in buying all Henri's sculptures. Quinn had opened the influential Armory Exhibition of Post-Impressionist works in New York in 1913 and won important cases regarding artistic legacies and the ownership of estates; by the 1920s he would amass the largest collection of European art in the world. Pound arranged Quinn's purchase of two of Henri's sculptures, 'Marble Cat' and 'Water Carrier' from the Omega workshops, for which he paid £42.10s on 7 February 1916. Sophie wrote to him shortly beforehand, accusing him of 'mystifying and tom-foolery', possibly 'double-dealing', in contrast to her own 'utmost sincerity'. Her mood was one of suspicion as she had already identified some forgeries at a New Bond Street dealer, some 'feeble imitations' with a squiggled fake signature, prompting her to authenticate Henri's genuine work by adding her own name to it.[19] Despite their attempts to be placatory, Sophie's tone towards Quinn and Pound remained confrontational, and she was determined to retain control of Henri's work, including the speed at which she dispatched it. 'Shall greased lightning move me to thundering speed?' she asked, adding that she would dispatch the statues to Quinn 'at present' because he was 'not in haste'.[20]

Eventually, prompted by Quinn, Pound asked to see the document proving the gift of Henri's work and possessions to Sophie, which the artist had signed in August 1914 before his first departure for war.

'When some of so-called friends of my late brother came to me,' she wrote in *Matka*, 'saying that his parents claimed all his possessions/ heritage through the French Embassy, I told them I had a document stamped, where Henri confirms having given me everything.' Pound advised her that she should have the paper validated and stamped at Somerset House and put into safe custody. Sophie did act upon this advice, travelling there with Pound, carrying the document, where she was told that 'no claim could be made against this act of donation.'[21] On December 11, after she had collected together 'thirty animal drawings, five studies of riders on horseback, eighty-four nudes, six drawings for vases, four small drawings, four modern drawings and two other studies', Sophie deposited them in the Westminster and London County Bank in Putney.

Sophie was keen to organise an exhibition of Gaudier's work and met with T.E. Hulme to begin the process of locating and sourcing his work. Conscious that Henri's mother had never liked her, she offered to give up her claim to his estate if it upset the Gaudier family, hoping his father might travel to England to meet her and together they might go through Henri's possessions. 'I said I wanted to give some statues to museums and was going to write to Henri's father asking him to come over so that we should dispose together of everything. I did so. Instead of answering me the parents wrote to the Embassy saying that they do not want to have anything to do or deal with "that woman".'[22] Her gesture of friendship, this attempt to connect with Henri's family, then elicited a letter from Germain Gaudier, expressed 'in a vulgar manner' in which 'the man menaces to come up to London and start a suit' and threatened her with the police. Sophie was upset and furious. As it transpired, though, old Mr Gaudier was unable to come to London so he entrusted Hulme with his suit instead. She began trying to organise the exhibition but the complicated question of who owned commissioned and purchased works, coupled with the difficulties of co-operating with Henri's friends, drew the process out through 1916 and 1917. As in other times of extreme unhappiness in her life, Sophie's thoughts turned darker:

Prey to my extreme misery, to a complete disarray, left totally alone in the world. Fate has dealt the final blow on me and I am left beaten and wiped out emotionally and physically. What in the world is left for me? Absolutely nothing, not even the certainty of a firm decision – suicide – for I am tormented by the choice in my destiny ... At this moment of utter distress, merciless beings with unrefined feelings came to me and inflicted blows to my pride and human dignity indiscriminately. These creatures who I know are very inferior in worth to me, who treat me like some tramp.[23]

Early in 1916, Sophie had been living in a 'hell hole' at Munster Road in Fulham, which had been the 'one road that (she) absolutely refused to go into' but had been driven there by fate. By May, she was 'out of the mess' thanks to a Miss Westwood, with whom she was living in Fulham Palace Road.[24] It was only intended as a temporary measure and soon she was feeling restricted and isolated, after having alienated Henri's friends, whose distance she interpreted as English reserve and rudeness. In September 1916, she moved to The Cot, Wotton-on-Edge in Gloucestershire, which was at 3, Wortley Terrace, on the edge of town. On the western tip of the Cotswolds, Wotton was twelve miles south of Stroud and twenty-two miles north of Bath, near the rolling green countryside of the Severn valley. Benefitting from the quiet surroundings and shielded from the disturbing daily news headlines, Sophie tried to complete her novels *Trilogy* and *Our Work*, which then stood at almost 400 pages. But it was difficult to work as her brain was 'in turmoil', roaming 'like a tiger in a cage'; at one moment she was 'full of life – exuberant, almost happy' and the next, 'utterly broken with sorrow and despair'.[25]

Sophie, the woman who may have never experienced full sexual intercourse, now became obsessed with the idea of making a physical connection with some 'lusty' local man. In March 1917, she was trying to inspire the 'moronic male population which squat in their holes around here like pigs' by using her eyes to make 'outrageous promises' and to interest them in her body by using 'the vivacity of my gestures and nervous and breathless speech'. She enjoyed teasing the men, who 'get all of a sweat with themselves charged with animal lust' and exposing them as 'the lustful boars they are'. Once they were interested, though, her 'entertainment becomes a nightmare' and she was 'tormented' by the idea of afflicting distress. 'Uncertain of offering physical love' she took the same line as she had with Gaudier, proposing a 'sisterly friendship and the spiritual protection of a devoted companion'. Sophie was clearly deeply lonely, hoping to attract a man to replace Henri, in the same sort of chaste-sisterly way, but unaware of how to gain his initial attention in anything other than a sexual way. This provocative sexuality, with the consummation withheld, need not necessarily have been problematic on its own, but its bizarreness drew attention to Sophie in unwarranted ways and created a climate of tension around her. In addition, her appearance was becoming increasingly odd, as she walked about the countryside in all weathers, 'barefoot, unwashed and dishevelled,' resembling a 'rag bag' of clothes, muttering to herself in a mixture of different languages.[26] Locally she was considered mad, a judgement apparently confirmed by her requests that her neighbours leave her alone and her complaints to the police that she was the target of harassment.

Her letters to the artist Nina Hamnett survive from 1917-18, when she seems to have considered the younger woman her closest friend, a connection to Henri and her lifeline to London. Initially, Sophie had been in touch with Nina about recovering Henri's drawings from the Omega workshops, still attempting to push the memorial exhibition to its conclusion. It was Nina who had first introduced Henri to the workshop's director and, in November 1915, Fry had written to Sophie on Omega headed paper offering to release a sculpture of Henri's to be kept in the Victoria and Albert Museum. She had also sent the museum another eight works and received a letter reassuring her that the two sculptures and six plaster casts would be well looked after.

In the early summer of 1917, Sophie invited Nina to come and stay with her, 'I am hungry like a wolf of intellectual society, being practically starved of spiritual company,' but added that it was hardly worth spending over a pound on rail fare unless she stayed a while. She urged Nina to 'come for a least some weeks and we shall lead a splendid bohème as I am myself turning out into little better than a tramp ... the Cot is big enough for us both especially that I live chiefly on the tops of the surrounding hills and only come down to sleep in the den.'[27] Sophie wrote to Nina that she had 'a bed (somewhat hard) some chairs and tables – only the rules and laws imposed upon my life by the Satans who reign.' She wanted to offer 'complete hospitality, however my resources are very minimal and my means to earn, because of the state of my health, almost none ... I cannot offer you to partake of my table most of all with the dearness of provisions – the house naturally is at your disposal (there are three rooms) and as I have no one to wait on me we will share the cooking tasks.'

Exactly when Nina made her visit is unclear, but she probably stayed at The Cot for two weeks in the autumn of 1917. Nina slept in a top attic on a short sofa, with her feet sticking over the end. At nights, Sophie would stand at the bottom of the stairs and shout up to her about art and philosophy; on one occasion at about three in the morning, she screamed out the question whether Nina would have 'gone off with Henri' if she'd had the chance. Nina shouted back that she would have and was a little scared about Sophie's reaction, but the moment passed. They spent their days walking. Sophie had the use of an upstairs room in a porter's lodge on a nearby great estate and she would lie on the floor there, eating nuts and throwing the shells on the floor. Nina was only allowed to join her on condition that she did not speak. Nina also recorded that she wore 'old-fashioned' clothes and was reading Casanova. Sophie used the visit to read aloud some of the poems she had written but was upset when Nina only praised her more light-hearted efforts and ignored the outpourings of her heart; in the end, Nina would distract Sophie from reading them by singing music-hall songs.[28] When she left to stay with Roger Fry, Nina felt 'rather shaken' by her visit and was told that she was 'quite mad to stay with lunatics'.[29] Sidney Schiff also visited Sophie, offering her money which she refused, and realised that she was deeply unwell.

In October 1917, Sophie was caught in rain on the way back from a walk to Ozleworth and was ill in bed again. She told Nina that 'not only has my illness returned after a dozen days, but it has continued for a week, I can neither take a bath or walk, think what misery for me who has only these two meagre physical pleasures.' This developed into an inflammation of the intestines but when Sophie visited the doctor, 'he got out of me everything to do with my birth, my ancestors without even taking the trouble to examine me. Without doubt I represented in his eyes a possible spy, not an individual who needed relief.' In November, she wrote that she was 'squashed into a great gelateous (sic) ball, a huge roll of dung which suffocates me ... it would take very little for me to drag fat Dick into this and give myself to his cruelty, his filthy ugly debauched form, toothless mouth and paunched belly.'[30] She must have looked terrible, as 'people around here are quite convinced that I am being very near the "other side".' However, her work sustained her, as 'I cannot afford to die before having disposed of Henri's works and having put some order into my scribbles.'[31] Nina was due to visit her again at Christmas but Sophie was forced to postpone due to illness.

Sophie ended up hating The Cot, which became a prison for her. It was difficult for her to stay clean as 'this slut of a landlady said nothing to me about the chimney not functioning at all.' She had spent two hours poking the fire to warm water for a bath and failed. Plus it was noisy. 'There is a racket about six o'clock in the morning and as I work until 12 or 1 in the morning, I can hardly sleep.' She became paranoid about her neighbours who would watch her comings and goings with amusement and not try to conceal their comments about her. She could hear every noise through the thin walls, including their fire being stoked, the cries of their child and perceived herself to be constantly tortured by them. She would leave the house early and return late, carrying a suitcase and sit in a field or barn all day. Upon her return, she heard her neighbours announce 'she's back!'[32]

In the spring of 1918, Sophie went up to London to attend Gaudier's memorial exhibition which was finally being held at the Leicester Galleries. She lodged with a Mrs Gilling for about eight weeks. She had hoped to write the preface to the catalogue but Bevan advised her this would seem too much 'in the family' so the task was given to Pound, who had recently published his own memoirs of Henri. Horace Brodsky recalled her wandering around the gallery like a 'wild caged animal', with clothes 'begrimed with food and mud' and her hair 'chopped short as if she had cut it herself with blunt scissors.' Only when cornered by a few old friends would she stand still and then 'her eyes were darting from wall to ceiling ... and her conversation clipped with short sentences interspersed with mutterings and asides in different languages.'[33] John Quinn spent over £500 on three sculptures, ensuring the exhibition was a financial success.

Between the end of the war in November 1918 and November 1922, Sophie's mental health deteriorated. An occasional visitor to London still, she appeared at the Leicester Galleries, where owner Oliver Brown recorded that she looked 'shabbier and more dilapidated than usual', carrying a large brown paper bundle. On another occasion, she was looking 'very ill ... wild and haggard' as she tried to take a hammer to a statue of Henri's, a cast of a Madonna, which she believed the sculptor would have wanted destroyed. To Brown, she seemed 'a sad figure ... evidently heartbroken at the loss of her companion.' He judged her kindly, to be 'a clear-headed and intelligent woman, well-educated and a good linguist but she had become obsessed by her devotion' to Henri and she 'could never recover from his loss.' Brown had been told 'she wrote good verse but she never showed me any of her own poetry'[34] although she asked him to order her some new book of French verse. He sent her the final payments due to her at the end of 1920.

In August 1921, Sophie left Gloucestershire and had a small holiday in Margate. Staying briefly at 41 Marine Parade, part of a long cream terrace overlooking the bay, she upset the other residents with her furtive glances and muttering, and accused the landlady of spying on her, before moving on to another hotel. Back in Gloucestershire her behaviour was increasingly erratic and she hoped to escape to France or Poland, writing to inform the Polish Consul that it was his duty to help her leave England 'before the damned English rob me of the wealth which was left me by my adopted brother.' She concluded the letter by cursing 'England and everyone who has committed the crimes of Satan' against her.[35] She made the last coherent entry into her diary in late August, when she crept past her middle-aged neighbour, asleep on his deckchair, to empty her slops in the drain beside him, resulting in a violent argument. Complaints against her were made and she was, from this point onwards, under observation by the local authorities. The last straw was a letter Sophie wrote on 11 July 1922, to 'The

Secretary at Home Office, Chief Scoundrel and Ruler of a Damned Race', given here verbatim:

> Mlle S S Brzeska hereby gives notice second and last that she wishes and ardently desires to leave this doomed hell of an island and will persist in her wish until she has been let free to leave it without having to undertake any more fruitless journeys. Mlle Zofia Brzeska, adhering to the God's Rhythm in pair contrary to the Devil's Rhythm of impair numbers expects not only to leave this country in August next about 10th but awaits to have all her journey expenses to Paris paid by the English government as well as £8,000 of damages for lost times, injuries sustained etc etc.
>
> In case the English government should fail to let go now and prolongate her stay until October, £16 of damages will have to be paid for if time means 'moon-ey,' for citizens of this country it means real gold for the undersigned. I shall not waste any more of this precious time in sending more curses I have a very 'influential Protector' and He will see to it that Justice be dealt out sooner or later. In case it should be decided to stop the devils game played on me and let me go I require at least a week's notice before my starting for the journey ...
>
> All these details are being given at this occasion in order to avoid any further correspondence on the matter plaintive having already lost too much time in elle correspondence without respondance in journeys most unpleasant etc etc She understands very well that the devil, chief ruler of England has to be pleased and so on. But it must be meant only for his subjects and faithful adherents to whom the undersigned shall never belong nor be counted to.
>
> Mlle Zofia Brzeska protests almost with utmost energy against her being considered a state prisoner and her communications with friends and relatives abroad being cut and interrupted. SGB.[36]

On 9 November 1922, Sophie was escorted from The Cot to the Barnwood House County Mental Hospital in Gloucestershire. Her landlady reported to Schiff that Sophie came 'rushing down the stairs, so fast that her two keepers could not keep up with her.'

She had wrapped a shawl about her face and started screaming.[37] The officer in charge described her as a 'very bad case indeed' from whom they could glean nothing of any sense. Opened in 1860, Barnwood catered for affluent patients who contributed towards their own keep and patients in limited circumstances who were treated at reduced rates. The charge for Sophie's upkeep was £56. 2s 4d per year and her assets, including Gaudier's legacy totalled over £3,800, according to a schedule attached to the affidavit offered by her solicitor.[38] Once admitted, patients were not permitted to leave. A number of activities were offered, including concerts, lectures, theatre and dances in the hall, as well as crafts, croquet, tennis, cricket and walking. There were also gardens with vegetable patches. Sophie died at Barnwood at 6.45pm on 17 March 1925. She was fifty-two. The cause of death was bronchial pneumonia. In spite of her wealth, recently recorded by the asylum, she was given a pauper's burial. After her death, Henri's biographer J. S. Ede wrote:

Many people will remember Miss Brzeska in the streets of London, a strange gaunt woman with short hair, no hat, and shoes cut into the form of sandals. She felt that the world was against her, and never for an instant did she forget the tragic loss of her 'little son'. He became for her the whole of her life, but a life consumed by remorse, in that she had not been to him a companion more complete, more lively and more sympathetic.[39]

17

Three Extraordinary Women

It is said that successful artists remember the days when they were poor with sad nostalgia. There can be no doubt about this. They have left in those places where they lived when they were young and poor all that was best in themselves ... When they leave poverty behind them they are also bidding farewell to a purity and a dedication which they will try in vain to find again ... Picasso's restless spirit, continually needing to delve and look further, could only develop satisfactorily in an atmosphere undistracted by glamour and wealth.[1]

The bohemian life was not an easy one. The lives of Sophie Brzeska, Ida Nettleship and Fernande Olivier were acts of consistent bravery in the face of censure, hardship and illness. Their freedom was bought at considerable personal cost. Sophie, Fernande and Ida each fell in love with an artist, a man who found significant fame, sharing their life and witnessing, even participating in, the creation of works that would enter the artistic canon. While canvases were being covered or stone carved, Sophie, Ida and Fernande were creating and maintaining a domestic and emotional foundation for the production of art; a home, a centre, an essential continuity and stability. But they rarely did so as passive witnesses. Not only were they facilitating their men's work, they were also acting as models, supplying food, comfort, guidance and attempting to engage in their own artistic pursuits. Few people today know anything about their painting or writing: their obscurity is partly a product of these men's colossal success as well as the limited machinery of culture, biography and history. Their aspirations have been forgotten, their efforts subsumed in domesticity. And yet they lived bravely, even radically.

Polish aristocrat Sophie Brzeska was to have her literary efforts frustrated through decades of privation and poor health, yet she continued writing stories, until insecurity and illness broke down her mental health completely. Illegitimate French beauty Fernande Olivier had the potential to become a writer or teacher before a chance encounter altered the direction of her life forever. Later, her artistic talent was eclipsed by the immense presence of her lover, on whose name she would continue trading as a way out of poverty. English middle-class Ida Nettleship sacrificed a promising career to be the muse of the man she loved, only to feel that she had failed, and to die young, worn down by a string of pregnancies. Yet their lives sing with determination and vitality. As frustrated artists, beset by the insurmountable obstacles resulting from their moment in time, they matter. As women, their stories tell a familiar and universal truth. They deserve to be brought out from the shadow cast over them by their more famous menfolk and allowed to shine. But they also beg the question of whether such sacrifice was worth it.

To the twenty-first century eye, the lives of Sophie, Ida and Fernande can read like relentless tests of endurance. Existing in pitiful and harsh conditions, often isolated and lonely, they can surely inspire sympathy in an era when women's lives have been altered forever by advancing technology, emancipation, contraception and drastic social change. All three found their choices affected by the struggle to balance domesticity with creativity and as a result, saw their early promise curtailed by the difficult daily business of survival. Children, poverty, ill-health, lack of opportunity and their devotion to a man got in the way. Yet this was the world as they knew it. The demands placed upon women were complex and constant. Although the laws surrounding marriage and divorce were changing, health provision was improving and the suffrage cause was advancing, such liberties did not fully penetrate even the most enlightened families. Nor could they change the basic dynamics of male-female relationships. Picasso was so jealous about Fernande that he sometimes refused to let her go out alone; Augustus John continually impregnated his wife and was irritated by the noise of their children; Sophie refused to submit to Gaudier's sexual requests yet feared he would be stolen away by another woman. The ability of these three women to fulfil their artistic potential was inseparable from their gender. For Ida, Sophie and Fernande, specific circumstances combined to create obstacles between them and their full artistic expression.

Inescapably, the late nineteenth century shaped their health. Born into financial dependence, Sophie and Fernande were perhaps better equipped to deal with later privations in adulthood, their survival partly due to a learned resilience the middle class Ida lacked. Poor diet, health and sanitation provided constant challenges in the adult lives of all three and, in some cases, the impacts were permanent, even fatal. An additional side effect for Fernande and many other women in similar deprived situations, was the irreparable damage to their reproductive abilities, through disease, violation or aborted pregnancy. However, in spite of the obvious suffering this caused, infertility meant they were never exposed to the huge risks of childbirth repeatedly faced by Ida and other contemporaries. Additionally, Sophie, Ida and Fernande found their developing sexual identity challenging; the transition from adolescence brought danger, discomfort and often disappointment. At varying points in their lives, all three suffered from a lack of control over their sexual activity and the physical and emotional aspects of their relationships with men. Ida was overwhelmed by John's fecundity, Fernande's beauty made her a target for predators and Sophie insisted on a platonic relationship with Gaudier.

Outside the confines of a protective family unit, the world they inhabited was fraught with dangers for young women; Ida and Sophie travelled independently but, as Sophie and Fernande's experiences testify, the more immediate threats to physical safety and virtue could be closer to home, even within it. Sometimes their choices, or lack of, caused them to be isolated from friends and family and their brave attempts to adapt to this loneliness were not always successful. In turn, each sought the consolation of more reliable and sympathetic female companions, who had shared similar experiences. This is not to suggest the development of a powerful solidarity or 'sisterhood'; their biographies make clear that these attempts at female connection could be disappointingly short-lived, sometimes rebuffed, marred by rivalry or frustrated by conditions beyond their control. None of them can be claimed for the suffrage movement. They did not fight for women's rights or make any stand that was politically motivated; they were essentially private individuals rather than spokeswomen yet, in their own way, they played a part in the redefinition of the boundaries that defined female lives. Each experienced specific moments when changing social and moral expectations informed their decision making and resulted in deliberate acts of defiance which, although frequently motivated by personal desire, expose a complex interrelation of individual and context. Millions of Sophies, Fernandes and Idas fought out their own personal battles before the minority stood up for them. What seems most strikingly and inescapably time-specific, was the power of men to define and limit their artistic achievement: their success being as durable as contemporary masculine understanding and generosity.

Separated by the passage of a century and vocal women's movements, it is easy to talk about wasted opportunities and romanticise these women as heroines sacrificed to male success. As artist Edna Clarke Hall put it in response to her critics, women's responsibilities lie equally with their children and '...in the development of the powers in herself which are her true expression.'[2] The early twentieth century does provide examples of comparable women who became successful artists as well as raising children: Bloomsbury's Vanessa Bell, poetess Frances Cornford, Ida's friends Edna Clarke Hall and Gwen Salmond, as well as Montmartre's Suzanne Valadon and the Impressionist Berthe Morisot – all persisted despite complicated personal arrangements. Yet there was also a significant number of successful women who remained single, delayed marriage, or did not have children, featuring on the fringes of these three lives: artists Ursula Tyrwhitt, Dorothy Brett, Dora Carrington, Gwen John, Nina Hamnett and Marie Laurencin; writers Virginia Woolf, Gertrude Stein and Katherine Mansfield. For some it was a deliberate choice, predicated upon circumstances or sexuality, whilst some exercised little control over their own fertility. Of course there are many others but, although equal success in the realms of domesticity and creativity was achievable, it was significantly more difficult than for the women of the later twentieth century. Possibly of the three, Ida came the closest to having what would now be considered the most successful, if short-lived, 'career', studying at the Slade throughout her teenage years. A handful of Fernande's pictures have been reproduced in biographies of Picasso and, until recently, Sophie's unpublished diaries and short stories languished in a Colchester library, unread. Their posthumous existence has been allied to the fame of those who directly affected their output but it is significant that they have been remembered primarily as women and not artists or writers.

The arena of relationships and gender expectations was difficult and complicated for Sophie, Ida and Fernande: all three rejected the marital ideals of their families in order to follow their hearts. Their quests for romance were not always successful, as their relationships expose the double standards of sexual behaviour, but nor did marriage guarantee security. Instead, these women sought to forge new family units and open relationships that allowed for greater sexual and personal freedom, although the idea often proved more fulfilling in theory than practice. The casual encounters and affairs of Sophie and Fernande were strikingly modern in comparison with the expectations of their upbringing and despite remaining faithful, Ida saw her marriage become a ménage à trois and John's infidelity was continual. The men's hold over these women was personal and sexual; their nature and the unshakeable single-mindedness essential for artistic dedication could unconsciously undermine the ambitions and identities of their partners. In each case though, it was a willing female companion who contributed to these men's determination, facilitating the production of art by providing domestic security as well as inspiring and modelling for some of the most recognisable works of the era. These paintings and sculptures could be produced partly because there was someone, a woman, providing emotional and domestic stability, but it could not just be any woman; Sophie, Ida and Fernande each made a choice to enter into a partnership dedicated to art. This unites them and makes them paradoxically remarkable and typical: they each made a choice. What influenced those choices and how far the women were aware of their options and the ensuing consequences is the substance of this triple biography.

Sadly, it is clear that each suffered as a result of sacrifices they made. Their ambitions and intentions were frequently compromised in meeting the needs of significant figures in their lives. Perhaps Sophie, Ida and Fernande could be accused of naivety on entering into such relationships, yet this overlooks the specific conditions of their upbringing, unfairly undermines their ability to make informed decisions and does not take into account the timeless nature of sexual attraction and the peculiarly individual choice any woman makes to become intimate with any man. Perhaps the men could be accused of selfishness; but they cannot be blamed for not being as enlightened as subsequent generations. Each had made a prior commitment to follow a course to which they felt destined and art history has since vindicated their 'selfishness'. It is unhelpful and anachronistic to speak here of blame and responsibility. What is perhaps more interesting, is that these three couples belonged to wider social milieux which have attracted such titles as 'bohemian', 'enlightened' and 'experimental', yet their lives show inconsistencies in the practice of this freedom and the impracticalities and unsuitability of some of their number for such a lifestyle. Often the price for this 'freedom' was paid by someone else, usually a woman: exploring experiments in bohemian living, Virginia Nicholson has gone as far as to call them the 'casualties of male egos'.[3] It was in 1958, on the death of Gwen Salmond, that Augustus John remarked on the promise of the women of her generation, 'but these advantages for the most part came to nought under the burdens of domesticity.'[4] For all three, their bohemianism was fragile and costly.

Finally, the theme of self-deception and storytelling emerges repeatedly in all three lives. With Fernande's name changes, the questions arising over her diary and her memoirs and with Sophie's retrospective re-invention of her past and her mental instability the most dramatic examples, each woman maintained a complex and personal relationship with truth. Even Ida's brave efforts to confront reality proved a heavy burden for the sheltered girl who had woven an innocent fantasy world around her childhood friends. Whether for pride or self-preservation, the circumstances of their lives led these three women towards deliberate, artistic acts of concealment and fantasy and other, less conscious self-deceptions. This should not surprise or deter a reader. Such behaviour is as timeless and untidy as human relations.

Arduous as their circumstances may now appear, these women's stories are radiant in places, awe-inspiring in their determination and frequently illumined by their ability to exercise their will and fight for their own happiness. In this way, they are more modern than their birth dates might suggest. Theirs is still a battle that is relevant today. Ida's life was cut short before she was able to gain the perspective of time and look back upon her early years. Sophie outlived Gaudier, but her ability to reflect upon her choices was later hampered by her poor mental health. So the final words go to Fernande who, in 1933, observed the disparity between the fates of the men and women she knew who had lived bohemian lives:

I know some of the women who lived with those artists, companions of the good and bad hours of their youth: and they are growing old alone too, with only their memories as constant companions.[5]

Appendix 1

Six previously unpublished poems by Sophie Gaudier-Brzeska

A Concert
The wind loosens its edges...
A concert's powerful tone...
The whistling of the trees agrees
With the breath of life that criss-crosses
The airs...
... Among this burst
The strongest expression of all
Introduces the timid cymbals
From a solitary cricket.

Originally written in French, transcribed by H. S. Ede, translated by Amy Licence. Composed following the death of Henri Gaudier-Brzeska, the focus on sound is a recurrent theme of Sophie's. Although she frequently found it difficult to live among other people's noise, she had an appreciation of the sounds of the natural world, which had a harmony captured in this extended metaphor, from the intense volume of the wind to the tiny contribution of the single cricket. Each element has a part to play, essential and vitalising, as if the poet draws inspiration, even draws life from the vigour she witnesses in the natural world. Sophie felt far greater sympathy with such an environment, rather than with people.

Pain

The pain is beautiful when she is lonely
Discreetly touching the cheek.
The pain is beautiful when it does not exaggerate
Does not laugh at our tears and does not play.
But when all the powers of heaven and hell
Strive to grind alone, O, misfortune!
Pain, you lose your taste and become vulgar
Still tearing the corpse of a heart.

La Douleur [translated above]

La Douleur est belle – quand elle est solitaire
Discrètement nous effleurer la joue
La douleur est belle quand elle n'éxagère
De nos pleurs ne se rit, et ne joue
Mais quand toutes les puissances du ciel et des enfers
S'acharnant a moudre en seul – ô malheur,
Douleur, tu perds ton gout – et deviant vulgaire
Déchirant encore le cadavre d'un coeur...

Originally written in French, transcribed by H. S. Ede, translated by Amy Licence. After Henri's death, Sophie captures the continual agony of her loss. There is an ambiguity in 'elle', as 'she' and 'it'.

Nocturne, 1915

It is a November evening.
A beautiful black horse
Awaits the agony
On the field of victory...
In one last effort
It rises and arches
Fighting against death
Because a company
Passes by.
The horse whinnies,
Cries for help,
But collapses at once into death.

Originally written in French, transcribed by H. S. Ede, translated by Amy Licence. Written just five months after Henri's death, it is difficult not to draw parallels with the final moments of the horse depicted here. By placing the focus on an animal, rather than a person, Sophie has drawn out the elements of beauty and nobility inherent in the creature, which has been drawn into the conflict of men although it has no place there, just as the art of the talented Henri was halted by war. The irony of the noble horse's death on the field of victory highlights the futility and senselessness of conflict, which reduces all to the impersonal, the 'company', who appear to pass unawares.

Muse

My Muse was conceived from suffering,
Born in the crises of pain,
Lulled by the idea of revenge,
Nourished by the milk of misfortune.

She was bathed in tears
Of bitterness, doubt and abandonment.
Those who revolt, who disarm,
And who disdain and defy opinion,

Come and sing with me the emptiness.
My Muse, child of despair,
Come what may, the stories
Must leave that part to the Devil.

Originally written in French, transcribed by H. S. Ede, translated by Amy Licence. Sophie's childlessness is highlighted in this bitter metaphor, which explores her 'motherhood' of her own muse, which she has brought forth as the result of her grief. Formerly casting herself in the role of Henri's mother, she has birthed her own replacement through her pain at his loss; a bleak and lonely mood which inspires much of her surviving poetry. It is also a sad parody of the act of creation, as she sexlessly engenders her own work of art.

Merry Christmas, 1915
Pianofortes bang by scores
Phonographs by dozens howl
Till my head is all in sores
Thousand voices brag and brawl

My nerves are wild, to madness strung
That rings bell and this blows horn
I wish to hell this horrid dung
And that damned Christ never had been born.

*Originally written in English, transcribed by Amy Licence.
Sophie was still in London when she composed this poem just six
months after the death of Henri Gaudier. It captures her life-long
desire for peace and quiet, while her living space is invaded by
the noise of others, at this time the jollity of festive celebrations
on the piano and phonograph, an early form of record player.
Her response is blunt, visceral, in her moment of despair, facing
Christmas alone in a country in which she did not feel welcome,
at a time of privation, ill-health and war. She damns the 'dung'
of the festive noise to hell and concludes with a sentence so
blasphemous for her era that it's publication at the time would
have elicited censure, even prosecution. This is clearly Sophie
at a low point: other poems contain more traditional, hopeful
religious symbols.*

Enviable Humans
I hear people say around me
"Life is very short:
Before we have time to taste its joys
Death already claims us."

Happy humans who run towards death
At such speed
Why must I wait so long for my knell
My life has lasted an eternity

Originally written in French, transcribed and translated by Amy Licence. Sophie captures the sense of alienation and difference she feels in comparison with those around her, who are speaking to each other, rather than to her. This is a symbolic distance, a deeper gulf than mere sentiment; their regret of the brevity of life and belief that it contains joy contrasts with her experience of suffering and desire for it to end.

Texts reproduced with the kind permission of the Albert Sloman Library, University of Essex.

Appendix 2

An extract from Sophie's unpublished comedy drama, 'Shining Tokens'

Scene 21.

(The porter's lodge in a magnificent park.)

Oiselle: It happened so that I was turned out of my house unexpectedly. And as the other cottage which I have taken is not ready yet for occupation, I am obliged to benefit by this hospitable roof.

Mrs R: Yes, but is it only a roof and nothing besides. How can you stop here without any furniture?

Oiselle: (Showing the empty box and a copper taken down in the scullery) You see, there is my chair and my bath tub.

Mrs R: Have you a bed at least or a table?

Oiselle: No, I use the windowsill as table and a bag of hay from the farm as a bed.

Mrs R: How long have you been here?

Oiselle: Only since yesterday. I stayed in G. for two days but there came a family with a pack of children and I prefer to sleep on the floor than to put up with their noise.

Mrs R: When do you think of coming to your new cottage?

Oiselle: In five or six days.

Mrs R: But how can you live like this for a whole week? I should die if I had to spend two days here. How can you cook?

Oiselle: Oh, I have a spirit lamp. You see, you are used to comforts and I am thriving on the simplification of life. I can put up with almost anything.

Mrs R: Don't you catch cold with your bare feet?

Oiselle: No, on the contrary, this is to harden me. If you wait a minute, I'll go upstairs and bring you the drawing of my brother which I promised you. (Goes.)

Mrs R: She's certainly very funny, but she seems happy, just the same.

Mr R: Or she pretends to be. Couldn't you let her have a room somewhere at the mansion?

Mrs R: Ssh, we don't know her. God knows who she may be. No, no, nothing of the kind.

Mr R: But she seems alright, well educated.

Mrs R: Ssh, ssh, here she comes.

Oiselle enters.

Oiselle: You see, I don't see any of these drawings under £10 or £15, but it will make me a pleasure offering one to you if you let me have the lodge for the whole summer. The forge is very beautiful and inspiring, the place very quiet, while my new cottage is on a noisy road like the previous.

Mrs R: Why did you take it then?

Oiselle: Oh, I have tried far many others but the landlords refused me everywhere. I suppose they are afraid of a foreigner. And I cannot pay a high rent, so the more enlightened landlords' abodes are not accessible to me.

Originally in English, transcribed by Amy Licence. As well as capturing something of Sophie's idiosyncratic English, this scene draws on autobiographical concerns. The constant need to find suitable accommodation, for peace and privacy, of extreme poverty and hardship and the difficulties of her nationality and relating to other people, are all brought to the fore. These details find an echo in the descriptions provided by Nina Hamnett, who visited Sophie in Gloucestershire in 1918, when she had the daily use of a lodge in a great park. It is illuminating that the Oiselle (Mademoiselle?) character is selling sketches of/by her brother, suggesting that Sophie may have used Henri's work as currency at times of extreme need.

Text reproduced with the kind permission of the Albert Sloman Library, University of Essex.

Acknowledgements

Thanks to the team at Amberley, to my editors Jonathan Jackson and Shaun Barrington, cover designer Aaron Phull and the rest of the team for their work in promoting this book, and others. I have been blessed with some wonderful friends: thank you in particular to Anne Marie Bouchard, Sharon Bennett Connolly, Jonathan Howell, Claire Ridgway, Geanine Teramani-Cruz, Tim Byard-Jones and Harry and Sara Basnett, for keeping me sane during the writing of this book. There have been significant others. I am also grateful for the help of John Peel at Manchester Art Gallery, Violette Andres at the Musée Picasso, Tanya at Yale Library and Nigel Cochrane at the Albert Sloman Library, University of Essex. Also to my godmother 'Lady' Susan Priestley, for her kindness and support. Thanks also to all my family, to my husband Tom and my sons Rufus and Robin, to Paul Fairbrass, Sue and John Hunt. Most of all, this book is for my mother for her invaluable proof-reading skills and for my father for his enthusiasm and open mind: this is the result of the books they read me, the museums they took me to as a child and the love and imagination with which they encouraged me.

Notes

Preface

1. McCully, Marilyn (ed) *Loving Picasso: The Private Journal of Fernande Olivier* Harry N Abrams 2001

Introduction

1. Siegel, Jarrold *Bohemian Paris: Culture, Politics and the Boundaries of Bourgeois Life 1830-1930* JHU Press 1999

1: Sophie

1. Gaudier-Brzeska, Sophie *Matka and Other Writings* Mercury Graphics, London 2008
2. Hamnett Nina *Laughing Torso* Constable 1932
3. Brodsky, Horace *Henri Gaudier-Brzeska* Faber and Faber 1933
4. *Matka*
5. The masculine form of the surname is Brzeski, the feminine Brzeska

6. https://pl.wikipedia.org/wiki/%C5%81%C4%85czki_Brzeskie
7. https://translate.google.co.uk/translate?hl=en&sl=pl&u=http://www.genealogia.okiem.pl/powstanies/index.php%3Fnazwisko%3DBrzeski&prev=search
8. http://www.ics.uci.edu/~dan/genealogy/Krakow/other/index.html
9. https://translate.google.co.uk/translate?hl=en&sl=pl&u=http://www.genealogia.okiem.pl/powstanies/index.php%3Fnazwisko%3DBrzeski&prev=search
10. https://familysearch.org/ark:/61903/1:1:X57C-LZD
11. Brodsky
12. Ibid
13. Ibid
14. Matka
15. Ibid

16. Ibid

17. Davies, Norman *Heart of Europe: The Past in Poland's Present* Oxford University Press 2001

18. Brodsky

19. Yezierska, Anzia *Hungry Hearts and Other Stories* Virago 1987

2: Ida

1. Booth, Charles *Life and Labour of the People in London*, Volume 1, 1889, Volume 2, 1891

2. Smith, Adolphe and Thompson, John *Street Life in London* Sampson Low, Marston, Searle and Rivington 1877

3. Orr, Clarissa Campbell Women in the Victorian Art World Manchester University Press, 1995

4. Frost, Ginger S *Living in Sin: Cohabiting as Man and Wife in Nineteenth-Century England.* Oxford University Press 2011

5. Ibid

6. Hopkins, Ellice (ed) *Life and Letters of James Hinton* C.Kegan Paul and Co 1878

7. DNB

8. Ellice

9. Ibid

10. Ibid

11. Ibid

12. Ibid

13. Ibid

14. Ibid

15. Ibid

16. http://search.findmypast. co.uk/results/world-records/ england-and-wales-births-1837-2006?lastname=hinton &eventyear=1855&eventye ar_offset=2

17. http://spartacus-educational. com/Wmarriage.htm

18. Murphy, William Michael *Prodigal Father: The Life of John Butler Yeats.* Syracuse University Press, 2001

19. Ibid

20. Ibid

21. Holroyd, Michael *Augustus John: The New Biography* Vintage 1998

22. Ibid

23. http://henryirving.co.uk/ correspondence.php?forena me=Ada&lastname=Nettle ship&address=&datemin= &datemax=&contentsumm ary=&doctype=&collectio nref=&notes=&docholder= &correspondenceid=&adv ancedsearch=advancedsearch

24. Ibid

25. http://www.dailymail.co.uk/ femail/article-1366616/ Victorian-beetle-wing-dress-worn-Ellen-Terry-display-50k-repair-job.html

26. http://www.jssgallery.org/
    Paintings/Ellen_Terry_as_
    Lady_Macbeth.htm

27. Thomas, Alison *Portraits of
    Women: Gwen John and her
    Forgotten Contemporaries*
    Polity Press 1994

28. Holroyd

29. http://search.ancestry.co.uk/cgi-
    bin/sse.dll?_phsrc=yxA371&_
    phstart=
    successSource&useP
    UBJs=true&gss=angs-
    c&new=1&rank=1&ms
    T=1&gsfn=Ida&gsfn_
    x=1&gsln=Nettleship&gsln_
    x=NN&MSAV=1&uidh=7e4
    &pcat=1891UKI&h=26890
    333&dbid=6598&indiv=1&
    ml_rpos=1

30. Ibid

31. Holroyd

3: Fernande

1. Merriman, John. M *Massacre:
   The Life and Death of the
   Paris Commune of 1871* Yale
   University Press 2016

2. Fulton, Charles C *Europe
   Viewed Through American
   Spectacles,* 1873 (Later, Palala
   Press)

3. McCully, Marilyn (ed) *Loving
   Picasso: The Private Journal
   of Fernande Olivier* Harry N
   Abrams 2001

4. Ibid

5. Ibid

6. Ibid

7. Ibid

8. Ibid

9. Ibid

10. Ibid

11. Ibid

12. Ibid

13. Ibid

14. Ibid

15. Ibid

16. Ibid

17. Ibid

18. Ibid

19. Ibid

20. Ibid

21. Ibid

22. Ibid

23. Ibid

24. Ibid

25. Ibid

4: The Widening World

1. Hyde Park Gate News

2. Woolf, Virginia *Sketch of the
   Past*

3. Ibid

4. Mulvihill

5. http://spartacus-educational.
   com/Wmarriage.htm

6. Ede, H.S. *Savage Messiah*
   Windmill, 1931

7. Ibid

8. Matka

9. Ibid

10. Ibid

11. Ibid

12. Ibid

13. Ibid

14. Ibid
15. Ibid
16. Ibid
17. Ibid
18. Ibid
19. Ibid
20. McCully
21. Ibid
22. Ibid
23. Ibid
24. Ibid
25. Ibid
26. Ibid
27. Thomson
28. McCully
29. 3rd empire book
30. McCully
31. Ibid
32. Ibid
33. Ibid
34. Ibid
35. Ibid

5: *Art School Ingénue*
1. Hignett, Sean *Brett, from Bloomsbury to Mexico, a Biography* Hodder and Stoughton 1985
2. Corbett, David Peters and Perry, Lara English Art 1860-1914: Modern Artists and Identity. Manchester University Press 2000.
3. Words by Augustus John, in an obituary of Gwen Salmond in 1958.
4. Woodeson, John *Mark Gertler* Sidgwick and Jackson 1972

5. Corbett
6. Ibid
7. Ibid
8. Woodeson
9. Ibid
10. Holroyd
11. Thomas
12. Ibid
13. Ibid
14. Ibid
15. Ibid
16. Holroyd
17. http://mv.ancestry.com/ viewer/9aca7f73-f8b3-43f8- bce9-a8db185cdeaa/8742896/ -281558670
18. Thomas
19. Ibid
20. Ibid
21. Woolf, Virginia *A Room of One's Own* 1929
22. Corbett

6: *New Found Land*
1. Fernande's diary.
2. Matka
3. Ibid
4. Ibid
5. Brodsky
6. https://en.wikipedia.org/wiki/ SS_F%C3%BCrst_Bismarck_ (1890)
7. http://www.gjenvick.com/ SteamshipLines/Hamburg AmericanLine/1890s- DeckPlans-CabinPlans- FurstBismarck. html#axzz4YaqCXs8

8. Moreno, Barry *Ellis Island* Arcadia 2003

9. http://www.gjenvick.com/PassengerLists/Hamburg-AmericanLine/Westbound/1900-10-07-PassengerList-Patricia.html#axzz4YaqCXs8N

10. Ibid

11. Roth, Henry *Call it Sleep* (1934) Michael Joseph 1963

12. Koren, John and King, William Alexander *Benevolent Institutions 1904.* (New York, by census.) Govt Print 1905

13. http://jdaresidence.com/

14. Matka

15. Meyers, Jeffrey *Katherine Mansfield: A Darker View* Cooper Square 2002

16. https://www.myheritage.com/research/collection-30289/poland-tarnow-roman-catholic-diocese-church-books-1612-1900?s=423773301&formId=master&formMode=&action=query&exactSearch=1&useTranslation=1&qname-=Name+fn.Michael%2F3+ln.Brzeski+fnmo.1+lnmo.3&qbirth=Event+et.birth+ey.1869+me.true

17. Cole

18. Ibid

7: Sex

1. Fernande's diary

2. Ibid

3. Ibid

4. Ibid

5. Krauss, Rosalind E *The Picasso Papers* Thames and Hudson 1998

6. Diary

7. Ibid

8. Ibid

9. Ibid

10. Ibid

11. Ibid

12. Ibid

13. Matka

14. Ibid

15. Ibid

16. Ibid

17. Ibid

18. Ibid

19. Ibid

20. Ibid

21. Ibid

22. O'Keeffe, Paul *Gaudier-Brzeska An Absolute Case of Genius* Allen Lane 2004

23. Matka

24. Hardwick, Joan *Immodest Violet: Life of Violet Hunt* Andre Deutsch 1990

25. Matka

26. John, Augustus *Chiaroscuro: Fragments of Autobiography* Jonathan Cape 1952

27. Holroyd

28. John, Augustus *Finishing Touches* Readers' Union 1966

29. Ibid

30. Thomas

31. Holroyd

32. Ibid
33. Ibid
34. Chitty, Susan *Gwen John 1876-1939* Hodder and Stoughton 1981
35. Holroyd
36. Thomas

8: *Liberation*

1. Fernande's diary
2. Ibid
3. Ibid
4. Ibid
5. Ibid
6. Ibid
7. Ibid
8. Ibid
9. Richardson, John, *A Live of Picasso Volume* 2 *1907-1917* Jonathan Cape 1996
10. Fernande's diary
11. Ibid
12. Buisson, Sylvie and Parisot, Christian. *Paris, Montmartre; A Mecca of Modern Art 1860-1920*. Terrail 1996.
13. Diary
14. Ibid
15. Ibid
16. Ibid
17. Ibid
18. Ibid
19. Ibid
20. Ibid
21. Ibid
22. Richardson Vol 2
23. Diary
24. Ibid

25. Ibid
26. Ibid
27. Ibid
28. Ibid
29. Ibid

9: *Fin de Siècle Paris*

1. Reynolds, Sian 'Running Away to Paris: expatriate women artists of the 1900 generation...' *Women's History Review*, Volume 9, Number 2, 2000.
2. Roe, Sue *In Montmartre: Picasso, Matisse and Modernism in Paris 1900-1910* Penguin 2015
3. Chitty
4. Roe
5. Chitty
6. Foster, Alicia *Gwen John* Tate Gallery publishing 1999.
7. Reynolds
8. Ibid
9. Holroyd
10. Thomas
11. Holroyd
12. Reynolds
13. John, Augustus *Finishing Touches*
14. Roe
15. Holroyd
16. Roe, Sue *Gwen John: A Life* Vintage 2002
17. Chitty
18. Brodsky
19. Ede
20. Ibid

21. Cole
22. Ede
23. Matka
24. Ibid
25. O'Keeffe
26. Ede
27. Ibid

10: Being Mrs Artist

1. Thomas
2. Ibid
3. Thomas
4. Ibid
5. Ibid
6. Holroyd
7. Ibid
8. http://interactive. ancestry.com/7814/ LANRG13_3418_3421- 0395?pid=20344901&bac kurl=http://search.ancestry. com/cgi-bin/sse.dll?indiv% 3D1%26db%3Duki1901 %26h%3D20344901%2 6tid%3D%26pid%3D% 26usePUB%3Dtrue%26_ phsrc%3DyxA386%26_phs tart%3DsuccessSource%26u sePUBJs%3Dtrue%26rhSou rce%3D8913&treeid=&per sonid=&hintid=&usePUB=t rue&_phsrc=yxA386&_phs tart=successSource&useP UBJs=true#?imageId=LAN RG13_3418_3421-0395
9. Holroyd
10. Sampson, Anthony *The Scholar Gypsy: The Quest for*

a Family Secret A and C Black 2012

11. Ibid
12. Ibid
13. Ibid
14. Holroyd
15. Ibid
16. Ibid
17. Ibid
18. Ibid
19. Thomas
20. Ibid
21. Ibid

11: Love and Poverty

1. Ede
2. Matka
3. Envelope 4, letter a Gaudier-Brzeska collection, Albert Sloman Library, Univeristy of Essex
4. Ede
5. Matka
6. Ede
7. Mastka
8. Denman, J Unemployment Statistics from 1881 to the Present Day unemploymentbackto1881_ tcm77-267536%20(1).pdf
9. Ibid
10. Ancestry.com
11. Ede
12. Ibid
13. Ibid
14. Ibid
15. Matka
16. Ede

17. Ibid
18. Fernande's diary
19. Ibid
20. Hobhouse, Janet *Everybody who was Anybody: A Biography of Gertrude Stein* Littlehampton Book Services 1975
21. Ibid
22. Richardson Volume 2
23. Wilson, Elizabeth *Bohemians, The Glamorous Outcasts* Tauris Parke 2003
24. Greer, Germaine *The Obstacle Race: Fortunes of Women Painters and their Work* Farrar, Straus and Giroux, 1982
25. Diary
26. John *Chiaroscuro*

12: *Ménage À Trois*

1. Holroyd
2. Ibid
3. Ibid
4. Ibid
5. Ibid
6. Ibid
7. Ibid
8. Greer
9. Ibid
10. Holroyd
11. Bagnold, Enid *Autobiography* William Heinemann 1969
12. Cole
13. Ede

14. Epstein, Jacob *Let There be Sculpture* Readers' Union. 1942
15. Ibid
16. Cole
17. Ede
18. Tomalin, Claire *Katherine Mansfield: A Secret Life* Penguin 2003
19. Ibid
20. Meyers
21. Ede
22. Cole
23. Ibid
24. Ede
25. Ibid
26. Ibid
27. Ede
28. Cole
29. Ibid
30. Ede
31. Ibid
32. Ibid
33. Ibid
34. Ibid
35. Ibid
36. Cole
37. Ibid

13: *Madame Picasso*

1. Diary
2. Roe, *Montmartre*
3. Richardson Volume 2
4. Diary
5. Ibid
6. Hobhouse
7. Diary
8. Ibid

9. Richardson Vol 2
10. Diary
11. Ibid
12. Ibid
13. Ibid
14. Hobhouse
15. Richardson Vol 2
16. Ibid
17. Brassai
18. Richardson Vol 2
19. Ibid

14: New Houses, New Homes
1. Holroyd
2. Ibid
3. Ibid
4. Ibid
5. Thomas
6. Hooker, Denise *Nina Hamnett: Queen of Bohemia* Constable 1986
7. Ibid
8. Ibid
9. Ibid
10. Ibid
11. Ibid
12. Cole
13. Ibid
14. Cole
15. Pound, Ezra *A Memoir of Gaudier-Brzeska* New Directions Publishing 1970
16. Cole
17. Ibid
18. Ede
19. Richardson Volume 2
20. Ibid
21. Richardson

22. Ibid
23. Stein, Gertrude *The Autobiography of Alice B Toklas* Bodley Head 1933
24. Ibid
25. Richardson
26. Krauss
27. Richardson

15: Mortality
1. Ede
2. Matka
3. Ibid
4. Ede
5. Ibid
6. Ibid
7. Epstein
8. Ede
9. Ibid
10. Pound
11. Ibid
12. Ibid
13. Matka
14. Pound
15. Cole
16. Ibid
17. Ibid
18. Pound
19. Cole
20. Holroyd
21. Ibid
22. Ibid
23. O'Keeffe
24. Roe, *Montmartre*
25. Holroyd
26. Ibid
27. Roe
28. Ibid

16: *Afterwards*

1. Olivier, Fernande *Picasso and his Friends* Trans. Heinemann 1964 (Original 1933)
2. Ibid
3. Ibid
4. Ibid
5. Ibid
6. Diary
7. Ibid
8. Ibid
9. Oiivier, *Picasso and his Friends*
10. Diary
11. Ibid
12. Matka
13. Ibid
14. Ibid
15. Ibid
16. Ibid
17. Ibid
18. Ibid
19. Cole
20. Ibid
21. Matka
22. Ibid
23. Ibid
24. Ibid
25. Cole
26. Ibid
27. Ibid
28. Matka
29. Cole
30. Ibid
31. Matka
32. Cole
33. Ibid
34. Cole
35. Ibid
36. Ibid
37. Ibid
38. Ibid
39. Ede

17: *Three Extraordinary Women*

1. Fernande's diary
2. Thomas
3. Nicholson, Virginia *Among the Bohemians: Experiments in Living 1900-1939* Penguin 2003
4. Corbett
5. *Olivier, Picasso and his Friends.*

Bibliography

Bagnold, Enid *Autobiography* William Heinemann 1969

Booth, Charles *Life and Labour of the People in London*, Volume 1, 1889, Volume 2, 1891

Brassai, *Conversations with Picasso* University of Chicago Press 2002

Brodsky, Horace *Henri Gaudier-Brzeska* Faber and Faber 1933

Buisson, Sylvie and Parisot, Christian. *Paris, Montmartre; A Mecca of Modern Art 1860-1920* Terrail 1996.

Chitty, Susan *Gwen John 1876-1939* Hodder and Stoughton 1981

Cole, Roger *Gaudier-Brzeska: Artist and Myth* Sansom and Company (Radcliffe Press) 1995

Corbett, David Peters and Perry, Lara *English Art 1860-1914: Modern Artists and Identity*. Manchester University Press 2000.

Cork, Richard *Wild Thing: Epstein, Gaudier-Brzeska, Gill* Royal Academy of Arts 2009

Crespelle, Jean-Paul *Picasso and his Women* Hodder and Stoughton 1969

Davies, Norman *Heart of Europe: The Past in Poland's Present* Oxford University Press 2001

Du Maurier, George *Trilby* 1894

Ede, H.S. *Savage Messiah* Windmill, 1931

Epstein, Jacob *Let There be Sculpture* Readers' Union. 1942

Foster, Alicia *Gwen John* Tate Gallery publishing 1999.

Frost, Ginger S *Living in Sin: Cohabiting as Man and Wife in Nineteenth-Century England*. Oxford University Press 2011

Gaudier-Brzeska, Sophie *Matka and Other Writings* Mercury Graphics, London 2008

Greer, Germaine *The Obstacle Race: Fortunes of Women Painters and their Work* Farrar, Straus and Giroux, 1982

Franck, Dan *The Bohemians: The Birth of Modern Art, Paris 1900-1930* Phoenix 2002

Hamnett Nina *Laughing Torso* Constable 1932

Hardwick, Joan *Immodest Violet: Life of Violet Hunt* Andre Deutsch 1990

Hignett, Sean *Brett, from Bloomsbury to Mexico, a Biography* Hodder and Stoughton 1985

Hobhouse, Janet *Everybody who was Anybody: A Biography of Gertrude Stein* Littlehampton Book Services 1975

Holroyd, Michael *Augustus John: The New Biography* Vintage 1998

Hooker, Denise *Nina Hamnett: Queen of Bohemia* Constable 1986

Hopkins, Ellice (ed) *Life and Letters of James Hinton* C.Kegan Paul and Co 1878

John, Augustus *Chiaroscuro: Fragments of Autobiography* Jonathan Cape 1952

John, Augustus *Finishing Touches* Readers' Union 1966

Koren, John and King, William Alexander *Benevolent Institutions 1904.* (New York, by census.) Govt Print 1905

Krauss, Rosalind E *The Picasso Papers* Thames and Hudson 1998

McAuliffe, Mary *Twilight of the Belle Epoque: The Paris of Picasso, Stravinsky, Proust, Renault, Marie Curie, Gertrude Stein and their Friends Through the Great War* Rowman and Littlefield 2014

Mailer, Norman *Picasso: Portrait of Picasso as a Young Man.* Little, Brown and Company, 2005

Meyers, Jeffrey *Katherine Mansfield: A Darker View* Cooper Square 2002

Moreno, Barry *Ellis Island* Arcadia 2003

Mulvihill, Margaret *Charlotte Despard: A Biography* Pandora 1989

Murger, Henri *Bohemians of the Latin Quarter (Scenes de la Vie de Boheme)* 1851

Nicholson, Virginia *Among the Bohemians: Experiments in Living 1900-1939* Penguin 2003

O'Brian, Patrick *Picasso* William Collins 1976

O'Keeffe, Paul *Gaudier-Brzeska An Absolute Case of Genius* Allen Lane 2004

Olivier, Fernande and McCully, Marilyn (ed) *Loving Picasso: The Private Journal of Fernande Olivier* Harry N Abrams 2001

Olivier, Fernande *Picasso and his Friends* Trans. Heinemann 1964 (Original 1933)

Orr, Clarissa Campbell *Women in the Victorian Art World* Manchester University Press, 1995

Pound, Ezra *A Memoir of Gaudier-Brzeska* New Directions Publishing 1970

Reynolds, Sian 'Running Away to Paris: expatriate women artists of the 1900 generation ... ' Women's History Review, Volume 9, Number 2, 2000.

Richardson, John *A Life of Picasso Volume 1 1881-1906* Jonathan Cape 1991

Richardson, John, *A Live of Picasso Volume 2 1907-1917* Jonathan Cape 1996

Roe, Sue *Gwen John: A Life* Vintage 2002

Roe, Sue *In Montmartre: Picasso, Matisse and Modernism in Paris 1900-1910* Penguin 2015

Sampson, Anthony *The Scholar Gypsy: The Quest for a Family Secret* A and C Black 2012

Siegel, Jarrold *Bohemian Paris: Culture, Politics and the Boundaries of Bourgeois Life 1830-1930* JHU Press 1999

Smith, Adolphe and Thompson, John *Street Life in London*, 1877

Stein, Gertrude *The Autobiography of Alice B. Toklas* Bodley Head 1933

Thomas, Alison *Portraits of Women: Gwen John and her Forgotten Contemporaries* Polity Press 1994

Thomson, Richard *The Troubled Republic, Visual Culture and Social Debate in France 1889-1900* Yale University Press 2004

Tomalin, Claire *Katherine Mansfield: A Secret Life* Penguin 2003

Wilson, Elizabeth *Bohemians, The Glamorous Outcasts* Tauris Parke 2003

Woodeson, John *Mark Gertler* Sidgwick and Jackson 1972

Yezierska, Anzia *Hungry Hearts and Other Stories* Virago 1987

Index